Coarse Fishing

Coarse Fishing

with

Matt Hayes

The Crowood Press

First published in 1995 by
The Crowood Press Ltd
Ramsbury, Marlborough
Wiltshire SN8 2HR

British Library Cataloguing in Publication Data

A catalogue record for this book is available from the British Library.

ISBN 1 85223 866 6

Designed by:
D & N Publishing
DTP & Editorial Services
Crowood Lane, Ramsbury
Marlborough, Wiltshire SN8 2HR

All photographs by the author, Mick Rouse and various contributors
Line drawings by Jeff Parrott.

Photograph previous page: a 10lb 5oz barbel caught on the Dorset Stour by the author.

Dedication
This book is dedicated to my long-suffering wife, Christine, who throughout our married life has been the driving force and inspiration for everything that I have done and will continue to do in the future.

Printed and bound in Great Britain by
BPC Hazell Books Ltd
A member of
The British Printing Company Ltd

CONTENTS

PREFACE

Of all the communication projects that I have been involved with, and these include magazines, newspapers, videos and television, this book is the most important to me. A book is permanent and many writers, myself included, are attracted to the idea of leaving the world with a permanent reminder of their existence. This would seem to imply that my motivations for writing this book are entirely egotistical. The truth is that this is largely correct, and I would also acknowledge that the commercial success of the project is important too. The reasons for this have nothing to do with financial considerations and are entirely due to one of my most loathsome character defects – people pleasing. As far as I am concerned, I would far sooner have you borrow or steal this book and enjoy it, than buy it and feel that you have wasted your money.

The book is a straightforward, no-nonsense, technically based work which makes no compromise toward reminiscences and angling stories. At times I have been plagued by anxiety as a result of this very fact, but after a great deal of thought, my conclusion is that you cannot write an authoritative instructional book on all of the major coarse fish species and include anecdotes. Accordingly, the style is unashamedly workmanlike, and, I hope that after reading it, you will at the very least learn something and at best improve your fishing skills.

Matt Hayes

ACKNOWLEDGEMENTS

Len Gurd and Stewart Allum for being the best mates any man could have; Shimano UK, Leslies of Luton, Max, Cliff and Ken at Fox International, Gold Label Tackle, Kryston Advanced Angling Products, and Dave Thorpe Bait Developments for their support; Terry Eustace, Kevin Crawley (Leslies), Dave Thorpe and Chris Nicolau (DT Bait Developments) not only for their personal support but for 'having faith', too; to Simon Roff, Keith Higginbottom, John McKenzie, Mick Rouse, Kevin Wilmott, Andrew James, Tim Paisley, Kevin Clifford and Peter Maskell for giving an aspiring writer a chance; special thanks to John Lofthouse, Simean Bond, Craig Brew, Barry and Sharon Jeffries at Shimano for not only their professionalism, but also being nice guys and good friends too; to Ernie and Sue from Becal for the hours spent slaving over a word processor, and Jeff Parrott for illustrating the book with such enthusiasm and skill.

To my fellow contributors and friends: Steve Burke, Dave Thorpe, Tony Miles, John Watson, Stu Allum, Bill Rushmer, Peter Stone and John Bailey; to 'Stoney' especially for his Foreword, for his good friendship and for being even 'greater' in real life than the legend that I had admired for years; to John Bailey for giving me the opportunity to write this book and the inspiration, through his own writing, to pursue my dreams as an angler; to Bernard Venables for creating the character of 'Mr Crabtree', a timeless angler who will outlive us all, and whose angling exploits fired a young boy's imagination.

And finally, to my late grandfather, Dave Massey, and to my father, John Hayes, for putting up with the impatient young angler and turning him into an impatient ageing fisherman!

FOREWORD

When the manuscript of this book arrived I knew it would be something special, for without being patronizing, Matt Hayes is also a bit special. When his articles first appeared in magazines I wondered, despite photographs of his big fish, whether this 'new' writer was as good as his writing suggested.

When we eventually met and fished together I realized any suspicions I had were unfounded: the man could fish. I marvelled at some of his rigs and attention to detail – I almost felt like a beginner. Equally important, his watercraft is second to none. But that isn't all; a friend after meeting Matt remarked, 'What makes Matt so special is he is so nice with it.'

So much for the man, what about the book?

Like many successful anglers the author uses the very latest in tackle. Whilst good tackle won't turn a poor angler into a successful one, a good angler using good tackle will put more fish on the bank. For instance, Matt recommends the use of Fox Supa-weight putty for backleading, not only in stillwaters but in rivers. This, he says, eliminates the problem of striking at line bites, foul hooking and consequently spooking fish, a common feature where barbel are concerned. He also advocates putty in place of shot when float fishing.

I read the manuscript in two sessions, less than planned but I could not put it down. Most times I nodded in agreement, then a sentence or paragraph would pop up which I had to read again. For instance, on 'Slow-Water Chub': 'It is my belief that slow-water chub are fish that have opted for a state of semi-retirement, free to live out quiet, untroubled lives away from the intense competition that shoal chub have to contend with.' Now that is something new, isn't it?

The advice given by his guest writers is thought-provoking. On perch, Steve Burke says that curry flavoured maggots are favoured by large perch and suggests that an outsize 'Stripey' may be the only perch in a water. Three years ago I weighed and photographed a 6lb perch netted from a pit which was finally drained. No other perch were present. And how nice to see that largely neglected species, the dace, receiving the attention it deserves (from Bill Rushmer).

During my lifetime I have read hundreds of 'how to do it' books. From many I have gleaned information which has helped put a bend in my rod. But this book will put many bends into many rods. It is a book to be savoured, especially by those anglers who, no matter how experienced, have the desire to become better and more successful fishermen.

Peter Stone

1 THE BIG FISH SCENE

SPECIMEN FISH FROM RIVERS
by Stewart Allum

Throughout the 1960s, 70s and early 80s, certain fairly rigid standards appeared to be set regarding the general and ultimate sizes of our principal river species. Whilst exceptional specimens such as 7lb chub, 3lb roach and 12lb barbel did of course exist, such was their rarity that only a handful of genuine captures were recorded throughout this period. I stress the word 'genuine' here, there being many false claims, 'guess-timates' and hoaxes reported in the angling press. A situation which, sadly, persists to this day.

For example, as a keen chub angler I monitored every report carefully and the plain fact is that between 1967 and 1985 I can only recall four properly photographed and authenticated river chub in excess of 7lb being recorded; the best documented was Jack Hilton's magnificent 7lb 2oz specimen from the Hampshire Avon in 1967. Indeed, all four of the above fish were caught prior to 1973, and it was to be more than a decade before a genuine river chub in excess of 6lb, let alone one of 7lb, was to appear again in the angling press. The only notable exceptions during this period were some exceptional stillwater specimens taken by Peter Stone, Phil Tew and a few other pioneering anglers, who had been experimenting with deadbaiting techniques in order to catch the elusive giants of the Oxfordshire gravel pits.

Where rivers were concerned, the largest authenticated seasonal captures were usually fish in the 5½ to 5¾lb bracket; even four-pounders were regarded as specimens. Indeed, these nation-wide results were mirrored in the catches made by chub study group members at that time, whose ranks included some of the most talented and experienced chub anglers in Britain. It was not until the latter part of the 1980s that genuine 6 and 7lb chub began to reappear in the angling press and in 1987, just to illustrate this point, the chub study group recorded its first river giant, a 6lb 4oz specimen taken by Alan Owers from the River Waveney.

Results since then have been absolutely staggering. During the 1993/94 season alone no less than six fully authenticated 7lb-plus monsters were reported in the angling press, together with many others over the 6lb mark. Neither were these fish restricted to the better-known chub rivers such as the Avon and Stour: one of the seven-pounders came from a canal, whilst 5 and 6lb specimens were recorded from rivers throughout the land, many of which had never previously shown such outstanding form. Many theories regarding this remarkable upturn in the average size of chub have been expressed, perhaps the most plausible being that many of these tremendous fish were born during the drought summer of 1976, a particularly good year for chub spawning. As these fish reached their normal maximum growth span during the late 1980s (when they would have been some eleven to twelve years old) they were treated to a succession of mild winters and low water levels, when much of the summer weed and an unseasonably high amount of natural food was still in evidence. This resulted in some of the larger, healthier fish going on to attain weights never previously recorded on such a massive scale. Whatever the reason, there has certainly never been a better time to go chub fishing – but what of our other river species?

A 3lb roach has always been every river angler's dream, and still remains one of angling's toughest targets. Almost every season, as far back as I can remember, a tiny handful of such fish have been recorded. Some rivers have always produced larger-than-average roach, in particular the Hampshire Avon, the Dorset Stour, the Kennet, Norfolk's River Wensum and the Bristol Avon; the usual pattern is for these rivers periodically to throw up a good crop of 2lb-plus specimens with perhaps the occasional three-pounder. Recent seasons, however, have shown a dramatic increase in the number of 3lb specimens recorded, and one river in particular stands head and shoulders above all others. I refer, of course, to the Hampshire Avon.

Many factors may have contributed to the unusually high number of big roach now being caught from this river. For decades the Avon was blighted by appalling mismanagement, which included excessive weedcutting, pollution from trout farms, disease, over-abstraction, the introduction of alien species such as rainbow trout, carp and bream, together with the drainage of water meadows. All combined to produce a river where the indigenous species did well to survive at all. The 1970s marked a particularly dreadful period, with even 2lb roach and 4lb chub a rarity in what had once been Britain's premier chalk stream. Fry survival amongst roach generally was very low, and for many years it was rare indeed to see any small- to medium-sized ones at all.

The last four or five years have been much kinder to the Avon. A more enlightened approach to weedcutting has seen higher summer levels with reasonable cover being left to shelter the young fry, whilst the past two mild, wet winters have topped up the chalk aquifers, keeping the river at a good level whilst washing away many of the pollutants which had accumulated over the years. Roach can live to a great age, certainly in excess of twenty years. Those surviving shoals from the 1970s and early 80s found themselves in a river where they had little competition from smaller fish and an abundance of natural food. Many have now reached specimen size, and the good news is that their offspring are finally on the increase, the last two seasons having seen a marked upturn in the number of smaller

roach being caught. Nature, it seems, has attempted to restore the balance in spite of man's undoing, though it remains to be seen whether this will lead to any lasting improvement in the Avon's fortunes.

Barbel, on the other hand, are relative newcomers to many rivers. They are another species which can live to a ripe old age. The River Medway, for example, is hardly an ideal barbel habitat; a narrow, sluggish river with a fairly silty bottom, it was originally stocked with barbel by *Angling Times* as a publicity exercise during the early 1950s. These fish have not bred very successfully; nonetheless a small localized colony still exists, and one of these survivors, probably one of the original Kennet stock fish, achieved legendary status in 1992 when it became Britain's first specimen to hold the official record at over 15lb in weight. Bob Morris, its captor, had caught the very same fish ten years earlier when it was already a 'double', which gives some

Stewart Allum with a giant barbel of 12lb 14oz – another species growing to record size in our rivers.

idea of the longevity of this species. This fish has since been recaptured at over 16lb in weight.

If barbel can grow so large in such a poor habitat, then what of those which exist in ideal barbel rivers such as the Avon, Stour, Severn and, latterly, the Wye, where they are a comparatively recent introduction? The average size of barbel on these rivers has, in fact, escalated beyond all comprehension during recent seasons. In 1983 when I caught my first double-figure barbel, a 10lb 14oz fish, it was large enough to win me several prizes as the heaviest specimen reported in the angling press that week. Nowadays such a fish, though still a fine example, would scarcely be worth reporting when compared to the 12lb, 13lb and 14lb giants now appearing regularly throughout the autumn and winter months, not to mention the increasing number of double-figure fish from previously unrated rivers. It would appear that our barbel are finally coming of age and that they, like the chub, have taken full advantage of recent climatic fluctuations.

So what does the future hold? With huge carp now appearing with increasing frequency throughout our river systems, together with specimen bream, zander and a host of other hitherto alien species which have benefited from various introductions over the years, the prospects for today's river specialist have never been more exciting or challenging. This could be the time to rediscover your river, for it may have changed a great deal since last you saw it.

When I considered the idea of asking a guest writer to cover the development of river fishing, Stewart Allum was the obvious candidate. This man possesses watercraft that simply makes me green with envy and his experience of river fishing, its development and the rise and decline of various river species, is second to none. The same comments regarding stillwater knowledge and expertise can surely be applied to the next contributor, Peter Stone. Who better than 'Stoney', an angler whose name has been synonymous with the growth and development of gravel-pit fishing, to write this introduction and to bench-mark the current state of our stillwater fishing in general?

STILL WATERS AND GRAVEL PIT REVOLUTION   by Peter Stone

My love affair with gravel pits is now approaching its thirtieth birthday. In those early days (the mid-1960s) the gravel pits in my area were few and far between, and the results as regards big fish by my friends and I were not outstanding. We caught plenty of fish, yes, but even I, always the optimist, never foresaw the kind of fishing anglers would be enjoying in the years ahead. Then in the late 1960s some friends and I cast our lines into T.C. pit. The average size of the tench – between 4lb and 5lb – stunned us, for we had never known tench fishing like it. At that time a 4lb tench was a big fish, and a six-pounder was a 'dream' one. How big would they eventually grow, we wondered, for the pit was less than ten years old.

A few years later another pit attracted our attention. As at T.C., the tench were of large average size – for example, one morning a fine specimen weighing 6lb 7oz slid over my net, an almost unbelievable fish; I was still reeling with excitement half an hour later when friend Pete Carpenter came round. 'I've had a six-plusser,' I said. 'I did better than that last night,' Pete replied, 'I had an eight!' *Eight pounds*! I could hardly believe it; just what was happening to the tench?

However, another pit close by was the jewel in our crown: two acres in extent with banks lined with litter it was not a pretty sight, but as we were to discover, hundreds of specimen roach and chub lived in the crystal-clear water. The roach population was enormous. The first year I kept a diary and recorded over 400 roach, taken by John Everard, Fred Towns and me, with only one under 1lb and several over 2lb. The following season I took ninety-six big roach in the first fortnight. But that wasn't all: the chub population was also large, with many four-pounders and the odd 'five' gracing our nets. It held big bream, too, but these eluded everyone. One evening fishing for roach the float dipped and I found myself into a 'slab' which pulled the scales to 8¼lb. It caused a sensation in both the local and national press, for in those days it was a very big fish indeed.

During the next few years great changes took place in the pits that my friends and I were fishing. The tench got even bigger, with seven-pounders common and a sprinkling of eights, and then on one memorable evening a 'double' slid over my net. Big tench were caught everywhere, as the four-pounders of the 1960s, big fish in their time, had grown on. It was a never-to-be-forgotten experience: a tench revolution had taken place. Writing on tench in *Stillwater Angling*, Dick Walker recalls a fight Pete Thomas had with a big tench. He concludes: 'Peter has always refused firmly to tell me how much *he* thinks that tench weighed but I am not so hesitant. I do not think it can have been less than 8lb.' Dick, great angler that he was, never caught a 6lb tench. This was not due to lack of skill, but simply because big tench were not around in any great numbers in his time. I tell this simply to illustrate the vast changes that occurred in the 1970s and 80s.

Then came the chub – and what chub! One day John Everard decided to try the second pit I mentioned: he caught three chub, at 4lb 12oz, 4lb 4oz and 3lb 13oz. We couldn't believe it; such chub from a stillwater were unknown to us. We immediately obtained permission to fish it, and never looked back.

Although by then we were catching plenty of 'fours' and the odd 'five', we did not see – or, to be truthful, *expect* to see – larger ones. But as the years passed it became increasingly obvious that enormous chub inhabited one of the pits where we were fishing. Another angler and Geoff Barnes both saw a brace in the same swim which they estimated to be over 10lb. I never saw them, though I certainly saw eight-pounders. But as we were to discover, they proved very, very difficult indeed.

Then another pit attracted our attention, the pit where I caught my 'seven'. That also held (and still does) enormous chub, fish approaching – and possibly over – double figures. I did not fish gravel pits regularly until the late 1960s so I don't know whether outsize chub were around in any great numbers before that time; what I *do* know, however, is that the chub in the pit where Geoff

saw two doubles put on weight very quickly, also that the pit was an old-established one, having been dug after the Second World War. When we first fished the pit, chub between 1lb and 2lb were present in considerable numbers and we watched them grow into four- and five-pounders very quickly. It was during this same period that the tench put on weight quickly too.

In 1973 I caught, by design, a bream weighing 10lb 1oz in T.C. pit. A few weeks previously rumours were rife that a double had been taken, which if true was certainly the first from the water, mine being the second. During the next two or three years I took more big 'slabs', and on one memorable day when fishing the margins with a float, I caught eight over 8lb including two 'tens'. But by then the word had spread, and because of increasing pressure from other anglers I left T.C. Later on T.C. produced fish to nearly 14lb.

But the sixty-four-thousand-dollar question remains: what caused the tench, chub and bream, and in particular the tench, to grow so big? Many theories have been put forward but in truth no one really knows. On tench, a respected angler/ writer maintained that the introduction of boilies by carp fishermen had played a part; but I am far from convinced. That may be so in some waters, but it most certainly wasn't in the pit where my friends and I caught so many sevens, eights and two doubles. Only a handful of anglers fished the water, none of whom used boilies. It was the same in the early days of T.C., where only a handful of anglers fished and when boilies were unheard of, but where the tench and bream were already big. The first time I walked around T.C. was when a neighbour told me about some 'large carp' he had seen. The carp were bream, and big ones. No one had cast a line into T.C. then, and I was one of the first to do so.

Chub, being predatory, wax fat on other species. The pit where I took my 'seven' holds a population of huge bleak, 6 and 7in (15 and 17.5cm) in length. Chub love bleak, and I believe those big bleak are partially responsible for the chub growing so big.

And carp. Here again there has been an explosion, one which the late Dick Walker would never have dreamed about. When Walker caught 'Clarissa' in 1952 a 20lb fish was a big fish, a fish much sought after by the then small band of carp enthusiasts. Even Dick, who looked far into the future, could not have visualized the carp scene of today.

I don't think carp can be put in the same bracket as tench, bream and chub in the context I am discussing, however. The carp in most of the pits today have been stocked and are not truly 'wild' fish to those waters; nevertheless they have put on weight very quickly, far more quickly than the carp natural to some lakes I know where the growth rate is far less. But why? Many of the pits are completely barren of weed, the bottom akin to a concrete road; yet the carp still put on weight rapidly. Strange.

For many pike enthusiasts gravel pits have given them exceptional specimens, especially pits which hold a population of big bream. My experiences have shown that pike put on weight quickly where bream are present, not only in pits but in rivers, too. I am not a dedicated pike angler, but one gravel pit gave me a fish of a lifetime. Geoff Barnes and I had gone chub fishing and before we settled down over our bobbins I decided to cast a plug around. 'I'll see if a big chub fancies this,' I remarked as I walked off. 'You'll probably catch a big pike,' Geoff replied. Four casts later he was proved correct, when a superbly conditioned specimen weighing 31lb 12oz slid over my waiting net.

Today gravel pits have sprung up everywhere. In my area alone there are well over thirty, with more being dug, and most contain big fish with chub and tench the dominant species. Why fish grow so big in gravel pits is an interesting question. Water quality is a major factor, likewise the insect population for fish to feed on; yet this also applies to many estate lakes, where a 5lb tench still remains a big one. Obviously there are other factors, but no one *really* knows the answer.

In *Gravel Pit Angling* (published in 1978) I wrote: 'Today gravel pits are in great demand and rightly so, for in them you can find sport of which you could only dream.' Prior to my gravel

The flat cap gives it away – 'Stoney', wearing his famous trademark, plays a gravel pit tench.

pit baptism I had many dreams, dreams which subsequently were realized – and this is also true for a great number of anglers. I also wrote in *Gamekeeper and Countryside* in 1978: 'Had anyone written a few years ago about catching *numbers* of seven-pound tench and *hoping* a 'ten', should it come, would not be gravid, he would have ended up on a psychiatrist's couch. Tenchwise, times have certainly changed.' For stillwater enthusiasts gravel pits have given a new dimension to their fishing. I myself have witnessed enormous changes over the last thirty years, and consider myself fortunate to have been around during this very exciting period.

2 FISHING TACKLE IN THE 1990s AND BEYOND

There is an old saying in angling that 'fishing tackle catches anglers not fish'. There can be no doubt, however, that the development of improved materials and manufacturing processes and their positive impact on the quality of fishing tackle available today has led to the downfall of increasing numbers of big fish. The best fishing rod in the world will not make a poor angler into a good one, but if an experienced angler needs to present a bait at 130yds (120m), the technology now exists to put fish at this range within his capabilities. The tackle scene as it is today is constantly pushing back boundaries and helping anglers to improve their results and gain maximum enjoyment from this great sport of ours.

Purists may scorn the current hi-tech boom in tackle and accessories. Surely though, their admiration for antique fishing tackle provides evidence that appreciating the qualities and workmanship of angling equipment is a preoccupation that will stand the test of time. One can imagine the descendants of angling's most staunch traditionalists extolling the virtues of a 1990s baitrunner fifty years from now. From a personal viewpoint, I have a keen interest in any innovations and developments that will help to catch more fish, or to enhance my contact with the angling experience.

For this reason, the following guide to the essential equipment that I use to pursue a variety of big fish from different types of venue is a vital part of this book.

Choosing the right fishing tackle to suit your needs is a very personal thing. I know several anglers who prefer to use equipment from a bygone era, such as split cane rods and centre pin reels. They catch plenty of fish, too, but using antique fishing tackle when modern technology is so far superior is not for me. I can only recommend what I use, and as far as I am concerned that means the most functional equipment available to me: namely, carbon fibre rods, fixed spool reels and a centrepin where its use is appropriate.

The complete modern-day specialist angler will possess several rod and reel set-ups, and with so many alternatives available it is important that we understand the fundamentals, the alternative being a very expensive mistake.

RODS

When choosing a rod, any rod, it is important to ask yourself a number of questions, namely: how far have I got to cast? What strength of line am I most likely to use? How big are the fish that I am most likely to catch? What type of action do I enjoy playing fish on most? And last, but not least, how much can I afford? Always try to buy the best tackle that you can afford; this policy is invariably worthwhile. There are several *key* components to all fishing rods:

Action
There are basically three types of action: 'through', 'progressive' and 'fast taper'. 'Through' action rods will bend through to the butt, adopting a hooped curve when placed under severe compression. The bend is even throughout the blank. Choose this type of action if you want to gain maximum enjoyment when playing your quarry.

'Progressive action' describes a rod that becomes progressively more powerful towards the butt. When maximum pressure is exerted, the rod will bend throughout its length, but it will possess extra strength from the middle downwards to bully hard-fighting fish. An excellent compromise action, most anglers like to use rods that fit into this category.

'Fast taper' rods are very tip-orientated. In truth, they possess very little in the way of action as such, the bottom two-thirds of the blank being very stiff, with the top third being very flexible by comparison. Personally I don't like fast taper rods because I consider that they take the pleasure out of playing fish, as well as increasing the risk of the hook hold failing at close range. There can be no doubt though, that if you want to cast a long way, you cannot afford to ignore them.

Test Curve

The test curve rating of the rod is important, too. The term 'test curve' describes the amount of weight necessary to bend the tip of the rod to ninety degrees. Thus, a 2lb test curve rod requires 2lb of pressure to achieve this effect. Test curves are important, the basic rule being that the higher the test curve, the stronger the rod will be.

Length

Length is vital. Most rods are either 11, 12 or 13ft long and everyone has his personal preference. Shorter rods will be correspondingly lighter and easier to control, but will lack the speed of response that a longer rod has when picking up line. There are occasions when it is necessary to use a rod at the maximum length possible. For instance, when I am trotting in 'boily', unpredictable currents, I like to use a 15ft match rod for improved float control. Nowadays there are even 20ft long models available, a testimony to modern technology since building a rod of this length is fraught with difficulties. Equally, there are times when I am more at home with a very short rod; when stalking for example, since poking a long rod through branches and thick undergrowth can be a positive hindrance.

There are other considerations too, and your final choice should only be made when you have fully considered exactly what you want the rod to do. Maybe you are a regular swim-feeder angler on big rivers, a situation that demands the use of a long rod to keep as much line off the water as

possible, to avoid the current dislodging your tackle too easily. Perhaps you are a trotting fanatic, in which case a light, responsive rod is a must.

I must again emphasize that I can only recommend what I use; the table overleaf illustrates my personal preferences as far as rods and reels are concerned.

REELS

Choosing the right reel is far from easy, given the technological advances that have been made in recent years and the sheer range of models on the market. All my fishing reels, with the exception of centre pins (yes, I do use them occasionally!) are made by Shimano, a company that has been very largely responsible for the advancement of the fixed spool in the last decade or so. Shimano manufacture reels to my dream formula, which is as follows:

Smoothness is vitally important. A good reel feels smooth when retrieving a cast or playing a fish; there should be no jerkiness or hesitation when the handle is turned. The smooth drag mechanism is absolutely vital if, like me, you like to play fish directly off the clutch as opposed to back winding; line should leave the spool constantly and without hesitation or jerkiness. A well-made clutch will tick like an expensive watch when line is pulled from it under constant pressure.

Balance, too, is very important, and the weight and shape of the reel that you choose should feel right when it is combined with the rod that you use. When buying a reel, try it out on your own rod. I also like reels to be stable, so that vibration and 'wobble' are minimal when the handle is turned at high speed. A stable and balanced reel will deliver improved control over hard-fighting fish.

Of equal importance are some of the more recent developments that Shimano have made. Spool design is particularly vital when long distance casting is involved. An aerodynamic spool design with a slight 'cone' profile will decrease line friction, giving longer, trouble-free casts, whether you are flicking out a light link leger or belting out a 3oz lead to 150yds (140m). The

The Shimano baitrunner – it revolutionized the fixed spool reel.

Shimano Aero System not only improves casting power, it also increases accuracy.

When I am bolt rig fishing I would not be without a baitrunner reel. The development of the baitrunner is the most significant advancement in reel design since the fixed spool was invented. For those of you unfamiliar with the concept, the baitrunner allows the clutch of the reel to be bypassed, simply by pushing a lever forwards. This puts the reel into 'free spool' mode, allowing hard-running fish to take line with minimum resistance and with no danger of the line flapping around or over-running. The baitrunner has become the carp angler's first choice, but I also find them indispensable for trolling, particularly when I am after pike on trout reservoirs.

For tench and barbel fishing or stalking carp, I like to use a reel with 'Fightin' Drag', a feature that allows the clutch mechanism to be altered while the fish is being played, by simply moving an easily accessible lever on the back of the reel. When the lever is returned to its central position, the clutch returns to a pre-set level. It is the perfect feature for coping with the adrenaline-pumping unpredictability of big, hard-fighting fish.

When trotting on a pacey river, I like the improved control that a centre pin reel gives. A centre pin allows the float to progress downriver without the jerkiness and 'stop/start' characteristics of a fixed spool. My favourite pin – a trotting special – was made for me by Pete Henwood at Specialist Tackle, Romford.

Finally, it is vital that you choose a reel that will hold an adequate amount of line. Most reels have spool capacities stated on their packaging. I would never use a reel that cannot hold at least 100yds (90m) of the heaviest line I am likely to use. When carp or pike fishing, the same rule is applied, but with a minimum requirement of 250yds (225m).

In summary, when you buy a rod and/or a reel it is absolutely essential that you have fully considered your exact needs. Remember that the most expensive is not always the best, and several makes should be compared before you make your final choice. I make no apologies for stating my bias toward Shimano products, since I can only talk about the tackle I use. I would openly acknowledge however, that there are a number of other companies making excellent products these days.

Rod

Style	Length (in feet)	Action	Test Curve
Short/medium-range carp	12	Through/Progressive	1¾–2¼ lb
Long-range carp	12	Progressive	2¾–3lb
Stalking carp	10–11	Progressive	2lb
Stalking river	11–12	Through	1lb
Stalking stillwater	12	Through/ Progressive	1–1¼lb
Legering: big river/feeder fishing	12–14	Progressive	1¼lb
Legering: medium/small river/ feeder fishing	11–12	Progressive	1lb
Legering: stillwater/feeder fishing	12	Progressive	1¼–1½lb
Float fishing: medium fish, rivers and lakes	13–14	Progressive	12oz
Float fishing: big fish, rivers and lakes	12–14	Progressive	1lb–1lb 2oz
Pike: stillwaters	12	Progressive	3lb
Pike: river	12	Progressive	2¼–2½lb

Reel

Type	Minimum Spool Capacity	Additional Features
Carp – fixed spool	15lb/250yds	Baitrunner big, wide spool
Carp – fixed spool	15lb/250yds	Baitrunner
Carp – fixed spool	15lb/100yds	Drag
Avon – fixed spool	10lb/100yds	Fightin' drag
Avon – fixed spool	10lb/100yds	Fightin' drag
Medium/heavy feeder/quivertip – fixed spool	8lb/100yds	Fightin' drag
Medium feeder/quivertip – fixed spool	8lb/100yds	Fightin' drag
Stepped-up Avon – fixed spool	10lb/100yds	Fightin' drag
Heavy match – fixed spool-centre pin	6lb/100yds	
Specimen float – fixed spool-centre pin	6lb/100yds	
Pike/carp – fixed spool	15lb/250yds	Baitrunner
Pike/carp – fixed spool	15lb/250yds	Baitrunner

BITE INDICATION

With the increasing specialization of angling styles, bite indication is becoming ever more sophisticated in an attempt to keep pace. But some of the best methods have been around for a number of years and remain to this day highly effective. The most basic of them all is sight fishing, that is, watching the line where it enters the water, or where water clarity and/or depth allow, watching the bait itself. A pair of polarizing glasses is the only extra accessory required but it is surprising how few anglers appreciate the degree to which polaroids minimize reflected glare from the surface of the water. I am a keen sight fisherman and rate this style more highly than any other where conditions allow it.

In recent years legering has become more popular, particularly with the rising popularity of carp and swimfeeder fishing. A float, however, is the most sensitive bite indicator available. Allrounders will carry two types, namely wagglers (for still- and slow-water fishing) and stick- or balsa floats (for medium- and fast-paced water). A selection of wagglers, including models with bodies, without bodies and in a variety of lengths, will cope with varying casting distances and the effects of wind strength and undertows. In flat calm conditions, an inserted tip will be more sensitive than a straight tip which is more suited to pacier currents and windy conditions. In extremely choppy conditions, a drift beater-type float, with its characteristic sight bob, is vital.

Stickfloats come in a variety of shapes and sizes. Small baits and precision work demand the use of a traditional stick model, while deeper or pacier water is more suited to the Avon type. For big baits and fast currents, a large balsa will deliver the control necessary to keep the bait at a constant depth.

Floats have also changed cosmetically in recent years, with clear, crystal-type floats becoming popular; the idea behind these excellent floats is that they are less easily seen by shy fish in clear and/or shallow water. And while it is important that the fish shouldn't see your float, it is equally vital that you can, and with as little eye-strain as possible. For this reason I always carry a selection with black and orange tips to suit varying backgrounds. Better still, in my opinion, are floats which have interchangeable tips and isotope attachment facilities so that varying light conditions can be coped with instantly; the range of floats by Drennan International are probably the finest in their field. Just recently Preston Innovations have introduced a new product which enables temporary change of float tip colour without ruining the float. The product is known as Pro-Paint and represents excellent value for money, particularly as it precludes the need to own two sets of floats with different coloured tips.

Finally, it is important that floats are shotted correctly, with as little of the tip showing above the water as possible. To an extent, conditions will dictate how far you can 'dot a float down', but the less tip that is showing above the water, the more sensitive the arrangement will be.

Float fishing is fine when you are presenting a bait within five or six rod lengths of the bank, but for distance work, legering is far more convenient. Leger bite indicators come in two basic forms, those found on the rod, such as quivertips or swingtips, and those that are separated from it, such as bobbins or monkey climbers and so on. On rivers I use quivertips or, in some cases the rod tip, exclusively. I always carry a variety of tips to cope with varying strengths of flow, my favourites being the push-in variety, and in a range from $\frac{1}{2}$oz to 4oz in $\frac{1}{2}$oz graduations. A properly matched quivertip will adopt a slight bend, but will not bend through to the top of the rod blank itself.

For after-dark fishing, I whip isotopes onto the quiver- or rod tips, using a method that I developed myself (*see* Fig. 1). I much prefer the disposable 'starlight'-type isotope to the 'life-time' models, the former being much brighter and less painful to watch.

Bobbins are my favourite indicators for stillwater legering; they are far more sensitive than their modern-day counterparts and I always insist that my bobbins should be as light as possible. In strong winds or undertows I prefer to use the 'fixed arm' type, since total sensitivity becomes

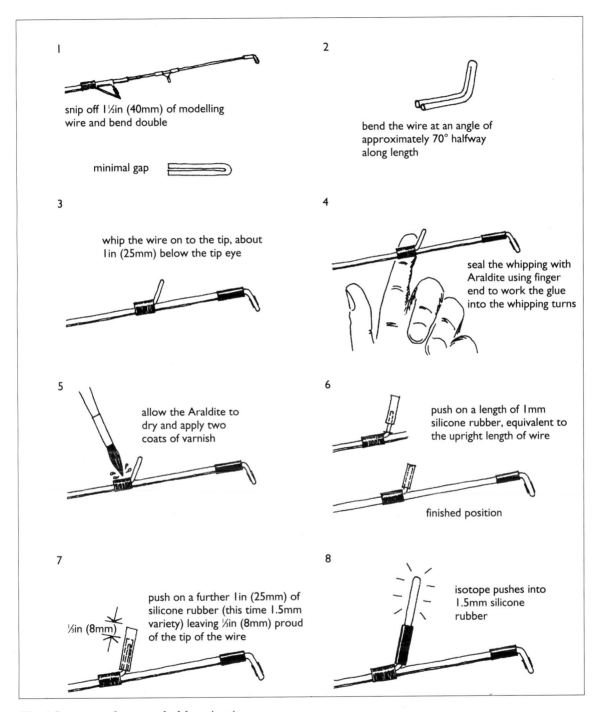

1

snip off 1½in (40mm) of modelling wire and bend double

minimal gap

2

bend the wire at an angle of approximately 70° halfway along length

3

whip the wire on to the tip, about 1in (25mm) below the tip eye

4

seal the whipping with Araldite using finger end to work the glue into the whipping turns

5

allow the Araldite to dry and apply two coats of varnish

6

push on a length of 1mm silicone rubber, equivalent to the upright length of wire

finished position

7

push on a further 1in (25mm) of silicone rubber (this time 1.5mm variety) leaving ⅓in (8mm) proud of the tip of the wire

⅓in (8mm)

8

isotope pushes into 1.5mm silicone rubber

Fig. 1 *Isotope attachment method for quivertips.*

Components: pliers, wire cutters, 1mm silicone rubber, 1.5mm silicone rubber, 1mm copper modelling wire (available from modelling shops), whipping silk, Araldite, varnish and paintbrush.

impossible. My favourites are commercially made models, the 'Swingers' by Fox International, which possess clear bodies and the facility to fit an isotope. When stillwater fishing I will also be relying on the secondary indication of a 'buzzer', so I am happy to use the permanently glowing isotopes.

The 'swing arm' or 'fixed arm'-type indicator is really little more than a stable bobbin. The arm stops the bobbin from swinging in the wind, while a sliding collar weight allows you to adjust the sensitivity of the bobbin simply by moving it up and down the stem. Long-range carp anglers generally tend to use this type of indicator at its heaviest setting so that 'drop back' bites, caused by the fish moving towards the angler, are exaggerated. Indeed, the use of very heavy bobbins to increase the resistance when bolt rig fishing has become very popular. This means that the best fixed arm indicators should allow the line to come cleanly away from the clip and cause minimum friction when a take is under way.

Monkey climbers seem less popular these days, but they are just as effective for carp fishing 'bolt-style' as they ever were. I have never rated them highly for sensitivity because there is always friction between the climber body and the needle on all the models I've tried. However, fished at the top of the needle to show both bolt takes and drop backs, they are perfectly adequate.

The latest generation of bite indicator is the 'tension arm', aptly termed the 'Springer' by Fox International. It is a highly specialized variety used for long-range carp fishing. Basically, this consists of a bobbin that is located on the end of a flexible quivertip stem. Fished under tension, 'Springers' show both 'runs' and 'drop-backs' dramatically and by increasing resistance, enhance the 'bolt' effect. Predator anglers prefer to use the 'drop-off' type indicator that allows the line to pull free when a run gets under way, but drops back when a fish moves towards the bank. Cut-down versions are ideal for perch fishing, while commercial models are produced for catfish, pike and zander.

Finally, it seems all stillwater anglers like the secondary indication of electronic bite alarms, or 'buzzers' as they have become known. Modern versions possess tone, volume and sensitivi-

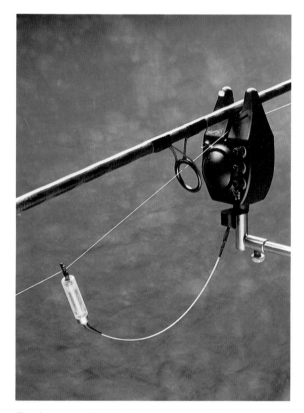

Tension arm – ideal for long-range carp fishing.

ty control to suit the needs of the user. The very latest versions by Fox also possess a remote, cordless, sounder box facility. Purists may scorn their use, but for long-session angling and night fishing they are invaluable. Their major advantages are that they allow anglers time to look for signs of fish, to enjoy their natural surroundings, and get some much-needed sleep at night, without the need to reel in.

LINE AND HOOKLENGTH MATERIALS

In the days before nylon monofilament was invented, anglers used silk, twisted animal hair and a host of other strange materials as fishing line. How times have changed. Or have they? Today, companies like Kryston are once again using braids and twisted materials to construct advanced presentation leader accessories! More of that later.

Mono has certainly improved, and today's nylon lines are built to very precise tolerances with increasingly fine diameter/breaking strain ratios. Low diameter/pre-stretched monos are becoming increasingly popular with anglers trying to stay one step ahead of the fish with advanced presentation. Diameter, however, is but one area in which line has improved, and increased abrasion resistance, improved limpness and decreased visibility have become equally important. For general, all-round applications I prefer the softest, limpest mono available for improved presentation and general 'castability'; my favourite brands are Berkley Trilene XL and Rod Hutchinson's 'Sabreline', both of which are limp, surprisingly abrasion-resistant, and extremely easy to knot.

Harsher applications demand heavier-duty lines, and I prefer Berkley 'Big Game' in breaking strains above 10lb and Trilene 'XT' from 4 to 8lb; both of these lines are extremely abrasion-resistant and yet possess surprisingly low 'memory'. Fluorescent lines are becoming more popular these days, especially for surface and snag fishing when being able to see your line at all times is important. Once again I use a Berkley product, 'Trimax', a superb mono that is highly visible in the air and yet barely visible in water. 'Trimax' is expensive, but it really does offer the best of all worlds, being limp, extremely castable and very abrasion-resistant.

Hooklength materials have also been developed and refined in recent years, to the point in fact that choosing the right one can be difficult. Most of the time I am happy to use nylon because it is relatively cheap, convenient and reliable, but in certain circumstances I will use more recently developed alternatives. Dacron was the first hooklength material to rival monofilament. In recent years it has become more or less redundant because other, superior materials are now available. Dacron's biggest asset is that it is much softer than nylon, but its abrasion resistance is poor.

Braided hooklengths such as Kryston 'Silkworm' and 'Merlin' are superb hooklength materials, being much limper than mono and many times more abrasion resistant. The success of braids has proved that the diameter of leader materials is largely irrelevant; what really counts is limpness, and the superiority of braids can easily be demonstrated by pinching a short length between forefinger and thumb, leaving a few inches proud. Whereas mono will remain upright, braids will 'flop over', giving a graphic illustration of their advanced presentation qualities. Drag them across a sharp surface, however, and you will notice that they are many times more resistant to abrasion than standard mono.

The ultimate in presentation must be 'multistrand', another Kryston development made from multiple fine fibres. Try the forefinger and thumb test, this time holding the material under water: whereas you will find it difficult to detect multistrand, nylon leaves a harsh, almost cable-like impression by comparison. The fibres, though fine, are also surprisingly tough, thus giving increased abrasion resistance. Multistrand is very prone to tangles, however, and to overcome this problem, the 'combi-link' has become popular. This involves knotting together one-third multistrand in proportion with two-thirds of another material, usually 'silkworm' or 'Merlin'. The ratio of the two materials is important, as is using the correct knot, the best one being the four-turn water knot (see Fig. 2a). Indeed, tying the right knot is

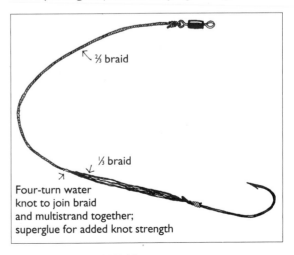

⅔ braid

⅓ braid

Four-turn water
knot to join braid
and multistrand together;
superglue for added knot strength

Fig. 2a The 'Combi-link'.

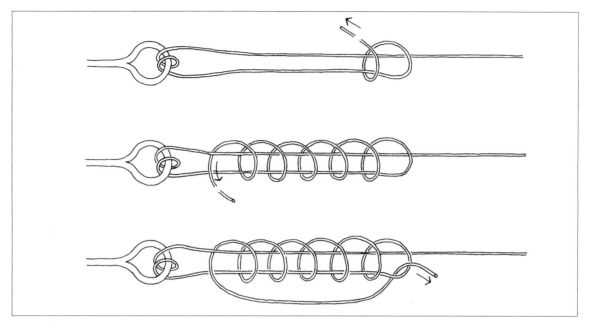

Fig. 2b. *Five-turn grinner knot.*

vital with any type of leader material, but never more so than with braids. Inferior knots such as the blood knot can be termed 'strangulation' knots, where the strangulation effect causes the knot to cut itself; and braids are exceptionally prone to this problem. With the right knot, however, they are incredibly strong, the right knot for swivels and hooks being the five-turn grinner, with the line passed twice through the eye (*see* Fig. 2b).

Popular as braids are these days, I personally still use mono most of the time, my first choice for the hooklengths being Trilene XL. However, for wary, pressured fish, or for snag fishing, I have no hesitation in turning to alternative materials.

SPECIALIST ACCESSORIES

The modern specialist scene has become characterized by the development of a huge range of accessories, rig 'bits' and camping equipment. It would be impossible to cover it all here, so I shall confine my comments to those accessories that I use myself; later I shall discuss the contents of my

tackle boxes, but to begin with let us consider some of the major items.

'Session' angling has become very popular indeed, with anglers spending several days, or even weeks at a time on the water; to do this comfortably you need the right equipment, the most obvious item being a bivvy. Nowadays there are many to choose from, and bivvy design has certainly progressed from the old canvas overwrap. Modern bivvies are aerodynamic, easy to construct and spacious. Stability, strength and water resistance are important too, although these qualities are difficult to evaluate when the bivvy is simply on display in a shop. If you intend to buy a bivvy, spend some time in a friend's first, and ask several anglers for their comments. Personally I like the Fox one-man model or Fox two-man version when space is desirable for longer sessions. For summer fishing when the weather is pleasant I dispense with the bivvy and use a large brolly with storm sides: two models spring to mind, the Fox Ultra 50 and the Nash Oval.

A good bed-chair is essential, and fortunately both Fox International and J.R.C. make a range to suit everyone's pocket. I use the Fox, and I

Tying the five-turn grinner knot (see following page also).

1. *Pass the line or braid through the hook or swivel eye.*

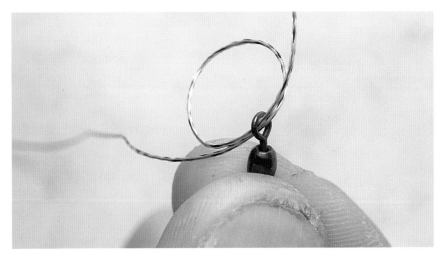

2. *Double back a length of line and trap it between forefinger and thumb.*

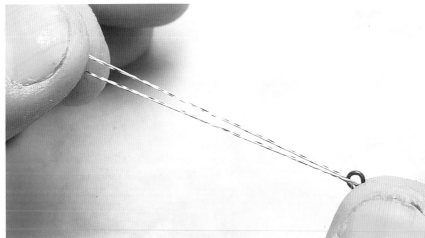

3. *Form a loop with the tag end.*

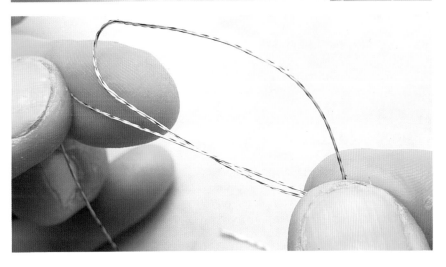

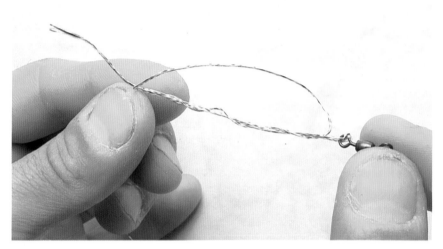

4. *Pass the tag end through the loop five times.*

5. *Pull the tag end to form the knot. Moisten the line and knot with saliva.*

6. *Pull the knot by tugging the mainline, not the tag end. Finish the knot with a small dab of superglue to prevent strangulation.*

always buy the top-of-the-range model – expense is no object when it comes to getting a good night's sleep! When I buy a bed-chair I assess it for strength, comfort and weight, and the Fox models are superb in all three departments.

For shorter sessions a 'low chair' is very useful. Sometimes, when stalking, I will sit on my unhooking mat, but when spending any length of time in a single swim, I'll take the chair. Again I use Fox; the latest models combine strength with comfort, and very importantly, they are light enough to carry long distances without causing fatigue. The adjustable legs are a valuable feature, and ideal for coping with uneven banks.

The next item to highlight is simple, relatively cheap, but to my mind absolutely indispensable: the Fox carp pillow, a fur-covered pillow with velcro straps for attachment to a bed-chair. Since purchasing this luxury item, all night sessions have become infinitely more tolerable!

Sleeping bags are particularly important in the winter months. Manufacturers tend to overrate them, in my opinion, the minus 30°C-rated bag being decidedly chilly when the temperature is minus 10°C, and so on. For summer and autumn I tend to use the minus 30°C version, while in winter I prefer the extra warmth of a minus 50°C! Once again, Fox International specialize in this type of product.

Thankfully, fish safety is becoming increasingly important these days, and the sales of unhooking mats, slings and sacks are soaring. Unhooking mats are vital when it comes to dealing with big fish. For UK and Continental use I like the Fox Classic Mat; as well as adequate padding, it also possesses carrying handles, velcroed sides to stop the fish slipping out when being transported to the water, and it floats! Buoyant unhooking mats can be 'floated' over deeper water, where you can then sink the front of the mat with your hand, thus allowing water to flood over both mat and fish. For retaining fish over a short period of time I always carry a couple of sacks, usually the largest models available to allow the fish maximum room. Look for a long, strong retrieving cord and a soft reliable mesh.

Another conservation-minded product that is enjoying wide European success is Kryston

'Klin-ik', a treatment that can be applied to hook-marks or any other damaged area of the fish's body. 'Klin-ik' speeds up the healing process and prevents infection setting in; its success is welcome news, and an indication of the more caring attitude that modern anglers are developing.

Moving on to the contents of my rucksack, I always carry a few marker floats and some home-made 'spods', torpedo-shaped devices that can be used for depositing particles at range. Ground pins for pegging down my bivvy or brolly will also be present, the best to my mind being the Fox 'T-peg' variety; these are extremely strong with corkscrew shafts and hard, durable handles for easy pegging out and removal. In one of the side pockets there will be a couple of spare bait droppers, made by Thamesly. I will also carry these in my stalker bag, since most summer trips will usually involve pre-baiting with hempseed.

When carp fishing, I will also be sure to have a cobra throwing stick for baiting with boilies at range. A stick is faster than a 'catty' for putting out any large amounts of bait, it is surprisingly accurate, and is capable of delivering a boilie in excess of 80yds (75m). Most of the time though, and especially at short to medium range, I will use a catapult and I only ever use one variety for loose feed, whether I'm firing out tiny particles such as hemp or large, dense baits such as boilies. My favourite 'pult' is made by Middy and consists of a U-shaped nylon/plastic frame, strong green elastic and an open construction mesh cup at the rear. Its only fault, like all other catapults, is the short life of the elastic, but for sheer accuracy and tight grouping of multiple baits it can't be beaten.

Now the inside compartments of the rucksack, and depending on the style of fishing I'm involved in, I will choose from one of three tackle boxes or a stalker pouch (more of this later). I have a box for carp, another for pike/perch, and one for general use, and rather than itemize the contents of each, I will confine my comments to some of the most frequently used items. Prominent in all three boxes is superglue. However did we get by without it? It can be used for repairing tackle, touching up knots, stiffening braid and sealing leaking accessories such as floats; it can even be used for fixing some baits to the hook, Chum mixer for example.

Swivels and link swivels are also common to each style of angling. I prefer swivels in sizes 7–10; as for links, I am less bothered about strength than the swivel proper, since the link isn't influential on whether I land or lose the fish. Being easy to use is my prime requirement, and I prefer the 'snaplock' type. Lure anglers, however, are in a different position since snaplinks are frequently used to allow rapid lure changes. Accordingly, the strongest links available are essential, and in this case I have no hesitation in recommending the Berkley Crosslok.

Beads are also a common item, and I use a mixture of hard beads (made by Gold Label) if I want the beads to slide on the line, and rubber shock beads (made by Fox) for knot protection. Rubber beads sit over the knot at the swivel and provide superb shock absorption, thus minimizing the risk of the knot weakening during a protracted fight.

One of the best items of tackle I have seen for years is the John Roberts low resistance leger ring; not too expensive but highly functional; it is the only attachment I now use for running leads. It has a large-bore internal ring and is made of hard nylon for minimum friction; there is a hole for the attachment of a swivel link, making it ideal for feeders and bombs of all varieties.

This brings us to leads: for general use, I prefer good old-fashioned Arlesey bombs in a range from ⅙oz through to 2oz. They are aerodynamic and very effective, their classic shape being as useful today as when they were invented by the late Richard Walker over thirty years ago. For very light work, especially on rivers, I always carry a few swanshot and I am happy to use as many as five on a light link before I put the bomb on. Light Arlesey bombs will cast further than shot, however, and I use them more frequently on stillwaters.

Floodwater fishing demands the use of heavier leads, and I like to carry a few flat leads since they hold position better in pacey currents than bombs; they are particularly effective for winter barbel fishing.

For carp fishing these days I use 'in-line' leads almost exclusively, and my favourites are made by that great and highly underrated carp angler, Dennis McFetrich. These are revolutionary, consisting of a superbly aerodynamic bomb which has 0.7mm semi-stiff tubing running through the body. At the bottom of the lead a rubber sleeve is bored out at both ends to take the tubing and a swivel attachment that has been specially designed not to 'lock up' – vital in the event of a 'crack-off' above the lead. The whole arrangement sits inside the bottom of the lead, meaning that tangles are absolutely minimal. All in all these leads are superbly functional, being well constructed, aerodynamic, with no rough edges and neatly finished.

Occasionally I use helicopter rigs, and for this style of fishing I employ a 'dumpy' pear-shaped lead because of its low centre of gravity (a factor that maximizes resistance to a taking fish, thus enhancing the 'bolt' effect). You might also like to consider 'tadpole' leads, another of Dennis McFetrich's inventions comprising a round lead with a very low centre of gravity, and special rubber attachments for achieving the helicopter effect. Regarding the helicopter rig, I always make mine up by using the Fox 'Helicopter rig'; this is a nice, straightforward, ready-made helicopter rig that utilizes the 'semi-fixed' principle, allowing the lead to break free of the rig in the event of a crack-off. This precludes fish having to tow around heavy leads if they subsequently pick up the bait.

Swimfeeders are a great alternative to legers, not only providing casting and holding weight, but also the option of achieving a tight carpet of loose feed in the vicinity of your hookbait. I use both varieties, the 'block-end' for small particles and maggots or casters in flowing water, and open-ended feeders which can be 'plugged' with groundbait for stillwater work. Drennan International produce a comprehensive range of feeders, my favourite being the feeder link (for light to medium block-end work), the oval-shaped block-end (for heavy work in major rivers), and the mini feeder (for block end work in very cold conditions). For open-end styles I like the cage-type feeders which have a very open construction and allow maximum water ingress. Nowadays the 'cages' are made of hard nylon/plastic, a positive development which helps to avoid distortion of the feeder when it is stored. In exceptionally heavy flows, clip-on weights or 'ski leads' can be used to ensure that the feeder holds bottom.

For attaching boilies and a host of other baits to hairs I use baiting needles and boilie stops; my favourites respectively are the Solar Tackle needle (croquet-hoop style) and the Drennan Boilie Stop. When buying a baiting needle make sure that it does not get progressively thicker towards the handle, since this will create a larger hole than necessary when large or multiple baits are being used.

Another item that I find myself using on a lot of fishing trips is a sliding rubber float stop. Originally these were sold for match style and pleasure fishing, for use as an alternative to a stop knot on the line. I like to deploy them for this purpose, but I also frequently use them in place of a stop knot on my hooklength; modern rig putties such as Fox 'Supa-weight' hold on to the line more easily if you give them something to 'bite' on. Sliding float stops come ready stored on convenient wire loops, and they are small and neat enough not to interfere if you decide to remove the putty half-way through a session.

I must add that 'Supa-weight' is the rig putty that I use. Its manufacturers, Fox, have applied a great deal of thought to producing the most durable putty on the market: it won't fly off the line easily, and its shelf life appears to be indefinite. And it *is* very heavy, being extremely dense for its size! Kryston Products produce a liquid putty called 'Magma', ideal for fine tuning terminal rigs. 'Magma' can be squeezed from the tube in which it is conveniently stored, to place tiny blobs of liquid onto your hooklength; after a short period these blobs will dry, leaving your hooklength nicely treated with several 'mini' weights to keep it flat on the bottom.

'Hawser' rig resin, also by Kryston, is a product that I use for permanently stiffening braids. When in a hurry I will use superglue, but to do the job properly I will use 'Hawser'. An inspection of my

various boxes the other day revealed that I seem to be sitting on a veritable EC 'mountain' of rig and silicone tube. I carry both the soft and stiff versions for a variety of uses, and in a range of sizes from 0.5 to 3.0mm. The various rig illustrations contained later in the book will demonstrate the multitude of uses I put it to.

For predator fishing I always like to carry some specialist items. First and foremost among these is wire for making traces: anyone who contemplates fishing for pike without wire is not fit to be called an angler. I use Berkley Steel Strand in 20lb breaking strain, this being the most reliable and easy-to-use wire that I know; it twists easily but does not kink badly, and gives a nice, natural presentation. A good pair of forceps is also essential and I carry a variety of sizes to suit the species I'm after, from short 6in (15cm) models for barbel and chub to 18in (46cm) models for pike. A 'deep throat' pike disgorger is also a must, particularly if the fish is very deep hooked. Full instructions on how to use the 'deep throat' are included with the item, which once again is the brainchild of that master of the 'neat' idea, John Roberts.

Finally as part of my standard pike-unhooking equipment, I also carry a pair of wire cutters with long handles in case, disaster of disasters, I have to cut the trace as close to the hooks as possible. To be honest, this has never happened to me (I always strike runs early) but it *can* happen, even to the most caring angler, so it pays to be prepared.

My collection of pike floats seems to increase by the year. For livebaiting I use the cigar-shaped variety with an internal central bore, while for deadbait fishing on stillwaters I prefer the weighted, bottom-end-only variety, known as pencil floats. Sunken floats are carried, too, and I use both round and cigar-shaped 'E.T.' polyballs in a variety of sizes for pike as well as perch. No pike float collection would be complete without an E.T. drifter float, large, varied floats for drifting out live- and dead-baits at range. I use mine in conjunction with another E.T. product, the 'Autogreaser', a neat little device that fits into one of the rod rings and automatically greases the line.

Most of the time for piking I use deadbaits, and a range of 'floater' sticks to insert into the bait are useful if you want to 'pop it up' or allow it to settle softly on the weed. Basically they are small, pointed balsa spikes with an eye at the thick end for the attachment of some light line so that the stick can be retrieved when unhooking the pike.

I rarely use Arlesey bombs for pike, preferring instead lightweight barrel leads, drilled bullets or even swanshot for casting weight. Sometimes, though, I will attach a heavy lead to a 'pike-safe' paternoster boom when livebaiting; these superb items of tackle prevent tangles and stop the pike from biting through the mainline above the wire trace if it lunges for the bait and misses!

Later in this book Steve Burke discusses fish finders more fully, so for the time being, suffice it to say that I own one for depth and feature finding in large waters and when trolling for pike. Trolling is an exciting method of fishing, and especially useful for catching giant pike on trout reservoirs.

Other useful items of tackle include boat rod-rests, a drogue for drifting, and a livebait cage. Finally, rather than cart a heavy, cumbersome tackle box around with me, whenever possible I will take my stalker bag and a (Gold Label) rig pouch. A surprising amount of gear can be stored in this superb fold-over pouch, including leads, hooks, putty, spare line, braids, shot, floaters, knives, beads and swivels.

Floater fishing equipment is included as standard. Gold Label floater floats are the best floater/controllers I have ever used, and I carry the full range, from the 'mini' to the 'Jumbo'. The large sight bob is visible from extreme range; when used in conjunction with line grease, it also helps to keep the line on the surface, enabling a good, clean strike to be made. The stem and body allow the controller to be precisely weighted with brass, making the floater superbly castable.

I fix mine to the top of my connecting swivel (which also accepts the hooklength) with another useful item, the tulip bead. Tulip beads allow leads (and controllers) to be attached semi-fixed style to the top eye of a size 7–10 swivel. A swivel link connects the lead or controller to the tulip bead, while the spigot end of the bead is made for accepting 2mm semi-stiff or silicone tubing to prevent tangles.

Finally, the 'bait band' is a recent concept that allows chum mixer to be attached to the back of a hook with minimum fuss. The band is made from hard rubber which grips the mixer very tightly, especially as it begins to expand in the water. A small hole located on a tab allows the band to be attracted to the shank, keeping the mixer free of the hook and preventing the bait from masking its point. As you would expect with such a 'neat' concept, John Roberts is once again the inventor.

Doubtless, there are a thousand other items that should have been included, but that is the beauty of modern, specialist angling: the wealth of equipment to enhance and improve your fishing. Long may it continue!

HOOKS

It has been said that a good hook is singly more important than any other item of tackle, since it is the direct point of contact with your quarry. Bearing this comment in mind, it is hardly surprising that hook designs have advanced significantly in recent years. One of the most notable advances has been chemical sharpening, a process that produces needle-sharp points, previously unattainable even with 'retouching'. Let me state here and now though, that I am very wary when it comes to chemically sharpened patterns, especially in 'hit-and-hold' or snag fishing situations. On a number of occasions I have witnessed some horrendous examples of tearing when fish have been held hard on hooks of this type. A couple of years ago I was regularly losing good barbel in a very snaggy swim because of hook-hold failure – until, that is, I changed to hook patterns. Of equal concern is the damage that this type of hook causes to a fish's mouth, so choose carefully.

As an all-rounder I use a variety of hook shapes and sizes according to the species and the prevailing conditions. Being a big fish angler, I rarely use fine wire patterns, preferring instead medium- to heavy-forged wire models. In the smaller sizes I like to use spade ends since I believe they give a superior presentation. Generally speaking, this is a situation in which I am happy to use the chemically sharpened variety, especially in sizes 14–20. My favourites are the Drennan 'Super-spade' and the Drennan 'Carbon Feeder'; both of these patterns have a short shank and beaked point to produce a very good hook-hold indeed, and I have never known one to break.

The hook which most frequently comes out of my tackle box in sizes 4–12 is the 'Jack Hilton' pattern made by Partridge of Redditch, a straight-forward, no-nonsense eyed hook designed around a tested pattern that delivers strength and reliability. I have yet to see one open out, and 'hook pulls' are minimal.

When carp fishing I use a variety of hook designs, depending on the rig that I am using. In open water I like the eyed owners or the Fox series two, both of which are short-shanked hooks. They are wickedly sharp, going in like no other hooks that I know, but I am reluctant to use them in weedy water because of the tearing problem. Pop-up baits are best suited to an out-turned eye, in other words one that is bent away from the point. The best hook that I have found for this purpose is the Rod Hutchinson 'Perfection' rig hook; pop-ups presented on this hook sit high in the water with the hook at a slight angle directly underneath them.

For carp fishing generally I prefer the Fox series one, a hook with an in-turned eye and one which, despite its extreme sharpness, produces a good hook-hold. When in very snaggy situations I use the strongest type that I can get away with; at the moment this is the Fox series 3 hook, a non-chemically sharpened model that won't let you down.

In recent years anglers have discovered that by changing the shape of the hook, they can outwit those ultra-wary fish that have developed hook ejection into an art form. The most controversial example has been the 'bent hook': these always 'flip over' when dragged across a fish's lower lip, digging in every time, but because they are very sharp, they are also capable of causing wicked damage to a carp's mouth, particularly as they

produce a 'corkscrew' effect under pressure. However, versions of the 'safe' bent hook have recently been developed, one of the most popular being the Jim Gibbinson 'line aligner', which utilizes rig tubing to extend the shank of the hook. The hook length emerges from the side of the tube, not the end, thus creating a bent hook effect except when pressure is applied, whereupon the arrangement straightens out. The same effect can be achieved by stiffening perhaps half an inch of the leader, directly above the hook eye, with superglue.

Nowadays I use a technique of attacking carp hooks known as 'snelling'. This superb method was demonstrated to me by Dave Chilton of Kryston. Instead of being tied on, the hook is 'whipped', the braid emerging from the back of the shank, an effect that creates a bent hook effect in its own right. Add glue to the first ¼in (6mm) of braid too, and the hook flips over every time. Its further advantages are that it is easy to tie, does not involve fiddling around with rig tube, and allows the angler to get the hairlength right with the minimum of fuss, every time. It is a superb arrangement, incredibly strong and it has never let me down. The ideal hook to use with the 'snelling' technique is the Fox series one with its in-turned eye, while on barbless-hook-only fisheries I will use the Terry Eustace 'Super Strong'.

NIGHT FISHING ACCESSORIES

Night fishing is becoming increasingly popular with specialist anglers. I am referring here to the sort of session that means staying on for a few hours after dark, not long session fishing which involves staying for a couple of weeks after dark! As long as you don't mind sitting on your own on a deserted river bank in pitch blackness, and the sounds of the night hold no fear for you, night fishing can be very productive, especially the first hour or two into darkness. However, this is certainly not something that youngsters should contemplate doing on their own, as the bankside can be a dangerous place at night time. And regardless of age, always make sure that someone knows where you are, just in case of emergencies. So, assuming that you have followed

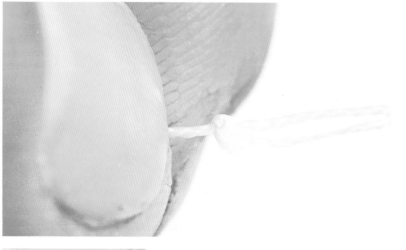

The knotless knot.

1. Tie a loop into the end of your hooklength (this will form the hair).

2. Pass the free end through the eye of the hook twice. Always pass the line through from the shank toward the point side.

3. Adjust the hair along the shank until it is the correct length.

4. *Trap the hair against the hook shank and wind the free end down, whipping over the hair in the process.*

5. *Stop whipping when you reach a position in line with the point of the hook.*

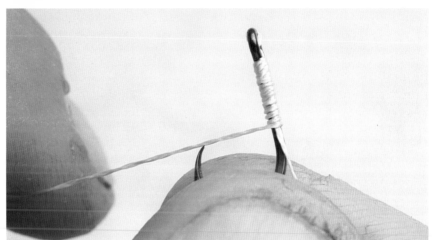

6. *Now pass the free end back through the eye of the hook, from the outside to the inside of the hook.*

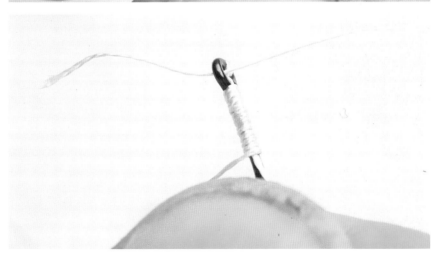

7. Finish the whipping off with superglue. Add a touch of glue to the braid.

the basic rules, let's take a look at the type of equipment required for a successful night session.

Torches

Give some thought to the type(s) of torch that you carry. I like small, thin torches which can be clamped comfortably between my teeth, and for this purpose, the mini-maglite type seems the best. Other anglers swear by the headlamp variety which allows totally 'hands free' fishing. I like to carry at least two torches when I am fishing, along with spare batteries, a small, fairly dim torch for rebaiting and unhooking fish, and a more powerful model which will help me find my way back to the car. Avoid floodlight-type torches that illuminate the bankside when you are fishing, and keep the torchlight off the water!

Tilley lamps should be avoided at all costs: they are anti-social, and are likely to cut down your chances of success by half. Whenever I *see* an angler with a Tilley lamp I cringe – although you can usually *hear* this sort first.

Isotopes

To detect bites at night, some form of isotope is a must unless you are prepared to touch leger. I prefer the Drennan 'Starlights' as these are much brighter than the permanently glowing variety; insert them onto quivertips and into floats and you can carry on fishing with a greatly reduced risk of eye strain. Most bite indicators have a slot for inserting isotopes, but quivertips will have to be adapted by whipping on a piece of silicone tubing an inch or so from the end of the rod. For float fishing after dark, Peter Drennan's superb range of crystallite floats are made with interchangeable bodies and tips, and are also designed to house one of his starlights for after-dark work; this is especially useful since it means you don't have to break down a successful rig and replace it with a 'special' night float.

Mobile Phone

When fishing on your own after dark the chances of breaking a limb, getting locked in somewhere or getting the car stuck are much greater than in daylight, the added problem being that other people are unlikely to be around to help you. Nowadays I always carry a mobile phone just in case of emergencies, and I recommend you use a model that is neat and compact so that you hardly know you're carrying it. Battery life is important and you should be able to find a make that lasts at least nine hours. The other advantage of a mobile phone is that if you catch a real 'biggie', you can call a friend out to photograph it.

Clothing

Taking the right clothes on a night fishing trip is essential, because even in summer the hours after dark can be decidedly chilly. In the warmer months I usually carry an extra sweatshirt and a

As night falls, there is an early success.

Rod Hutchinson bib and brace which is warm, waterproof and allows exceptional freedom of movement. I also carry a 'Hutchie' waterproof jacket in case of rain. In winter a good pair of thermal boots and one of the latest one-piece suits are essential. At the moment I use the Leslies of Luton 'minus 40' one-piece and I have never been cold in it, but superb outfits are also made by Rod Hutchinson, Wychwood and Fox International. In the pockets of my one-piece a pair of neoprene 'fingerless' gloves are permanently stored away, too, for those nights when the frost really cracks down.

Night Fishing Tips

1. Always set up during daylight unless you know the river bank very well.
2. Never night fish on your own if you are not a strong swimmer.
3. Lay your tackle out neatly around you so that everything comes to hand easily.
4. Avoid using a torch whenever possible so that your eyes become accustomed to the dark.
5. When you do use the torch, do not shine it on the water, and make sure it is a relatively dim one.
6. Take plenty of warm clothes (even summer nights can be cold), a warm drink, and plenty to eat.

3 THE BAIT SCENE

It was inevitable that fishing baits would undergo something of a revolution when specialist angling started to become popular in the 1950s and 60s. The two biggest developments in bait have been centred around carp fishing, specifically in the form of particles and boilies. Surprisingly, however, baits for species other than carp have changed very little in many respects, and it is only in recent years that anglers like myself have attempted to apply carp bait technology to baits in general.

NATURAL BAITS

Natural baits have always been effective fish catchers, primarily because fish are educated into eating naturally occurring food items from the moment that they are born. Natural baits require no pre-baiting, they are instantly accepted and rarely invoke fear in fish. No wonder they are still among the best baits that a big fish angler can use.

Worms are probably the most basic bait of them all, and there isn't a popular British coarse fish that swims that will refuse a well presented *lobworm*. Wherever possible I like to use lobworms in bunches on a big hook, usually a no 4 or a no 6, to create a 'Medusa's head' effect. Other types of worm include the *redworm*, a small lively variety that can be found in compost heaps. 'Reds' are particularly effective when fished over particles, particularly hemp, on a range of hook sizes from a no 16 for a single worm to a no 10 for a bunch of three or four. *Brandlings* are another species of worm found in compost heaps, easily identified because of a

Lobworm, perhaps the greatest fishing bait of all time, and prawns, a great change bait for chub, tench, carp and barbel.

series of characteristic yellow bands located around their body. Personally I don't rate them very highly and regard 'reds' as being far superior. It is important to remember that the major attraction of worms lies in their lively, wriggling action, and it is vital to present them as naturally as possible. For this reason I always hook them only once, usually about a third of the way down their body from the head. Nipping the tail off worms will increase their appeal, since this allows the natural, attractive juices of the worm to escape.

Slugs are another superb natural bait, particularly for chub. Unpleasant they may be, but hooking a freshly collected big, black 'slurper' on a size 4 and freelining it down the current can provoke ferocious bites from old 'rubber lips'. Being dense, slugs rarely require additional casting weight, and they are durable too – just nick the hook into the slug's skin, either in its back or tail, and you will get plenty of casts from it.

Crayfish used to be a very popular chub and barbel bait, and still would be if they were obtainable. Nowadays, however, true British 'crays' are becoming very rare, a sure sign of the unhealthy state of many of our rivers (crayfish thrive in clean water). The American signal crayfish is on the increase in the UK, but these are generally far too big to use with confidence.

One of my favourite naturals is the *prawn*. Peeled prawns from the supermarket are a tremendous bait for chub, barbel, tench, carp, bream and perch. Being white, they are highly visible and probably the best 'sight' fishing bait (whereby the angler watches the bait itself for bite indication) available, next to bread. I have always found prawns to be instant, wherever I have used them, and they are particularly deadly when fished over a bed of hemp.

When discussing natural baits, what could be more natural than a *live* or *dead fish*? It is a well known fact that pike, perch, zander and catfish enjoy fish baits, but other species will accept them with relish, too; chub and barbel in particular are highly susceptible to small natural deadbaits like gudgeon and minnows.

It would be impossible to list every natural bait here that has caught fish, and moths, grasshoppers, even bees dapped on the surface have tempted many a chub, for example.

STANDARD BAITS

There are certain baits that fall outside the 'natural' category that have nonetheless stood the test of time. These are bread in the form of both crust and flake, luncheon meat, cheese, and maggots and casters (which could, arguably, fall into the particle category).

Bread is a tremendous bait: chub, roach, dace, rudd, barbel, tench, carp and bream all love it. It has two major benefits, namely colour and buoyancy; and although it smells fairly bland to us, I have no doubt that fish can pick up its aroma very easily, judging by the results I have enjoyed with bread after dark. For presenting a bait at the bottom the soft flake pulled from the inside of a fresh loaf is superb, and by leaving the bread rough and 'fluffy', you will enjoy more takes. When hooking flake, pinch it lightly around the hook shank, and avoid 'over-squeezing' it so that it appears as natural as possible.

Bread crust is an excellent bait to present off the bottom, popped up by one or several inches; like this it absolutely stares fish in the face – they can't miss it, and they rarely refuse it. Being very buoyant, it is also highly manoeuvrable, especially in a lively current, thus allowing your hook to be worked into inviting and normally inaccessible nooks and crannies. Crust is also a tremendous surface offering for carp, rudd and chub: fished on a greased line, it is quite heavy enough, after a 'dunking', to be cast without the need for additional weight on the line.

One of bread's great advantages is its flexibility: it can be used on a variety of hook sizes, from a tiny pinch of flake on a size 14 to a great big chunk on a size 2.

Luncheon meat is truly one of the all-time 'great' big fish baits, and barbel, chub, carp and tench simply love it. It is convenient too, and can be used straight from the tin, either cut into

Luncheon meat and cheese paste – great baits that have earned 'classic' status.

cubes or torn off in chunks. Most anglers prefer the 'cube' method but when your quarry becomes wary, changing the shape of the bait works wonders. I either tear mine into chunks, or punch out 'tubes' of meat with an apple corer; these can then be diced into bite-sized 'cylinders'. For very wary fish, luncheon meat or sausage meat *paste* can be made by kneading the meat together with breadcrumbs or groundbait. Try adding a dollop of Marmite to spice it up. Like other standard baits, luncheon meat can be presented on a variety of hooks, from a large cube, chunk or lump of paste on a size 4, to a tiny cube on a size 12 to fool shy-biting fish. The main point to remember when hooking meat is to leave the hookpoint exposed so that it can penetrate the fish's mouth without being impeded by any lumps of fat or gristle.

Cheese is another all-time great bait, a favourite with chub, barbel, carp, roach and tench. It can be used straight from the packet or block in its natural form, although it is far more effective as a paste (natural cheese hardens in cold water) and the addition of some Danish pastry mix in a two-thirds cheese to one-third pastry ratio will avoid this problem. I like to dye my cheese paste (usually red) by adding a teaspoon of powdered carp dye; also half a teaspoon of synthetic cheese flavour per pound of paste will compensate for the diluting effect of the pastry. Try fishing cheese paste on a limited range of hooks from sizes 4 down to 10 according to the species you are after.

Finally, this section cannot end without a mention of *maggots* and *casters*. Their major drawback is that they are not selective and are prone to the attentions of nuisance fish, but use them on a venue which contains mostly big fish, and they are deadly. Even in waters with mixed populations, regular feeding with maggots or casters is virtually guaranteed to pull the big fish in; eventually the specimens will establish dominance, and a 'big hit' of big fish could be on the cards. They are excellent too, as a loosefeed over which to fish a bigger bait. One of the most deadly baits that I know is a 'Medusa's head' of lively, wriggling maggots: simply superglue live maggots (by the 'fat' end) to a cork ball and fish them a few inches off the bottom on a hair rig. This method has accounted for a large number of winter carp in particular, and seems to score heavily on 'curiosity' value alone.

ARTIFICIALS   by Steve Burke

Lure fishing in the UK is currently undergoing a revival – indeed it's true to say that it has probably never been as popular as it is today. It doesn't appeal to everyone, but as you're reading this piece I'll assume you're already hooked or interested in having a go!

If I had to use one word to describe lure fishing, it's 'fun'! Unlike sitting behind a set of bite alarms, you're always active and mobile. You'll also cover a lot of water, and therefore fish, and you can often induce even an inactive fish to hit a lure. Additionally, as you're hunting the fish rather than trapping them, even very short sessions are viable.

Tackle

If pike are present, the most important item of tackle is a wire trace. Failure to use wire will sooner or later mean another dead pike. Also make sure that your snap or snap swivel has a rounded U-shape end rather than the common V-shape as the lure can then move freely. Line strength should be sufficient to avoid leaving a lure in the fish, which means at least 10lb breaking strain if pike are present and heavier in snaggy conditions.

Reels are a matter of personal choice, mine being a fixed spool that I'm totally familiar with and which, unlike a multiplier, can cast all weights of lure including the lightest. However, avoid reels with very high gear ratios as they make slow retrieves difficult.

The correct choice of lure rod is very important and ideally you need a selection. For surface lures, especially jerkbaits, you'll need a short rod with a stiff tip to work the lure properly. Otherwise, whilst power in the butt is needed, a soft, sensitive tip is vital to show tentative takes. Indeed, American divers have watched up to fifteen takes in one retrieve without the anglers being aware of anything at all! For this reason I often use my own 'Quiverspin', which was developed from a 2¼lb test curve rod and which incorporates a special quivertip to show the difference between weed, the bottom and the tiniest of takes. On occasion even double-figure pike will move the quivertip just ½in (12mm)! The tip also enables a wider variety of different weight lures to be cast, but generally you'll need a rod of approximately 1lb test curve for every 1oz you'll be casting. I prefer a long rod of 9 to 10½ft, especially for bank fishing, where long casting and also keeping well back out of sight may be required.

Because lure fishing is so mobile you need to travel light. A landing net is, of course, essential, but make sure it's of a wide mesh design to avoid hooks tangling. An unhooking mat (mine has a shoulder strap and doubles up as a weigh sling) will protect your catch, and also you when sitting or kneeling. For short sessions, everything else, including a selection of lures, goes in the pockets of my fly fishing waistcoat, whilst for a longer trip I'll also take a Flambeau box with a carrying strap containing extra lures plus food and drink.

Types of Lure

Shortage of space means that I can only scratch the surface of this fascinating subject. For a more comprehensive classification I would recommend another Crowood Press book, *The Encyclopaedia of Lure Fishing*, which contains details of many of the lures currently available on the UK market. The authors are Chris and Sue Harris who also run Lures Direct – their catalogue is superb and well worth getting hold of.

Plugs

These fall into three types: surface plugs, floating divers and sinkers. An explosive take on a surface lure is one of *the* most exciting moments in angling – I defy anyone to remain calm in these circumstances! Surface lures tend to be best in summer, particularly early and late in the day. The secret is not to be in a hurry to start the retrieve or to recast. Indeed, each cast should ideally take several minutes.

Floating divers are probably the most versatile of lures, particularly in snaggy areas when you can retrieve them just above, say, a submerged weedbed. They run to a set maximum depth dependent on their design (usually the larger and more horizontal the lip, the deeper the plug will dive) and thus you'll need a selection to cover a range of depths. There are several types of floating divers, each with different actions. In general slim plugs have a more realistic action, whilst fat ones put out more of a throb. The strongest action of all comes from the banana-shaped plugs, which are excellent 'search' lures for large expanses of water.

Sinking plugs are useful in deep water or confined spaces and are either sinking versions of floating divers or else 'vibrators', which I find are especially useful when the fish are well on the feed.

Spoons

Possibly the oldest type of lure but still extremely successful, spoons come in all shapes and sizes. Those made from heavy-gauge metal can be cast a long way and sink quickly, whilst the thinner ones tend to have better actions and allow slower retrieves. Rather than retrieving at a constant rate, spoons are invariably most successful when fished erratically, and in fact many takes occur 'on the drop'.

Weedless spoons, which have a single rigid hook protected by a weedguard, are not used to any great extent in the UK, possibly because only small ones are freely available. However, I find them devastatingly successful, especially when they are fitted with a plastic tail, which increases the action and further protects the hook from snagging.

Spinners

Often considered beginners' baits, spinners catch big fish too – witness Gareth Edward's former record from Llandegfedd! Larger models are very successful for US muskies, a bigger cousin of our pike, and are now becoming available over here. These often incorporate a bucktail dressing, which lessens the chance of line twist and stops the spinner sinking too quickly. Otherwise, unless you're using a special design such as a 'weight-forward' spinner (typified by the classic Voblex), you'll be well advised to use a ball-bearing swivel and anti-kink vane to combat line twist.

Spinnerbaits

These are nicknamed 'flying coathangers', having one or more spinner blades on one arm and a weighted hook on the other, usually dressed with a rubber skirt. Despite looking nothing like food, they certainly catch fish, and are particularly useful in snaggy areas as they rarely get caught up.

Choose a single-bladed model to fish deep, a twin-bladed design to fish shallow, and one with propeller-shaped blades to retrieve at high speed on the surface. If necessary, replace the swivel with a ball-bearing version so that the blade spins even at very low speeds. Unless the arms meet in a loop you may also need to add a piece of silicone rubber at this point to stop your trace sliding down the arms.

Plastic Worms

These are particularly productive for the smaller species, but pike love them too! Especially in cold conditions they'll often outfish conventional lures as they can be worked extremely slowly. They can also be made almost totally weedless by twisting the hook and inserting it back into the worm. However, as with all weedless lures, you'll have to strike harder, and even then you'll miss more takes than normal. Finally, I've had most success fishing plastic worms sink and draw with a shot right next to the hook.

Colour

Here there is much disagreement with many authorities offering completely opposing advice. My own depends on whether you're trying to *imitate* natural prey or *attract* by flash. When imitating with, for example, a plug, I use light colours in bright conditions and vice versa. Conversely, when using a metallic spinner or spoon I'll do the opposite, choosing a dull finish when it's bright and so on.

Fluorescent colours are useful in murky water, especially if they're matched to the colour of the water. For instance, fluorescent green shows up better than any other colour when the water is stained green by algae. Finally, at night when the lure is silhouetted against the sky I find black much the best bet.

Method

The three most important factors in lure fishing can be remembered by the initials LSD, which stand for location, speed and depth (of which location is dealt with elsewhere).

Speed

As a guide, the higher the water temperature the higher the speed of retrieve needed, down to a mere crawl in winter when baits will often outfish lures anyway. Different lures, especially plugs, work best at different speeds but beginners invariably retrieve too quickly. The best type of retrieve will vary from day to day; sometimes a constant speed is best, but often stopping and starting, which better imitates a disabled fish, is more productive, especially for pike.

Depth

This is where even experienced bait anglers are most likely to go wrong, invariably fishing much too shallow – even though they wouldn't dream of fishing a bait way above deep-lying fish! Whilst fish may be at various depths, those willing to feed are often in a well-defined depth band. This is particularly so with perch, whose swim bladder arrangement means that they can't sustain rapid depth changes. However, whatever the quarry, it's important to ascertain the optimum depth to fish. This can quickly be done with lures simply by changing a floating plug to one which dives to a different depth, or with a sinking lure using the 'countdown' method. With this you count to a progressively higher or lower number as the lure sinks before beginning the retrieve.

Trolling

Undoubtedly the most neglected lure fishing method, trolling can be devastatingly successful where allowed. Its great advantage over casting is that the lure spends far more time at the taking depth. To make the lure move erratically you can steer an S-shaped course, or, often even better, allow the lure to bounce on and off the bottom. Floating plugs with big lips are best for this as they rarely get snagged, and also, unlike sinking lures, you can keep them at the right depth regardless of the speed of the boat. An electric outboard will enable you to hold the rod, and as relatively few fish hook themselves, especially at low speed, will much improve your catches.

Attitude

Each trip will bring a different combination of conditions and the key is to establish the successful pattern(s) of the day regarding where, how and which lure you fish. I have a motto 'if at first you don't succeed, try something *different*'. So don't fall into the rut of mechanically plugging away with the same old lure, otherwise your concentration will wander and you'll soon get bored.

Mind you, I can't think of anything more boring than sitting behind a set of bite alarms for hours on end! Give me the excitement of lure fishing any day!

My Top Ten Lures

The best lures depend on the waters you're fishing, especially their depths. However, these ten I wouldn't want to part with!

Arbogast, JITTERBUG	In black, my favourite surface lure, a real classic
Rublex, FLOPY	Small, barely floating banana bait, brilliant in the original rubber material
Rapala, SHAD RAP	Versatile floating diver that tantalizingly suspends at the depth it's cranked down to
Storm, LITTLE MAC	Outstanding trolled at 12ft (3.5m) for pike, but like many slim plugs not for perch
Luhr Jensen, KWIKFISH	Banana-shaped plug 5in (12cm) in size trolls to almost 20ft (6m) and is devastating for specimen perch as well as pike

Mann's 30+	The deepest diver I've ever used. Violent action and excellent for pike
Abu ATOM	Brilliant slow retrieve spoon on which I've had loads of big perch and pike
Johnson, SILVER MINNOW	Superb but hard to find US weedless spoon that's even better when fitted with a plastic tail
Mepps AGLIA	Excellent all-round spinner that's given me pike to almost 20lb, plus many big perch
Blue Fox BIG BASS	Very successful spinnerbait available in sizes up to ⅞oz

FLAVOURS AND ADDITIVES

Walk into the carp department of any decent tackle shop and immediately you will be overwhelmed by a veritable barrage of scents and smells. This nasal assault will contain an intriguing blend of aromas, some of them hideously unpleasant, others warm, welcoming and positively fragrant. From 'Strawberry Nectar' to 'Monster Crab', the list is almost endless, and all emanating from a mind-blowing collection of small bottles. If anglers from twenty or thirty years ago could have been transported forwards through time by a warp in the space/time continuum they could be forgiven for believing they had gone backwards, into the bowels of a secret medieval witch's cave.

Flavours are here to stay, and the potential that they undoubtedly possess for improving coarse fishing baits in general is almost unlimited. It is therefore rather puzzling that the development of additives and flavours, which could do so much for match, pleasure and general specialist anglers, has remained the almost exclusive province of their creators: the carp anglers. The same comments can be applied to the other two single most important developments in fishing baits: particles and boilies. The non-carp angler, it would seem, is indifferent to such products – or could it be that things have developed so quickly and to such a high level that the whole subject is utterly confusing to most people? I like to believe that it is the latter, so I will relate my own experiences in the hope that they may elucidate matters.

Firstly, let me say that my comments are directed toward the all-rounder and not the carp specialist. (For a more in-depth look at some of the carp-related products on the market, the section on carp baits in Chapter 11 will provide a more detailed examination.) Secondly, my experiences and conclusions are not scientifically based. Despite the fact that I have caught numerous specimen fish on flavoured baits, there are probably only a handful of occasions when I can say with almost 100 per cent conviction that a 'plain' bait would have been unsuccessful. But then again, I know for a fact that flavoured baits certainly do no harm. And I would state with absolute certainty that regardless of the circumstances of an individual session, over the course of a whole season, flavoured baits *do provide an edge*.

Which Types of Bait can be Flavoured?
In my experience there is virtually no limit to the potential of flavours. Maggots, bread, cheese paste, luncheon meat paste, luncheon meat cubes – all of them can be flavoured in one way or another. In the case of certain baits, the flavour is applied to the raw product, for example bread and maggots; with others it can be included in the cooking process – particles, fried luncheon meat.

The absorption of a flavour by uncooked baits can be improved by coating them in the liquid additive and then freezing them; in the process of thawing, the flavour will be sucked in through the skin of the bait. Even maggots can be treated in this way, and many anglers believe that dead, flavoured maggots are better than live ones. In any event, experimenting in the kitchen can yield all manner of weird and wonderful results (including failures!).

Flavour Types

Most of the flavours on sale to carp anglers are synthetically based, manufactured on chemical bases, the foremost among these being propylene glycol and ethyl alcohol. What really matters, however, is that there are basically five different types of flavour, namely fruit, fish (sea food), dairy, spice and savoury. As a general guideline regarding inclusion levels I would recommend that unless you are cooking baits, you use half of the manufacturers' recommended dosage level for a pound of boilies to each pound or pint of bait. Cooking burns off some of the flavour, and by operating at half the manufacturers' recommended level you should be on safe ground. *Never*, under any circumstances, should you exceed the recommended maximum level because too much flavour will actually repel rather than attract fish.

Sweeteners

Most fish have a sweet tooth, a fact that most anglers already recognize when they add a tablespoon of sugar to a pot of boiling hemp. Indeed, natural sweeteners such as sugar and liquid molasses make good bait additives. Man-made alternatives are many times more powerful, however, the best known of these being saccharin. But saccharin has a slightly bitter backnote, and the products sold specifically to carp anglers are not only more highly concentrated, they are sweeter, too. Most baits will benefit from their inclusion, including the savoury, spicy and fishy ones because sweeteners make the bait more palatable. As far as dosage levels are concerned, I would give the same advice for sweeteners as I have for flavours.

Palatants

'Palatant' is simply a buzz word: a few years ago palatants were known as 'flavour enhancers' and in truth, that is exactly what they are. Their use in fishing baits outside boilies is somewhat limited at present, but groundbaits spring to mind, and I have used palatants to improve the taste of cheese paste, luncheon meat paste and fried luncheon meat. There are a number of palatants on the market of various flavours.

Dyes

Dyes are not flavours as such, but they can be described as additives in so far as the addition of dyes to change the colour of popular baits can give these a new lease of life when results begin to taper off on untreated offerings.

Supermarket Additives

The products that I am about to recommend could add a new dimension to your shopping trips! Of all the additives available in supermarkets the spices are the most interesting for angling purposes. Proprietary curry mixes in powder form such as tandoori masala and madras are superb for spicing up luncheon meat (try frying the meat in them) and maggots. Turmeric and curry powder are both tremendous roach and perch pullers in winter – the powder can be added to a pint or two of maggots, and is especially effective if you also add half a teaspoon of Rod Hutchinson's 'Megaspice' flavour to each pint.

Double-strength tomato soup is the ideal medium in which to cook black-eyed beans, a tip that bait-master Rod Hutchinson has been advocating for years. And when making cheese paste, an excellent product to bind it with, in my opinion, is frozen Danish pastry mix as this helps to make the paste soft and pliable. Its other advantage is that it stops the paste hardening in water. I could go on, but have a good look round the supermarket shelves yourself and you'll soon have plenty of your own ideas!

Flavours for Individual Species

The carp is deliberately omitted from this section because it will eat just about anything vaguely palatable. For further information regarding carp baits, *see* Chapter 11.

Barbel

Barbel have definite preferences as far as flavours are concerned. Spice additives seem to be the most popular, with savoury an obvious alternative; their reaction to dairy, fruit and seafood flavours is lukewarm.
Recommended additives: 'Supa Spice' (Dave Thorpe Bait Developments); Nutra Spice range

A near 9lb barbel caught on flavoured sweetcorn.

(Nutra Baits); 'Cajun Crawfish', 'Megaspice' (Rod Hutchinson); 'Indian Spice' oil (Kevin Nash); strawberry (various), tutti-frutti (various), curry packet mixes (supermarkets), cayenne pepper (supermarkets and Indian food shops), Frankfurter sausage (SBS).

Bream

Bream respond well to most flavours, but the dairy and fruity aromas appear to be the best. A few years ago Duncan Kay recommended that amyl butyrate was very attractive to bream, and I am inclined to agree that flavours based on amyl butyrate and amyl acetate are prime bream catchers.

Recommended additives: 'Pineapple Nutrafruits', 'Banana Nutrafruits' (Nutra Baits); strawberry (various); 'Pear of Bananas', Esterblend 12', 'Ester pineapple' (Solar).

All the above flavours will work in isolation, but they are probably even better when blended in a 2:1 ratio with Rod Hutchinson's all-time classic 'Scopex'. Rod also makes a 'bream attractor' in spray form, and given his track record it has to be a winner, especially for groundbait.

Chub

Chub are relatively easy to please, and all of the various flavour types mentioned appeal to them. Spice additives are probably the least attractive. Recommended additives: 'Monster Crab', 'Compound T.F.', 'Seafood Blend' spray, 'Crayfish', 'Seafood Sense Appeal', 'Dairy Sense Appeal', 'Scopex' (Rod Hutchinson); 'Fish Frenzy', 'Kalamari Squid', 'Sour Cream' (Dave Thorpe Bait Developments); 'Grouper', 'Lobster Thermidor' (Kevin Nash); strawberry (various).

Perch

Perch really seem to respond to spicy flavours, particularly in winter.

Recommended additives: supermarket curry powders; 'Megaspice', 'Ultra-spice' (Rod Hutchinson); 'Supa Spice' (Dave Thorpe Bait Developments); 'Ace worm extract' (limited availability).

Roach

Roach appear to share similar tastes to bream, but if anything their palate is more catholic. The big surprise I have had when fishing for chub with fish-flavoured baits has been roach 'trouble'.

As well as the list of recommended bream flavours, I would add the following: 'Fresh Kipper' (SBS), 'Seafood Blend' spray, 'Crayfish' (Rod Hutchinson); 'Fish Frenzy' (Dave Thorpe).

There is certainly room for further experimentation with fish flavours for roach, especially when bread is the hookbait.

Tench

Tench have very definite flavour preferences but their tastes are quite wide reaching. I have based my recommendations not only on experiments with specific flavours for tench, but also on 'accidental' captures made whilst carp fishing, which indicate the tench's preference for a boilie combined with a particular flavour. In my opinion Rod Hutchinson's 'Maple Cream' is far superior to anything else I have used for tench (including Rod's own 'Tench Attractor' spray!).

Recommended flavours: 'Maple Cream', 'Mega Maple', 'Scopex' (Rod Hutchinson); 'Pear of Bananas', 'Caramel Toffee' (Solar); 'Toffee Cream Élite', 'Banana Nutrafruits' (Nutra Baits); 'Sweet Damson', 'Sour Cream' (Dave Thorpe Bait Developments).

NOTE: Banana flavours are exceptional when blended with 'Scopex' on a 2:1 basis.

In Conclusion

My experiments with flavours and additives are still in a formative stage, and it is not possible to discuss them any more fully here; but let me assure you that flavours really do work when they are used *over a period of time*. I hope that, as a result of reading this section, some of you will be encouraged to give them a try.

THE BOILIE PHENOMENON

The subject of boilies is discussed more fully in Chapter 11, the carp section; here, I will simply comment on the development of boilies as a general fishing bait and try to place them in their proper context, which is as but one weapon in the angler's armoury of baits. It is tempting to think of boilies as the ultimate, the wonder bait, so diverse is the sheer number of flavours and ingredients that can be used to make them. Indeed, the development of boiled baits since the early days has turned carp anglers into mad alchemists, constantly juggling with the latest blend of additives to turn base mixes into the single, golden bait that is irresistible to carp.

It was Fred Wilton who was responsible for the earliest experimentation with boiled baits. Using products derived from milk protein, he produced pastes that were bound together with liquidized eggs to produce a hard-skinned, round bait that resisted the attentions of 'nuisance' species. Carp responded to this new-found food source with gusto, particularly if the offerings were flavoured with artificial attractors. Wilton's original theory was founded on a belief that high protein baits would be sought out by carp in preference to other food sources since they could subconsciously or otherwise recognize the nutritional superiority of such baits. This theory was extended in later years and led to the production of high-food-value baits; these concentrated not just on protein content but included other food sources in an attempt to produce a bait that satisfied the carp's nutritional requirements in terms of fats, carbohydrates, vitamins and minerals.

It is argued by many that this process went too far. Running parallel to the development of new diverse base mixes such as bird foods and fish meals, and literally thousands of flavours, oils and palatants, anglers began to add vitamins and amino acids to the bait. And yet, at the same time, other anglers enjoyed phenomenal success with inferior baits based on semolina and soya flour. In retrospect, it seems that the issue of whether or not carp were ever able to detect the nutritional superiority of one food source over another is somewhat academic, and the plain fact is that so many boilies have been introduced into many of our lakes that for fish to distinguish a 'good' boilie from a 'bad' one must be impossible. Some anglers have begun using distinctive and unusual flavour 'labels' to differentiate their nutritionally superior baits from the competition, but whether it works or not is debatable. Nevertheless, the use of high-food-value food baits is certainly a favourable development that can only be good news for the carp.

A worrying development in recent years, however, has been the over-use of certain attractors such as fish oils which may be detrimental to the health of the carp. This is typical of the 'big fish or bust' mentality of many of today's carp anglers, but the common sense route here must be 'everything in moderation'. I don't believe that fish oils are bad for carp *per se*, but an exclusive diet of just one commodity cannot be good for anything or anybody. What is certain is that carp, tench and to a lesser extent, chub and barbel love boilies, and as a bait they offer definite advantages. These include the following:

Size

You can make boilies to whatever size you want. Small 6-12mm baits are ideal for tench, chub and barbel, or as a particle-style mass bait for carp. Large boilies in the 14–24mm size range can be used to avoid the attentions of small, so-called 'nuisance' fish.

Texture

Tench, barbel, chub and bream prefer boilies with a softer texture. Boiling times limited to up to 2 minutes will produce a firm outer skin with a soft inside. If you want a rock-hard bait for carp only, boil them for 2½ minutes or more.

Colour

A bright-coloured bait can be made by adding special dyes, and boilies like this will stop cruising fish in their tracks. More subdued, natural colours can be used to fool wary fish that are used to bright-coloured baits.

Flavour and Taste

The sky is the limit as far as flavour and taste are concerned. A never-ending supply of dairy, fruit, spice, seafood and savoury flavours, palatants and extracts should help you to create your own winning bait and stay one step ahead of the fish.

The three major types of boilies: milk protein, fishmeal and birdfood.

Buoyancy

Cooking processes and ingredients can be controlled to produce a totally flexible degree of buoyancy – sinking baits for resting on silt or weed, the choice is yours.

The use of boilies is becoming increasingly popular these days, but anglers who use them to the exclusion of particle, natural and standard baits will miss out on a lot of fish. Try to think of boilies as just another (albeit effective) bait, and consider carefully your reasons for using them before you mount one on your rig. To some extent, unless you are plagued by 'nuisance' fish, they should be the final step in the bait ladder, especially on under-fished waters.

PARTICLES

Anglers use the term 'particle' to describe a whole range of mass baits including pulses, beans and nuts. The popularity of particle fishing, or mass baiting as it is sometimes known, has increased dramatically in recent years, following some outstanding success using the technique. Particles are also relatively cheap when compared to other baits; thus whenever huge pre-baiting campaigns are considered, they are usually top of the list.

In their natural environment fish are quite used to seeking out rich concentrations of naturally occurring food sources. Invariably these will be small food items such as bloodworm or shrimps, and the richer the concentration of food, the more popular the feeding area will be. It is therefore hardly surprising that the introduction of particle baits in dense, tight concentrations has proved to be so effective.

My favourite particles and the methods for preparing them are as follows:

Hempseed

Hemp is the greatest fish attractor of all the particles. Small, dark, rich in oil and with that appealing little white kernel, if I was restricted to one loosefeed or groundbait for the rest of my life, it would be hemp. Carp, tench, roach, bream, barbel and chub simply love it.

I prefer not to drain hemp off, but instead leave it to stand and cool in its own rich, oily juice. I cannot understand how the practice of rinsing off hemp in cold water originated; it might give the hemp a fresh, shiny appearance, but in my opinion the loss of its attractive oil is detrimental.

To prepare hemp, soak it overnight in cold water and bring it to the boil the next morning. After a period of simmering, the distinctive little

Hempseed – the greatest fish attractor of them all.

white kernels will appear; at this stage pour it into a bait bucket, and take it to the water still warm.

Sweetcorn

Sweetcorn is highly convenient because it requires no preparation. Young anglers today take sweetcorn for granted and probably cannot imagine how devastating the 'yellow peril' was when it was first used as a bait for carp in the 1970s. Lake records, personal bests and phenomenal catches were the result, before its widespread use caused a downturn in sport. Nowadays corn is a well-accepted bait for bigger-than-average fish – roach, carp, tench, bream, chub, barbel and rudd are always greedy for corn.

The problem with corn is that after heavy use it is prone to 'blowing', and fish learn to recognize its bright yellow coloration as a danger signal; but when this happens, a switch to a dyed flavoured bait will improve catches. In the old days I used to dye and flavour my own, but 'Pescaviva' fishing sweetcorn has made this practice a thing of the past. For a start, it is available in 'peel off', resealable cans, easy to open and there is no waste. There is also a choice of three colours: yellow, orange and red. The list of flavours is impressive, and the dye/flavouring process is long lasting and very natural to the taste. The list of available flavours includes vanilla, strawberry, cherry, banana, tutti-frutti, yoghurt, honey, cream caramel, fish and, of course, natural. This is a superb product that has added a new dimension to an already great bait.

Groats

Groats are small, wheat-like seeds or granules that absorb water and flavours like a sponge. There is no need to cook groats, simply soak them in water plus a flavour or additional attractor for a few hours. Carp in particular love groats, and the killer combination appears to be groats soaked in condensed milk and water. The milky white cloud that surrounds the carpet of needle-like white groats when prepared in this manner has to be seen to be believed. Carp are known to enjoy the taste of milk anyway, and the visual and aromatic appeal of this combination is deadly. Being so tiny, groats cannot be used as a hookbait easily, but I have always fished boilies or other hookbaits over them to good effect. It is also interesting to note that groats are a popular and effective winter mass bait, probably because they do not rely on oil as their primary source of attraction and due to the quality of their visual attraction.

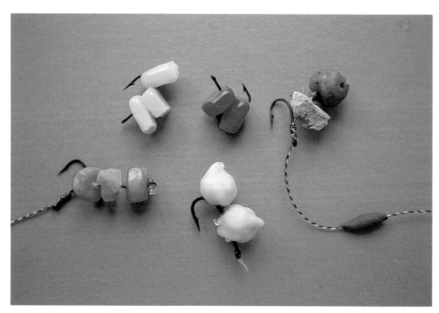

Particle hookbaits properly presented.

Peanuts

Peanuts are, I believe, the most instantly effective of the 'large' particles. Carp love them, and although other fish can be caught on peanuts, I regard them primarily as a carp bait.

To prepare peanuts, soak them in water for a minimum of forty-eight hours, making sure that you keep them covered in water throughout the whole soaking process by topping up the supply every now and again. Peanuts can absorb a phenomenal amount of water, and will swell up to twice or even three times their original size.

Use peanuts sparingly, restricting the loosefeed to three or four pouchfuls around each hookbait. Try to think of them as boilies, and you shouldn't go far wrong. My favourite way of preparing peanuts is to let them soak until they 'ferment'. They might smell awful to us, but the carp love them!

Tiger Nuts

'Tigers' are less instant for carp than peanuts, but they appear to enjoy a very long life once they have been established, whereas peanuts are prone to 'blowing' quite quickly. You will never make tiger nuts soft however long you boil or presoak them. To prepare them, boil them for an hour or so in water with a few tablespoons of sugar added to it. This gives them a sweet taste and is an extra, attractive dimension to their 'crunchy' consistency which carp appear to love. A great selective bait, for carp only.

Black-Eye Beans

'Black-eyes' make superb loosefeed and hookbaits. Their flat-sided shape helps them to lie on top of silt and weed, where that distinctive black ring sits staring lovingly at passing fish. Tench and carp love black-eye beans. They can be prepared simply by boiling for twenty minutes or so. To improve their taste and appearance try one of Rod Hutchinson's tips, which is to boil them in double-strength tomato soup.

Maple Peas

Maple peas are a superb hookbait to use over hempseed for carp, tench, chub and barbel; they are also a good carp, chub and tench attractor in their own right. To prepare maples, simply boil them until they are soft enough to accept a hook. However, do not, under any circumstances, rinse them otherwise you will wash off the outer skin. In any case, the warm oil of maples is a big attractor *per se*, and it is most satisfying to be able to fire maples out when they are still warm and the oil is at its thinnest for rapid dispersal in water. To improve the taste of maple peas, add some table sugar to the water they are boiled in.

Tares

Tares are very similar to maple peas in so far as they make a great hookbait to use over hemp. Prepare them and use them in the same way as maples.

Sinking Trout Pellets

These may not be classified as particles officially, but I certainly use them particle style. Trout pellets make a great loosefeed for carp and tench, being 'fishy', oily, dark and particle-size.; the best are those which contain fishmeals, rather than soya products. They require no preparation; simply take them out of the bag and fire them into the lake.

Trout pellets make poor hookbaits, being crumbly by nature, but make a soft paste by adding hot water to ground pellets and you have a real winner! Boilies work well when fished over T.P.s, but better still are those made by chopping up sausages of boilie paste extruded from a bait gun. This produces a trout pellet-shaped bait that will last for hours on the hook, and you can choose whether you have pop-ups or sinkers by boiling the pellet-shaped boilie for as little or as long as you like.

Chum Mixer

The discovery of Chum mixers as a fishing bait had two profound effects; firstly, it extended the principle of particle fishing to the surface, and as a consequence carp and chub were caught in great numbers on it. This prompted anglers to buy Chum mixer in enormous quantities, a phenomenon that continues to this day, since it is still purchased in huge volumes. It is this, no doubt,

Dyeing and flavouring Chum mixers.

◄

1. Here's the equipment you need: Chum mixers, kettle, old mug, teaspoon, carp dye, Dave Thorpe's Lump liquid.

▶

2. Measure out a pint of mixer.

◄

3. Add a teaspoon of powered carp dye to the dry biscuits. Add a teaspoon of DT Lump liquid and half a teaspoon of flavour to a cup a fifth full of hot water. Pour the liquid over the mixers.

▶

4. Now blow air into the bag and twist the top.

which has led to the irrefutable conclusion formed by the marketing department of the Mars Food Company (the makers of Pedigree Chum) that every household in Britain owns at least three dogs.

Chum mixers are, and have been for a decade, the number one surface-fishing bait. You can use them hard or soft, flavoured or unflavoured; my favourite way is to dye and flavour the mixers as per the picture sequence.

As a final comment on particles, I would first say never use raw particles: always soak and/or boil them first, as failure to do this could cause damage to fish. Secondly, one of the biggest limitations of particles is that they cannot be fired out with a catapult beyond a few rod lengths at best (though later in the book Dave Thorpe describes how to fish particles at range using a technique known as 'spodding', *see* Chapter 11).

5. Shake the bag until the sides go clear and the biscuits are evenly coloured.

6. The finished mixers, dyed and flavoured.

4 LOCATING FISH ON STILLWATERS

The two basic principles that lie at the heart of fish location are shelter and food. Fish like to feel comfortable in their surroundings, and shelter offers security from predators, while a natural food larder will be constantly exploited by fish of all species. So it is hardly surprising that the best swims of all are usually sheltered areas near to a food larder. If you can think in terms of these two basic concepts you will undoubtedly catch a lot of fish, because location is the key to successful angling.

The subject of river fish location is no less important than that of fish location on stillwaters, but rather than attempt to generalize, finding fish on rivers is dealt with in the chapter for each specific river species. However, there are fundamental rules and techniques which govern the successful location of all stillwater fish, and for this reason it seems appropriate to deal with this subject in its own right.

Stillwaters are many and varied, and no two lakes are ever the same; but broadly speaking stillwaters can be divided into categories, namely ponds, estate lakes, reservoirs and gravel pits. Each category will generally correspond to certain characteristics – although there are always exceptions.

STILLWATER CATEGORIES

Ponds

Small stillwaters are relatively easy to read. Generally speaking they are rich in plant life both above and below the surface: overhanging trees and bushes will provide shade and shelter for fish, while weedbeds will provide not only security but also a reliable food source. All kinds of weedbed will be natural holding areas for fish:

lilies, reeds, bistort and 'crowfoot' being amongst the most common (and the most productive). Baits presented close to, or even in the weed itself will produce plenty of bites.

Lakes

Estate lakes are amongst our most beautiful stillwaters; dug in the seventeenth and eighteenth centuries, estate lakes were the water gardens of the wealthy, privileged classes. At one end of the lake a feeder stream will be the source of the water and the remnants of the stream bed itself will usually be a very good fish-holding area or patrol route. In some cases it will run for most of the length of the lake, and is well worth mapping out.

The stream end is likely to be shallow, silty and probably surrounded by reed fringes. This type of area is usually very productive in early summer. Estate lakes usually become progressively deeper towards the dam wall and as late summer turns into autumn, many fish will migrate to areas between 6 and 15ft (1.8 to 4.5m) deep; in winter the deepest area, at the dam, will be favoured. Lily pads, crowfoot and reeds are very common in estate lakes, and wherever you find them, the chances are that you will find fish.

Reservoirs

Reservoirs usually possess very similar characteristics to estate lakes, and similar rules of location apply; however, you will probably encounter less surface weed growth because of the greater depth. Thick, soft, bottom weed is common in this type of water due to its clarity, and fishing can sometimes be difficult. There will almost certainly be greater variation in depth, and this presents interesting possibilities: an old stream bed may still be present, as will deep holes and troughs, and these are natural fish patrol areas. Frequently reservoirs will be flooded without the prior removal of buildings and other countryside features such as hedgerows and fences; these are obvious fish-holding spots, and in spite of being hazardous in terms of fish losses, they are invariably productive.

Pits

Gravel and other types of pit – notably sand, clay and brick – are a modern-day phenomenon. Frequently choked with weed in places, they are nevertheless full of natural food; gravel pits in particular are very much *the* specimen fisheries of the 1990s and beyond.

The depth variation in gravel pits can be dramatic. During extraction, troughs and gullies will frequently be dug in order to exploit a rich seam, and this leads to the creation of what anglers know as bars (long, thin, shallow strips) and plateaux (larger, table-shaped shallower areas). Fish like to patrol along bars, and will feed both on their surface and at the base of them, while a plateau is frequently a dining table

of the highest quality. The most productive spots invariably tend to be naturally weed-free areas, usually small patches where the fish's feeding activities have exposed the gravel. This is somewhat fortunate, since bait presentation is thereby much improved.

The biggest feature on any gravel pit will be the margin. Try to think of it as one long continuous bar, and you will begin to appreciate the value of a bait lowered off the rod tip.

Some gravel pits possess visible above-the-water features, reedbeds for example, or perhaps the most dramatic example of all, islands. Islands have always been accepted as reliable fish patrol routes, and they are well worth casting a bait to.

PLUMBING AND MAPPING

To understand truly a stillwater, you should do two things before you even contemplate fishing it. Firstly you should watch and observe. Try to spend as much time at the water as possible, preferably at the prime time for surface activity,

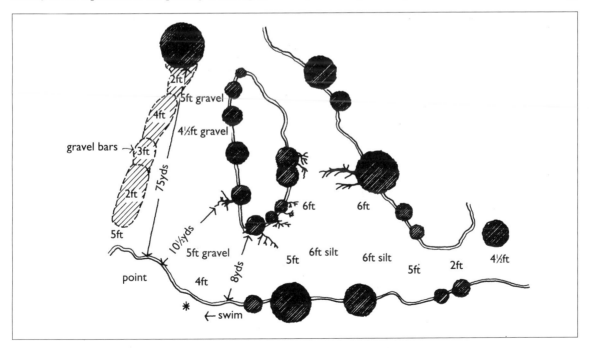

Fig. 3 A typical map showing a lake's features.

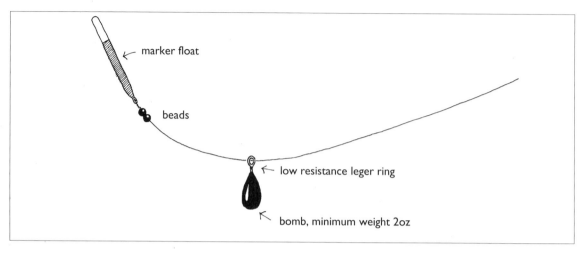

Fig. 4a Plumbing tackle: relatively weed-free water.

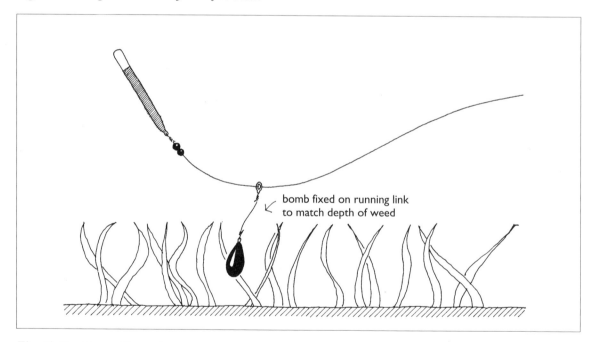

Fig. 4b Plumbing tackle: weedy water.

that is at dusk, constantly searching for signs of fish and plotting their movements. Having done this, pay further visits to the water with a plumbing rod, a compass and a few sheets of paper; this is the armoury of more traditional feature-finding methods and the object of the exercise is to map out the lake, noting both its above- and below-the-surface features. Begin by drawing the lake as close to scale as you possibly can, marking on it the clearly visible features. Plot also the points of the compass so that you can assess the effects of any winds likely to be present during future fishing sessions. The north-east corner of the lake will be one of its most important areas since fish tend to respond well to mild, south-westerly winds both in summer and winter; southerly winds too,

The author's feature-finding float set-up.

each foot off, the depth can be accurately identified by stopping the count at the point that the float hits the surface. Important clues regarding the nature of the lake bed in front of you can also be picked up using the same set-up. For example, if when you retrieve the float it is carrying fragments of weed, you will be able to determine the presence of a weedbed. Indeed, casting the lead around and dragging it slowly across the bottom can reveal a surprising amount about the bottom of the lake. If the lead comes back very freely, almost as if you are dragging it through custard, you have found silt. Sharp raps and taps on the tip indicate gravel, while a sharp pull round on the tip followed by a rapid slackening of the line indicates the presence of a bar. Weed, of course, creates a heavy, dense resistance.

Time spent in identifying fish-holding features will repay your efforts many times over on future fishing sessions. Successful anglers never fish 'blind' because they understand that a bait placed in the wrong area might just as well be cast up a tree. And when it comes to presenting baits in swims it is simply not good enough to be *near* a 'hot' area: feet, even inches can make an enormous difference to your results and I have lost count of the number of occasions when a cast made a couple of feet short of a feature has resulted in a complete absence of runs, while an accurately placed cast has resulted in hectic action. Proof indeed that the old adage 'a miss is as good as a mile' has a great deal of truth in it.

FISHFINDERS   by Steve Burke

Fishfinders are a very emotive subject. Some say they are essential time-savers on large waters, whilst others consider they are cheating (although this charge was once levelled at fixed spool reels!). However, if you think that you can motor around until you see a big fish on the screen, drop a bait on its nose and catch it, you are very much mistaken. And even if you do find a big fish, having a fishfinder won't get that fish to take your bait – only you can do that!

What a fishfinder can do is tell you where not

can be excellent, while north-westerlies can be regarded as better in summer than in winter. Easterly, north-easterly and south-easterly winds are bad news for anglers because they are usually cold and have a chilling effect on the water.

Begin by plumbing the water and make a thorough search of the area, casting in a fan shape at increasing distances from the bank. Each swim should be properly investigated and you should make a note of the depth, the nature of the bottom, and any features such as bars, snags and weedbeds. Try to mark out the extent of the feature by lining up its extreme limits with objects on the far bank such as trees, buildings and suchlike.

My basic plumbing tackle is illustrated in Fig. 4. A large marker float is used, but first slide a 2oz bomb onto the line, followed by two large rubber shock beads. Complete the set-up by tying on the float. After casting, wind down until the float is tight against the lead. Pay line off the reel (or baitrunner) a foot at a time. By counting

A fishfinder is a valuable asset when it comes to locating potential fish-holding areas.

to waste your time fishing. It will also indicate the depth, and the position of bars, drop-offs, snags, weedbeds and so on; the better units will also tell you the bottom hardness. Knowing that you are fishing on silt, for instance, means that you can change your rig and bait so that the latter remains visible. Again, find a hard patch on a soft-bottomed water and it is bound to be a hotspot. There are, of course, other ways of determining all this information but none are as quick or as accurate as a fishfinder. Naturally a fishfinder will also show fish, give an idea of their size, and indicate how deep they are (rarely on the bottom!). It will even show shoals of fry – find these, and predators won't be far away. Last but not least, using a fishfinder regularly will teach you a great deal about the movements and habits of fish.

Choosing a Fishfinder

Many anglers spend more than they need on a fishfinder, because of two common misapprehensions: firstly, the higher cost of the expensive models is largely to buy extra power to penetrate deeper depths, and this is a facility which the coarse angler simply doesn't need. Secondly, unless you have a long way to walk to your boat, there is little point in spending an extra £60 or so on a 'portable' model. These work off lantern

batteries which often don't last very long, and certainly work out very expensive to run. Standard models are actually smaller, but need a separate 12-volt battery. You can buy a small motorcycle battery if weight is a problem, or better still a 'deep cycle' battery from a caravan dealer and this will have a carrying handle. Both these types of battery last for ages and moreover can be repeatedly recharged.

The latest innovation is a 3D display which is helpful if you are fishing a water with a very uneven bottom or you want to position your boat over, say, a bend in a stream bed. However, perhaps the most useful extra is a side-scanner, which enables you to look under boats and trees and find undercut banks. It also avoids the boat going over fish in shallow water and spooking them. A side-scanner will even enable you to use your fishfinder from the bank! As a specialist supplier of fishfinders I hope this catches on, but even so I am not completely comfortable with the ethics.

From my comparative field testing of dozens of models, I would always recommend Eagle and Humminbird brands. Finally, make sure that you get a full UK guarantee, as fishfinders can and do break down, and sending your unit abroad for repair is both expensive and time-consuming.

5 BARBEL

When my parents decided to move house from the hustle and bustle of a busy Black Country town to the peaceful tranquillity of a quiet Shropshire village, they were making a choice that would have a major impact on my angling career. No less than 30yds (27m) from my bedroom window, the River Severn was clearly visible at the bottom of the garden. The Severn, as most of you will know, is one of the most prolific barbel rivers in England, and from the moment that I hooked my first fighting specimen, I became a barbel fisherman forever.

Whether you fish for barbel on a big, powerful river like the Severn or the Wye, or whether smaller, more intimate rivers like the Great Ouse and Dorset Stour are your choice, basic tackle requirements remain the same. Barbel are powerful fish whose long, irresistible runs and sheer tenacity will test even the most powerful equipment.

TACKLE

As far as rods are concerned, I prefer a progressive action that is forgiving enough to absorb the lunges of a big fish, but has enough power in reserve to pile the pressure on when it is needed. For general light to medium leger work and for heavy swimfeeder use, the Shimano 12ft Stradic feeder rod takes some beating. At twelve feet long, it is the perfect length for keeping line off the water when powerful currents are present and for setting a hook at range. The Stradic possesses two push-in quivertips of 2oz and 3oz – perfect for general barbel work. For flooded rivers and legering in powerful currents, I use a 12ft stepped-up Avon with a 1¼lb test curve. As I write, I am developing such a rod with Shimano, so watch this space!

Trotting enthusiasts will enjoy the hidden power of a 12 or 13ft specimen float rod, and there are a number of models currently on the market, available from specialist rod-building companies.

Reel choice is particularly critical with barbel. A good, reliable slipping clutch is absolutely essential, and if you can afford it, a reel with Fightin' Drag is tailor-made to cope with the sheer, uncompromising power of a big barbel in a heavy current. My first choice is the Shimano Aero GTM, a reel that possesses both of these features. For trotting, I like to use a centre pin whenever I can. Pins deliver a degree of float control that is impossible with fixed spools, paying out line freely and without any 'jerkiness' or hesitation, and whether you are running a float through or 'holding back', pins are a delight.

As you would expect, I like to use the strongest, toughest line available when after barbel and as far as I am concerned, that means Berkley Trilene XT. 'XT' stands for extra tough, a fitting description for a line that can withstand abrasion better than any other I know, and yet is soft, limp and very castable. Wet knot strength is crucial, since barbel will exploit any weak spots in your tackle and 'XT' breaks well above its stated limit, every time. For general legering I use 8lb, and carry a spare spool of 10lb for use in snaggy swims.

For hooklengths and trotting, I use another Berkley line, Trilene XL, which stands for 'extra limp'. XL is very soft and supple and yet it possesses surprising abrasion resistance. I always carry spare 100yds (90m) spools of it in 4lb, 6lb, 8lb and 10lb with a minimum hooklength of 4lb. I have never found it necessary to go any lighter for barbel, and I believe that to do so is irresponsible and positively invites breakages. My most frequently used barbel mono hooklength is 6 or 8lb and I catch plenty of fish, I can assure you, without having to go lighter.

A selection of legers from ⅛oz to 2oz, Partridge Hilton hooks, a selection of feeders, shock beads, and a range of braided hooklengths complete my terminal tackle requirements. I also always carry bait droppers for depositing maggots, casters and particle baits, while a couple of spools of PVA string are useful for presenting luncheon meat 'stringers'.

SUMMER BARBEL FISHING

Location

It is a common assumption that barbel will always be found in fast, shallow water, and while this is sometimes the case, in my experience big barbel prefer a medium and evenly paced current with reasonable depth (4 to 10ft [1 to 3m] is ideal). Like any other species, barbel like cover and this could be provided by a weedbed, an overhanging tree or a sudden change in depth (a 'depression'). They are also fond of directional changes in the current. These areas are known as *creases* and are created when slower-paced water meets a faster current. *Bends* are a frequent cause of creases, as are shelving river beds. Barbel take advantage of the fact that a crease area is, in effect, a giant food trap. Food items swept along by the fast current are often deposited in the slower area, and when normal water levels prevail barbel often position themselves right on the crease itself. In drought situations they may move across to favour the paciest water, since this will provide the best oxygen access, while floodwater will push them into quieter, more comfortable areas (more of this in the winter section in Chapter 5).

Weedbeds are very reliable barbel-holding areas. On faster rivers, ranunculus (streamer weed) provides barbel with security and food, while slower rivers are often full of cabbages – and on this type of water cabbages are synonymous with barbel.

Depressions in the river bed provide barbel with cover, and they also act as a food trap; they are therefore the recipe for a perfect barbel lie. The depth change doesn't have to be great, as little as 1ft (30cm) can be enough, but as a general rule, the more dramatic the drop-off, the more the barbel will like it.

Overhanging trees, particularly willows, make good and aesthetically pleasing barbel swims. A bait trundled right underneath the canopy will produce barbel bites, but the root area of the tree will be even better still, particularly if it is under-cut. Indeed *undercut banks* make very good barbel swims, and the most likely place to find them is on the outside of bends where the current has eroded its way into the bank.

Baits for Summer Barbel

A number of baits can be used to catch barbel, and they can be broadly divided into three categories: particles, naturals and standards. It is my experience though, that only a handful of the baits that I have tried over the years have been instantly effective. Barbel are extremely conservative in their tastes, but if you *can* establish a new food source, it tends to enjoy a long life. Standard baits like cheese paste and luncheon meat are classic examples: both are instant, even on virgin fisheries, and loved by barbel; they are particularly effective after dark and in coloured water when used on a large hook, usually a no 4 or a no 6. At the height of summer when clear water predominates, however, barbel can become wary of large baits, particularly cubes of luncheon meat; introducing free offerings in daylight can be the kiss of death, and often a single hookbait over a bed of hemp produces better results. Eventually though, even this may be refused. This is therefore the time to change the shape of the bait, either by tearing it off in chunks or punching out tubes of meat with an apple corer.

Changing the taste of the meat can produce a significant improvement in results, too. I like to fry mine in a hot curry powder, adding a teaspoon of a spicy synthetic carp flavour during the frying process; Dave Thorpe's Supa Spice is good, as is Nutra Baits' 'Cassia' essential oil. My favourite 'hot meat' special involves frying a tin of meat in two large tablespoons of cayenne pepper. I also like to add one teaspoon of Dave Thorpe's 'The Howler' palatant, a sweet, spicy powder which really peps the meat up. The finished product is a hot, spicy version of luncheon meat with a red outer skin and a rough texture.

Results using hot, spicy baits have been spectacular on those stretches that have been 'hammered' on normal meat, while cheese paste also seems sufficiently different to keep the 'tip' flying round. 'Pepperami', a hot spicy sausage with a tough skin, is a superb barbel catcher and an excellent alternative to luncheon meat. It is not always instant, but my results with it, particularly when fished over hemp, justify its inclusion as a 'classic'! Eventually, though, you may find that large standard baits simply fail to work at all during daylight hours. Put them on after dark and they are as good as ever, but try them in the daylight and in extreme cases I have seen barbel not only refuse them, but physically spook from the swim at the sight of them.

Now is the time to try natural baits, and the two finest in my opinion are lobworms and prawns. Lobworms will catch barbel regardless of the water's colour or height and the time of day – being natural they will never spook fish, and I

rate them very highly indeed. My favourite way to use them is to present them in a bunch, usually two or three worms on a size 4 or 6 hook over a bed of hemp. Prawns, too, are excellent, but have a much more limited 'shelf life', probably because of their bright coloration. For a while though, barbel will go potty on them and I buy them in frozen and peeled form from the supermarket. Other naturals include small live- and deadbaits, but since I have never used these extensively, I feel I am not qualified to comment.

It is never wise to be dogmatic about baits, but I will say this regarding hempseed: put hemp into a swim anywhere near barbel and they will eat it. It's as simple as that, and I *never* go summer barbel fishing without at least four pints of these magical seeds for company, and a gallon is better. Hemp is *the* barbel attractor *par excellence*. It can be prepared by pre-soaking for a few hours before bringing it to the boil – and here's a tip: do not drain the excess water off hemp, but leave it to soak in its own attractive, oily juices after cooking.

The primary function of particles, or mass baits as they may be termed, is to attract. Maggots and casters perform very well in this respect and are second only to the magical hemp. However, one of the problems associated with particles, and hemp in particular, is that fish tend to

The unmistakable head of a barbel; with its underslung mouth it is not difficult to imagine where it does most of its feeding – on the bottom.

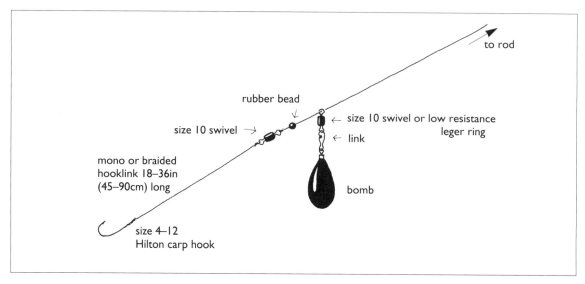

rubber bead

size 10 swivel →

← size 10 swivel or low resistance
leger ring

← link

mono or braided
hooklink 18–36in
(45–90cm) long

bomb

to rod

size 4–12
Hilton carp hook

Fig. 5 *Standard barbel leger rig.*

become preoccupied with them. Barbel are particularly prone to this, refusing to take any non-particle-sized offerings that the angler may be using as a hookbait. In this situation there is no choice but to use particles on the hook. Maggots and casters are good, while maple peas, tares and sweetcorn are particularly effective over hemp. A light scattering of your hookbait over the hemp bed is all that is required; over-baiting with bright particles like sweetcorn can be detrimental to success, particularly with pressured fish. Barbel will not tolerate large quantities of corn, and their wariness after being caught on it increases. A switch to red or orange sweetcorn will often improve results in these situations.

In extreme cases of preoccupation with hemp, maple peas are very good and lend themselves to hair rigging. Obviously hempseeds would be a good choice, but until recently they have been difficult to present on the hook – that is, until Kryston invented 'Bogey', a revolutionary clear, sticky substance that can be used to present balls or flat 'wedges' of hemp. To get the best out of 'Bogey', roll it in the dry seeds, boil the ball of bait and then cool it quickly under a cold tap to produce a hookbait comprised of cooked, rather than dry, seeds.

Rigs

I use a variety of rigs for summer barbel fishing, though the one I most frequently adopt is relatively straightforward (*see* Fig. 5): a basic leger tackle that can be used to present a variety of baits from large standards and naturals through to particles. The leger weight is varied according to the amount of weight required to hold bottom and reach the desired casting distance. For gentle flows, Arlesey bombs as light as ⅛oz may be sufficient, while powerful currents might justify legers up to 1½oz in weight. One of the most important aspects of the rig is the low resistance leger ring, marketed by John Roberts. Unlike small swivels and standard leger beads, the diameter of the bore on this small but valuable accessory is large enough to allow the leger to slide freely and is particularly useful for avoiding 'clogging up' by bottom debris, weed and suchlike. The rubber shock bead prevents damage to the knot by the swivel, and is far more effective than standard 'hard' beads in this respect.

Choice of hooklength material is yours. In open water I tend to use 6–10lb Trilene XL, while snaggy swims demand the use of a braid, usually 12lb Kryston Silkworm Ultrasoft. Barbel that have been subjected to heavy angling pressure will also respond well to braids, and the extra softness/limpness of silkworm produces a far more natural presentation than mono. More and more these days, I find myself turning to silkworm to increase the number of bites I receive and to provide extra abrasion resistance in snaggy areas.

Particle hookbaits are often better hair-rigged than side hooked. As a rule I am not fond of hair rigs for barbel, but there is no doubt that they allow particles to behave more naturally and, most importantly, they prevent hard baits from masking the hookpoint.

One of the behaviour characteristics of barbel that have received heavy angling pressure is that they often feed on hemp to the exclusion of other food items. Anything heavier than a grain of hemp naturally fails to respond in the same way as the tiny seeds. When cautious barbel feed on hemp they have a habit of swirling food into suspension, a feat they achieve by fanning their pectoral fins and sweeping their tails across the general area. Baits weighted down by hooks may be steadfastly ignored, particularly if they remain nailed to the bottom. The answer to the problem is to neutralize the weight of the hook by adding a buoyancy aid to the hair (*see* Fig. 6). My favourite rig is to sandwich a small 'poly pop' (available from the carp counter of local tackle shops), which has been coloured black with a Pentel pen, between two tares. The same thing can be achieved with maple peas by using a slightly larger piece of polystyrene and a brown pen. Hookbaits can either be fished 'popped up', by weighting the rig down with some Fox 'Supaweight' putty, or the poly pop trimmed back with some nail scissors until the hookbait sinks – but only just. This technique is known as critical balancing, and it can also be achieved with sweetcorn by using yellow, orange or red rig foam. Simply cut out a sweetcorn-sized piece of foam and trim bits off it until the arrangement begins to sink. A complicated balancing act? Maybe, but it has accounted for a number of double-figure barbel that I am convinced I wouldn't have caught otherwise.

When barbel become truly preoccupied on hemp, the other problem that has to be overcome is line bites, caused by the barbel bumping into the line as a result of their feverish feeding efforts. Line bites can be surprisingly violent and the dilemma that they create – whether to strike or not – is infuriating. The result of striking a line bite is usually a spooked fish, and rather than a satisfying lunge on the rod tip, a hasty strike is usually rewarded by the dismal sight of a single, large barbel scale fluttering on the hook. So line bites must be avoided at all costs if we are to strike only at the real thing. My solution is two-

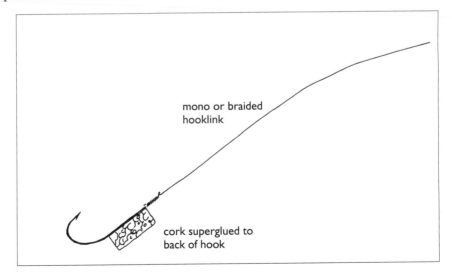

mono or braided
hooklink

cork superglued to
back of hook

Fig. 6 Barbel rig: buoyant hook.

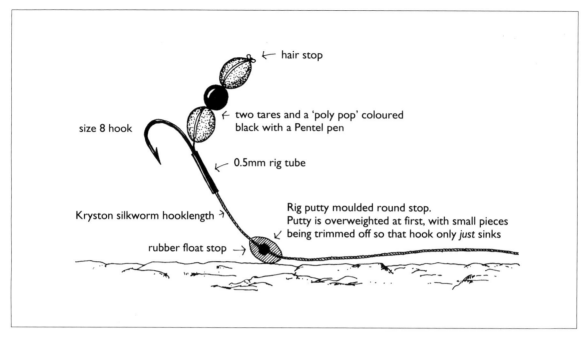

Fig. 7 *Pop-up particles.*

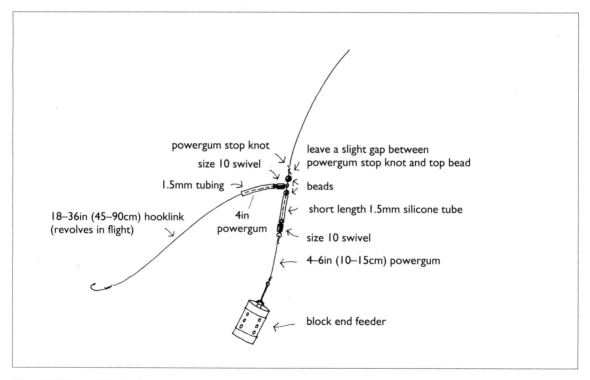

Fig. 8 *'Helicopter' feeder rig.*

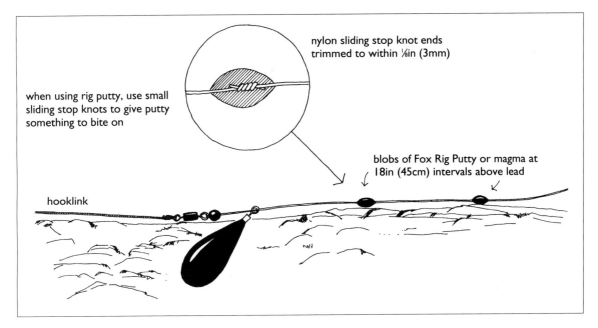

nylon sliding stop knot ends
trimmed to within ⅛in (3mm)

when using rig putty, use small
sliding stop knots to give putty
something to bite on

blobs of Fox Rig Putty or magma at
18in (45cm) intervals above lead

hooklink

Fig. 9 *Semi-fixed bolt rig.*

fold. Firstly I change from a light running lead to a heavy, semi-fixed bolt rig. I usually use a 1¾oz to 2oz lead in conjunction with a short hook-length of perhaps 12in (30cm) or so. Bites on particles using this rig are dramatic to say the least and cannot possibly be mistaken for anything other than the real thing! Finally, to avoid the risk of line bites, additional weight is employed above the lead in the form of a carp angler's backlead, or the use of two or three sausages of 'Supa-weight' putty placed up the line. This effectively nails several vital feet of line behind the lead to the bottom and out of the way of the barbel's fins and tail (*see* Fig. 9).

On faster-flowing rivers, a swimfeeder can be used to deliver a mixture of casters/maggots and hemp to great effect. The rig is simple and is shown in Fig. 8. Two important rules apply, however. Firstly, make sure that the feeder lands in the same spot every time in order to build up a carpet of bait. Secondly, make sure that it is heavy enough to settle and hold where it is cast, and not several yards away, otherwise feed will be emptied all over the river. Bites on heavy feeder rigs are violent in the extreme, so beware! One of

the most effective ways of fishing a heavy feeder is to use an upstream presentation.

Trotting for barbel can be very effective, particularly on faster flowing rivers. The basic float arrangement is simple: with a bulk shotting pattern to keep the bait down in the water and at a steady speed. 'Stick'-type floats, fished 'double-rubber' style are the best choice, and heavier patterns such as Avons, balsas and 'chubbers' give the degree of control necessary to catch barbel. Baits should be presented so that they trundle along the bottom, and if you can slow them down by 'holding back', so much the better.

The key to successful trotting lies in float control (presentation) and feeding. Always feed before you cast the float, and keep the bait going in at regular intervals, preferably every cast. Indeed, even while you are playing a fish – keep feeding! Remember too, that if you are using a mixture of maggots or casters and hemp, that the hemp, being denser, should be fed separately and correspondingly further down the swim than the maggots/casters (so that they land in the same place).

Laying on with a float is a deadly method for barbel, particularly in deeper, steadier stretches.

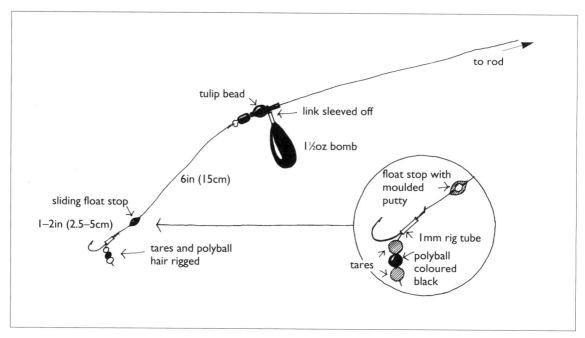

Fig. 10 *Barbel bolt rig.*

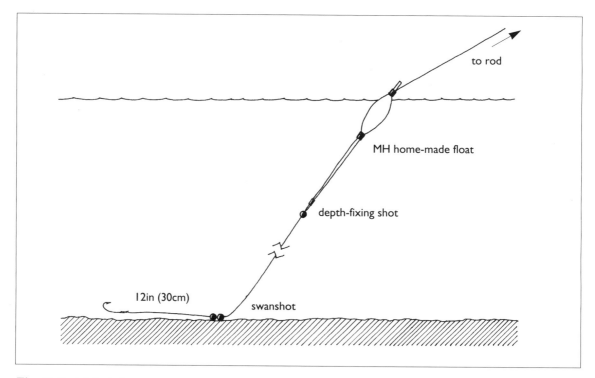

Fig. 11 *Barbel float rig.*

I like to use a float particularly for presenting baits near to cabbage beds, because the angle of the line, being direct from the float, is much steeper, allowing the bait to be located right amongst the stems and roots of the weedbed. Small differences like this can mean the difference between success and failure, since barbel are loath to leave cover in bright daylight. The other advantage of a float is that it provides a visual warning of an impending take. This is vital in snaggy areas, since a prepared angler will be in control of his quarry right from the start.

I like to make my own barbel 'laying-on' floats out of swan quills and balsa float bodies; robust and buoyant, they can be used to present baits in surprisingly strong currents. The tip of the float is made from a push-in 'plug', perhaps 2 to 3in (5 to 7.5cm) long, of painted peacock quill. I prepare both black and orange versions to cope with the varying light conditions. As an additional bonus, I make the bore which receives the tip exactly the right size to take not only peacock quill 'plugs', but also the largest size of 'starlight' available; this means that I can fish after dark simply by changing the tip from peacock to starlight, without having to break the tackle down. Believe me, the sight of a big luminous float-tip wavering and dipping before it finally shoots away under the water in decisive fashion, is heart-stopping stuff in the dark.

Approaching Summer/Autumn Barbel

My favourite way of catching barbel is essentially a mobile one. On arrival at the river and before assembling my tackle, I will bait several swims. The groundbait is invariably hemp, which I introduce via a bait dropper near to likely holding areas. I always try to choose a patch of clean gravel as close to cover as possible, and for an initial baiting half a pint of seeds is about right.

I then rest the swims for about an hour before revisiting them all with the dropper and the hemp bucket. My rod will remain in its quiver, but this time I also introduce a smattering of the chosen hookbait. After a further half hour 'rest', each swim is revisited for another 'top up' of bait, usually three or four droppers full.

Now, and only now, will the rod be tackled up. After a further twenty-minute 'settling' period, I will make a cast with the lightest leger I can get away with (to minimize disturbance) into all of the baited swims. At this stage I am not looking for real bites, I am hoping for line bites, and those swims in which 'liners' materialize will be baited up yet again before fishing proper can commence.

This whole programme can be curtailed if you are fortunate enough to be on a small, intimate river with clear, relatively shallow water; a pair of polaroids will enable you to observe first-hand whether barbel are visiting the baited areas. They can be difficult to spot, but the practised eye will soon grow accustomed to identifying the two orange pectoral fins and their 'ghostly' sandy shapes, moving nervously over the bait. And if you are patient, you will be treated to a valuable insight into barbel behaviour that will justify the

A double-figure barbel from the Great Ouse caught on flavoured luncheon meat.

seemingly long-winded nature of this complicated baiting programme.

At first, the fish will feed nervously, remaining in the swim for only brief intervals before leaving, then returning to recommence feeding. With each successive visit the feeding spell will increase in its duration, although it will never be long enough for the barbel to remain until all the food has been eaten. Nonetheless, their confidence will increase with each successive visit. You should also notice that over a period of time, if they remain undisturbed, the biggest fish in the shoal will eventually establish dominance over the smaller ones.

I hope you now understand the reasons behind the baiting programme. By demonstrating patience, not only are the chances of catching a barbel increased, the chances of catching the biggest fish in the shoal are also dramatically improved. Fishing can now commence as normal, and if line bites become a problem, take the measures that I described earlier. And, as a final tip: if you are able to observe the barbel coming into and out of the swim, always introduce your hookbait between visits to avoid spooking the shoal. This is especially important with semi-fixed bolt rigs.

WINTER BARBEL FISHING

Even as recently as twenty years ago, barbel were thought to be an unreliable winter quarry. Nowadays our increased understanding of barbel behaviour means that they are widely recognized as being *totally* predictable in their behaviour during the colder months.

Winter Barbel Behaviour

Barbel feed regularly in winter, but an area of controversy still exists regarding the point at which they cease feeding. I have read articles by 'experts' suggesting that barbel will not feed in water temperatures below 4°C; indeed, some have even gone so far as to suggest that for barbel to feed in temperatures lower than this figure is biologically impossible. My own experience

suggests that this is not the case, and as recently as last winter I caught barbel when the water temperature was less than 2°C. The critical point, however, was that the temperature of the water was increasing. I openly acknowledge that I will not normally go barbel fishing if the water temperature is less than +4°C. If it is greater than 6°C, and rising, I will move heaven and earth to be out fishing for barbel! And at over 6°C, winter barbel are very active indeed.

Winter barbel activity is undoubtedly linked more closely to temperature gradient than to absolute temperature. Tony Miles and Trefor West have suggested in their excellent book *Barbel*, that they would much rather fish with a temperature of 4°C that is rising, than 7°C and falling. I agree entirely with this viewpoint, and also with their conclusive statement that the best feeding conditions for winter barbel are provided by an influx of warm coloured water. Conditions like this are usually the result of wet, south-westerly airstreams with their accompanying characteristic mild weather.

Try to think of winter barbel as thermometers. Rising temperatures and an increase in water coloration will see a corresponding increase in activity, while declining temperatures and increasing water clarity usually herald a downturn in sport.

Locating Winter Barbel

After the scouring effects of floodwater and frosts, winter rivers are noticeably less characterized by cover, many of the weedbeds of summer having been swept away. To compensate for this, however, the water will be highly coloured, and this in itself provides barbel with all the security they need to forage confidently in 'open' water. Many of the holding areas will be the same as they are in summer, principally because they can provide a regular food supply. But other areas will now be visited regularly, too, as food becomes scarce, and in short, winter barbel could turn up almost anywhere where the current is to their liking.

The subject of current strength is vitally important when it comes to locating these fish in winter. Some say that during floods, barbel remain in their traditional haunts, and that their streamlined shape leaves them untroubled by turbulent, fast currents. Whether this is true or not is irrelevant, because my experience suggests that winter barbel have distinct preferences as far as flow rates are concerned. On flooded rivers in particular, identifying swims that possess the correct flow rate is critical. It is my belief that barbel prefer areas with slow- to medium-paced currents, and these are usually found in the marginal sections of a river carrying floodwater. The higher the flood, the closer they will move into the bank, and I have caught countless winter barbel in a flood by placing a bait in an area that is dry when the river is at normal level.

The best winter barbel swims that I know usually coincide with a bend or a partially submerged bush or tree. Slack water will always be located on the inside of a bend or directly behind the submerged bush, and the further out from the bank you cast, the faster the flow gets. I believe that barbel constantly seek out evenly paced currents moving at a comfortable speed; thus as floodwater increases or decreases they will move correspondingly closer or further from the bank until they find an area to their liking. Swims like these are highly favoured because they allow the fish to enjoy a comfortable existence regardless of river conditions. At normal level my comments

regarding summer barbel would apply, and the crease between fast and slow water is usually the 'hot' area; of equal significance is the fact that barbel will be tightly grouped and are often loath to move very far. In cold conditions particularly, a bait as little as 3ft (1m) away from the holding spot could be ignored. As a general rule, the lower the water temperature, the greater the degree of bait positioning accuracy required.

Baits for Winter Barbel

There are only four baits that I ever use for winter barbel: luncheon meat (usually bacon grill), cheese paste and lobworms and maggots. Quite simply, in warm, coloured water, barbel will respond best to a large 'smelly' bait both during daylight and after dark. Meat and cheese paste are my usual choices, purely out of convenience, but lobworms are just as good where eels are not a problem. In low clear water, particle-sized baits are better, although at this time of year hempseed holds nothing like the same attraction for barbel as it does in the summer and autumn, a phenomenon probably caused by the difficulty that hemp's natural oil has in emulsifying with cold water. Maggots are a much better bet, and unless water temperatures are very mild (above 8°C), I don't bother to carry hemp at all.

Luncheon meat is a great winter barbel bait. Where the barbel become wary of it, try punching it into cylinders with an apple corer or tearing it into chunks.

Rigs

My standard winter barbel leger rig is very simple, and basically the same leger tackle that I use in summer. The main difference is that I will probably employ a luncheon meat 'stringer' to deposit a few samples of the chosen hookbait in a very tight area (assuming that a holding spot has been identified). For presenting maggots I will use a swimfeeder, but in winter the large heavy feeder will be dispensed with, to be replaced by a small to medium block-end. The key to winter barbel fishing is regularity of feed, not total quantity. A regular stream of maggots over a few hours will eventually attract barbel if they are in the vicinity, but I rarely use more than 4 pints (2.2 litres) in a day.

Winter Barbel: Diverse Approaches

The two approaches I make to winter barbel are fundamentally different, and both are linked to the prevailing weather conditions. Thus, if the weather is mild and the river in good condition – that is, with steady or rising water temperatures and a good colour – I will opt for mobility. In these conditions, location is absolutely para-

mount. I *know* that the barbel will be feeding somewhere and my first task is to try and get a bite. This will involve the systematic search of several swims with a single hookbait, and I am confident that if I put a bait in front of a barbel it will take it. Every swim will be searched thoroughly, yard by yard, and only when I am satisfied that a bait has been presented in all likely areas will I move on. The best way to search a swim in this manner is to use a leger that will hold in the current, *but only just*. By drawing on the mainline and lowering the rod tip, the rig can be bumped along for a few yards before being allowed to settle. Bites will rarely materialize 'on the move' so it pays to adopt a 'stop/start' technique, whereby the bait is allowed to settle for a couple of minutes before it is moved on.

In winter, upstream legering is often more effective than 'downstreaming'. By casting upstream and balancing the leger with the current so that it only just holds bottom, a very sensitive presentation is achieved. Quivertips are ideally suited to this type of work, and a healthy bend in the tip is essential. This will help to exaggerate even the very shyest of bites, since the tip will straighten

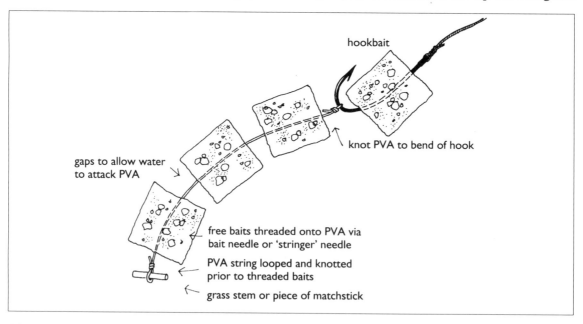

hookbait

knot PVA to bend of hook

gaps to allow water
to attack PVA

free baits threaded onto PVA via
bait needle or 'stringer' needle

PVA string looped and knotted
prior to threaded baits

grass stem or piece of matchstick

Fig. 12 PVA'd free offerings.

The author with an 8lb-plus winter barbel caught on a trip with his father.

dramatically when the bait is picked up. Of greater importance is the fact that barbel will feel absolutely minimal resistance, leading to bolder, more confident bites. This technique is also deadly for feeder fishing both in summer and winter.

On a low clear river, the only genuine prospects of good barbel sport will come with experience of _known_ holding areas. This is particularly so in cold weather, and in these circumstances, unless you know where the barbel 'live', fishing will be very hit and miss. However, informed judgement will usually be rewarded with a fish or two eventually. The main problem will be that feeding periods will be very limited; quite often they take place after dark and I have known winter barbel to feed well into the hours of darkness on many occasions. At night, luncheon meat, cheese and worms are excellent baits and a mobile approach can be considered, but during daylight the only viable approach will be with a swimfeeder and maggots. Regular casts, probably every twenty minutes or so, are the key to success, and it may take several hours for the first tell-tale knocks on the quivertip to materialize. Try to stick to a single likely area and keep everything 'tight', especially your casting and the positioning of the feeder.

Handling Barbel: A Final Plea

Barbel are our most sporting river fish, and it is in all our interests that they are handled properly. Barbel give their all during the fight and they should _never_ be retained in keepnets. Ideally they should be supported, head upstream in a flowing current, until they demonstrate enough strength to swim away unaided. If you intend to retain barbel in the _short_ term – and I do mean _short_ – there are two viable alternatives: the first is to place them head upstream in the margins, safely supported in the mesh of a large, open frame landing net. Better still, in my opinion, is the Gold Label pike/barbel tunnel. This uniquely constructed framed sack is wedge shaped so that it never collapses on fish, water pressure causing it to adopt a stable, open profile. Oxygen inflow is at its maximum and the barbel is well supported in the current. Traditional carp sacks should _not_ be used. With all the money that we spend on rods and reels, it is worth investing in the barbel's future by purchasing a tunnel. In this way, healthy barbel sport will be guaranteed for generations to come. Also, with the increasing number of stock programmes being carried out by both the NRA and individual fishery owners/managers, the future for the species looks like a bright one.

6 BREAM

A big bream is an impressive looking fish. Forget about the disappointing fight that bream up to 5lb are associated with, because a *big* bream will give a good account of itself and cause you to draw breath when you see it on the bank. I sincerely believe that bream over double figures are probably the hardest specimen fish of all to catch consistently. And when a huge, deep bronze-flanked bream finally rolls into the landing net you will know that it has been hard earned.

So far, truly gigantic bream have evaded me. To be fair, I have never fished a big bream venue, and must confess to being rather reluctant because of the long biteless sessions that are synonymous with specimen bream campaigns. However, the fact that I have never accidentally captured one indicates to me that a game plan is essential to catch giant bream with any regularity. It is therefore my intention in the future to make the sacrifice and to catch one of these awe-inspiring creatures.

In the meantime, I will describe the way in which I fish for big bream in small rivers – and although river fish cannot compete with stillwater bream in pure size terms, they are a worthwhile challenge in their own right. I have also persuaded Tony Miles, one of the country's top bream experts, to bring his essential knowledge to this book.

BIG BREAM FROM SMALL RIVERS

Mention an intimate small river with its characteristic bends, glides, overhanging trees and prolific weed growth to the majority of anglers, and the chances are that they will conjure up visions of hectic sport with dace, roach, barbel and especially chub. The last thing that will cross their mind is the possibility of a bream to 6lb or more. The fact remains, however, that whenever bream find their way into small rivers and streams they appear to flourish. But the attraction of small river bream goes beyond pounds and ounces because the approach required to catch them is angling in its purest form: stalking.

Location
When after small river bream forget everything you have ever learned about fishing for them on stillwaters and big, slow-flowing rivers, and imagine instead that you are fishing for barbel. For a start, you will need some polarizing glasses to help you spot the unmistakable dark shapes of a small group of big fish when they bask just underneath the surface, as they inevitably do on a warm day. Basking bream look almost black in the water, rather like large, elongated leaves, drifting slowly or holding a stationary position in the current. Visually identifying fish will give you an enormous head-start, obviating the need to explore countless swims with fishing tackle before you find them.

But bream will not always show themselves on the surface, and sooner or later you will have to come to terms with establishing their favourite haunts. In my experience the following features are reliable bream holding areas:

Cabbage/Lily Beds
These are classic bream swims, and are commonplace on many of our small rivers. Cabbages tend to grow in water between 3 and 8ft (0.9 and 2.4m) deep over a firm bottom. Look for them in some of the steadier runs with an evenly paced current which ambles along at a slow walking pace. If there are cabbages and bream in your river, the chances are that they will frequently coincide.

Bends

Bends are followed by bream wherever you find them in moving water. In extremely low water conditions, the outside of the bend where the flow is at its paciest might harbour a small shoal, but generally speaking the steadier water on the inside of the bend, or the crease where the faster water meets the slow, are more reliable.

Depressions

Holes in the river bed are called 'depressions' nowadays, but whatever the terminology, a sudden change in depth creates a food trap of the fish order: food that is swept along by the current gets trapped in the depression and inevitably the area becomes favoured by many fish, including bream.

Weir Pools

Weir pools hardly seem the most likely place to find bream, but they love them. Besides, weir pools are not all foaming water and unpredictable currents, in which case it is easier to recognize the advantages that they offer bream. Take the back of the pool for instance, an area that will be characterized by a steeply shelving river bed and a steadily flowing current: bream definitely like these areas and the rich feeding prospects that they offer. If your small river contains a good head of bream and a weir pool, the weir pool will almost certainly be one of the best swims on the river.

Overhanging Trees

Despite the fact that bream tend to roam the river in search of food, on hot days especially, the cool shade offered by a large overhanging tree, especially a mature spreading willow, could provide a temporary rest area. Not swims to spend vast amounts of time in, but worth a cast or two.

The Shallows

Evenly paced shallow glides are possibly the most unlikely sounding areas for bream. Bream have a reputation for enjoying deep water, and whereas I wouldn't class them as a deep-water species, nevertheless areas as shallow as 2ft (60cm) in depth make poor bream swims during daylight.

But not so after dark. Bream are reliable nocturnal feeders and they will move considerable distances to exploit rich feeding areas, especially those neglected during daylight. I have caught many bream on shallow glides less than 4ft (1.2m) deep, but each and every one of them has fallen to a bait presented after dark.

Baits

This is another area which contravenes the bream-fishing textbook. To begin with, forget about groundbait – use it on a small river, and all that you will succeed in doing is spooking the shoal for the rest of the day. You might think that groundbait introduced the night before a session would encourage the bream to feed heartily the following day, but you would be wrong. For some reason, even the appearance of a large carpet of groundbait on the bottom appears to unsettle these contrary fish. Holding a shoal of bream without groundbait is probably an alien concept to many bream anglers, but it pays to remember that bream shoals on this type of fishery are likely to number between five and ten fish. Loosefeed is a far more practical proposition. It can be introduced regularly without the alarming effects typical of a barrage of groundbait, and it can be fed 'little and often' to keep the bites coming.

Many stillwater bream experts have reported that bream do not like hemp. While acknowledging that this might be true for specimen gravel pit or reservoir fish, I can assure you that small river bream love it. A pint of hemp is my favourite loose feed and I always use it with total confidence, quite sure that if the bream are around they will eat it. Other obvious candidates include maggots and casters, with the emphasis on the latter because they don't crawl away. Indeed, a mixture of casters and hemp is an ideal loosefeed that will not only occupy the bream, but will also offer a good option for hookbait in the form of the casters if the bream refuse to pick up large hookbaits. Generally speaking though, I have few problems in getting bites on big baits fished in combination with 4 or 5lb hooklengths and sizes 6 to 10 hooks. Sweetcorn, lobworms and bread flake are my favourites, fished either singly or in cocktails, but on well-known barbel stretches luncheon meat takes some beating. Contrary to popular opinion, bream love luncheon meat, especially when they have developed a taste for it.

Remember, too, that a sprinkling of your chosen hookbait introduced over the hemp will improve the chances of a 'pick-up', and I like to scatter a few lumps of flake, grains of corn or pieces of broken worm at random.

Tackle

Two rods are required for small river bream: for legering, a medium feeder rod between 11- and 12ft long with a progressive action will be ideally suited to open water work when 4 to 6lb reel line will be used. Try to choose a rod with a choice of quivertips – 1½oz, 2oz and 2½oz glass tips are the ideal selection.

In snaggy swims I like to float fish. Instant bite registration puts the angler in control, and a bite on float tackle rarely comes unannounced.

The author with a typical bream from a small river.

Preliminary line bites prior to a 'take' are commonplace, and provided that your tackle is powerful enough, few fish should be lost. I like to use a 12ft specimen rod with a 1¼ to 1½lb test curve; a rod like this will be well matched to the 6 and 8lb reel lines that are necessary in snaggy, confined swims.

As far as reels are concerned, a medium-sized fixed spool reel capable of holding at least 100yds (91m) of 8lb mono will suffice, provided that it possesses a good slipping clutch mechanism. Personally I favour the Shimano G.T.M. or Symetre because of their superb aero spool design, a feature which delivers long, accurate casts, even with light link legers and strong line.

Since bream in small rivers are often found in extremely snaggy areas, I am also particular about the line I use. In open water this will be Trilene XL in 4lb test, an extremely limp nylon with virtually no memory which feels silky smooth to the touch. In snag-infested swims and for fishing across weedbeds, Berkley Trilene XT is my favourite because of its superb abrasion-resistant qualities, all-round castability and knot strength.

Other than this, a selection of shots, Partridge Hilton and Fox Series 2 hooks in sizes 6 to 12, Drennan Superspades in sizes 14 and 16 (for caster hookbaits), Kryston braided hooklengths (for abrasion resistance), light Arlesey bombs, forceps and bait droppers (for laying down beds of hemp) and balsa or crowquill Avon floats, complete my special tackle requirements.

Rigs and Tactics

I have already indicated that the successful small river bream angler will adopt a mobile approach. Forget about turning up to a 'hot swim', 'filling it in' and sitting back to wait for the inevitable 'ton-up' session to start. Instead, carry the minimum of tackle, bait a handful of likely looking swims, keep them topped up with bait, and fish them in rotation until you find some bream. The signal that you have found bream will be obvious enough, especially if you are fishing over a bed of hemp. Line bites are commonplace, even from a small group of fish when they are actively feeding over a dense carpet of bait. On the other hand, you might even catch a bream first cast if the swim has been prepared properly.

The first cast that I make into a swim will undoubtedly be with leger tackle, a light swanshot paternoster or link leger to minimize disturbance being the favourite, even if it is a swim better suited to an approach with float tackle. Unless I can see bream in a swim I will be testing for line bites, and when I get one I will immediately withdraw the tackle and replace it with a float if appropriate. Obviously, if it is an open water area or a far bank swim, I will persevere with the leger tackle and in this situation I will leave the leger in place until I get a proper bite. There is generally no problem, either, in distinguishing a line bite from the real thing: a 'liner' will cause the quivertip to nudge round quickly with all the initial hallmarks of a good bite, but it will spring back to its original position equally quickly. Other forms of liners include 'knocks', 'taps' and 'nudges' on the tip.

A real bite, however, will pull the tip positively round and it will either hold its position for a second or two or simply keep going. Either way, strike!

The leger tackle that I use for bream in small rivers is very simple, comprising a basic link leger with swanshot (SSG) used in place of an Arlesey bomb. The advantage of shot over traditional leger weights is that they can be precisely balanced to match the flow by adding or subtracting individual shot; you have finally got it right when the rig will hold its position in the swim but can be dislodged by drawing a few inches of line in front of the butt ring. The hooklength is usually 24in (60cm) long, and will be made from 4lb Trilene XL for use in open water swims or 6lb, 8lb or even 10lb Kryston Silkworm if there are snags present (see Fig. 13).

On a small river, however, perhaps the most exciting and effective way of catching bream is on the float. What could be more satisfying than watching a traditional crowquill or balsa Avon float waver and dip at first, before finally gliding away and disappearing from sight? It's real Crabtree stuff and personally I love it!

This is 'laying on', a traditional style of float fishing that is ideal for presenting a bait in the

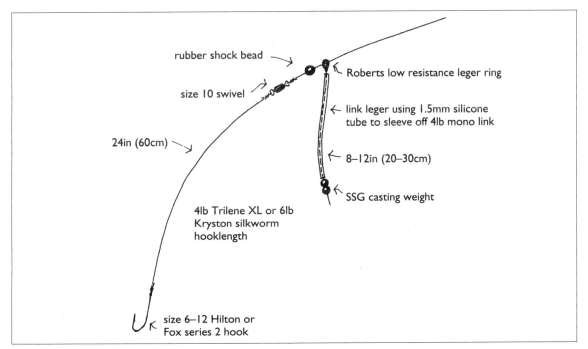

Fig. 13 Bream link leger.

margins as well as over the edge of a bed of cabbages or lily pads. But the advantages of this approach go way beyond pure aesthetics. Legering across thick, marginal weedbeds is fraught with problems: first of all, it is difficult enough to get your hookbait to lie near to the edge of the weedbed (probably the most likely place to produce a bite). And even if you do, the line will enter the swim at a sharp gradient, bite registration will be poor and striking will be ineffective. A float though, is ideal for this type of swim, especially if you grease the main line to keep it on the surface. The float can be made to lie hard against the outer 'pads' of the cabbages or lilies with the hookbait lying right next to the cover. Bite registration will be instant, and a timely strike, sweeping the rod upwards, will put you in immediate contact with the fish. A typical scenario would be as follows:

The float rig is cast out and drawn back until the float is touching the edge of the weedbed. The terminal tackle swings down in an arc underneath the float, settling hard against the root area of the weedbed. After a few minutes the float begins to waver, disturbed from its half-cocked lazy position by the activities of bream below. A few bubbles burst to the surface and the float dips sharply, but it bobs back to the surface immediately. A 'liner'. Indications like this continue for a frustrating couple of minutes or so (it seems like an hour) before finally the float bobs, dips and slides confidently across the surface, disappearing as it does so. The answering strike meets with solid resistance and the first bream of the day is on...

When the fight commences you will appreciate the value of using an 8 or 10lb Kryston Silkworm hooklength. It is not the fighting power of the bream that is the problem, for even a fit river bream is small and cannot be described as a 'scrapper', but the abrasive nature of the cabbage beds spells danger for taut mono lines. The

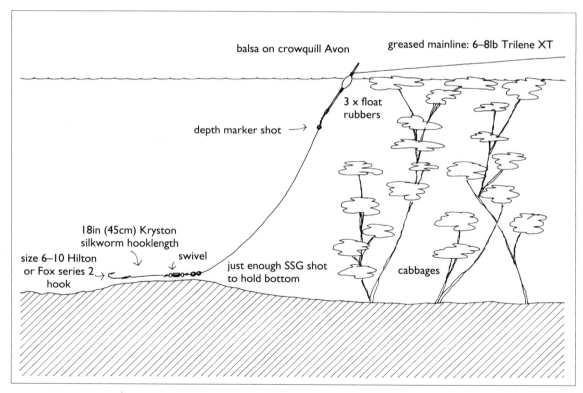

Fig. 14 *Laying on for small-river bream.*

object of the exercise is to get the bream out of the weedbed as quickly as possible, and the extra security of a braided hooklength is essential for bullying tactics like these.

In Conclusion

You will not break any national records fishing for bream on small rivers, but you might surprise yourself and catch a personal best. Specimen-sized bream, between 6 and 10lb or more are being caught with increasing regularity from the Upper Welland, Waveney and Great Ouse. Only last year I learned of the capture of a double figure fish in a match held on the Ouse!

Providing that you can tune your thinking to the size of individual fish rather than the 'big bag' syndrome, you will not be disappointed. In fact, disappointment will be the last emotion that

This catch of bream from a small river was taken on a float.

comes to the surface when you slip the net under a deep, slab-sided bronze bream from a river that you could almost jump across...

SPECIMEN BREAM
FROM STILLWATERS   by Tony Miles

Over the last fifteen or so years, most of the really enormous bream caught have been taken from gravel pits, and it is these fish and fisheries with which I am most familiar. However, other massive fish have been taken from natural lakes, meres and reservoirs, and although I know less about this sort of bream fishing, much of what I say about pit breaming will apply. The main difference will be in the location procedure. On the whole, lakes and reservoirs have far fewer features than the average gravel pit and are much richer; this means that the features which are present are more likely to hold feeding fish, and that the shoals of fish will be bigger. Where features are few and far between, shoals of big bream often graze like sheep, moving round in large numbers, frequently following defined patrol routes. Numbers of fish dictate that there is a far greater chance of individuals showing themselves by breaking the water surface, and this is a further aid to the location process.

A large head of big bream will also demand proportionately greater quantities of bait than the gravel pits of my acquaintance, which generally have a low population density. So when you read what I have to say about loosefeeding, apply it with regard to the numbers of fish in your water; my preparation of a Queenford swim with two tins of corn, for instance, when I would expect no more than half-a-dozen fish to visit me during the night, would be highly inappropriate if your water contains shoals of upwards of a hundred big bream.

Location of Gravel Pit Bream

If the bream on your pit are prone to rolling, then obviously you must take advantage of that; there is no better location tool than your own eyes. However, most pit location is a painstaking affair of mapping the contours of the water, and then

Bream like this beautiful double-figure specimen are a reward for dedicated bream enthusiasts like Tony Miles.

trying to interpret how they will affect the location and feeding behaviour of the bream. During the mapping process, I am looking for gravel bars and plateaux, areas of extensive bottom weed and areas of clean bottom. I want to know where the bottom composition is gravel, mud or silt, and in particular, which of the features accompanying a change in depth are naturally weed-free. Unlike tench, bream show a distinct tendency to favour naturally weed-free areas. Dragging has never proved very productive, either; both I and my friends have had very poor results after manual weed clearance.

For the actual mapping, I shall assume that you do not have access to a boat and echo sounder, which obviously make this laborious job so much quicker. First of all, set up a sliding pike float and a heavy lead so that you can comfortably map out to maximum casting range; the stop knot is made with 'power gum' (*see* Fig. 15a). Initially set the float at a fairly shallow setting, say 4ft (1.2m), and then cast the required distance to the left hand extremity of the swim, noting a feature on the horizon so that you can reproduce the cast each time. If the float alights in water deeper than 4ft

(1.2m), it will obviously disappear. Now start working the float back towards you in a series of long sweeps, perhaps taking in 3 yds (2.7m) of line at a time. After each sweep, give a little slack to allow the slider to work properly, and repeat this procedure until the float has been completely retrieved. If at any point during the retrieve the float crosses water of less than 4ft (1.2m) in depth, such as over a gravel bar, it will pop to the surface, and one feature will have been located. Continue this process at steadily increasing depth settings, and casting in several directions, and you will gradually build up a mental image of what you have in front of you.

Having located the position and extent of each feature roughly, it is now necessary to assess each one more accurately, and for this I use a second rod, rigged identically. Cast the first rod to the feature to be more closely examined, and leave the float in place as a focus point; then cast the float on the second rod all around it. If your casting accuracy is good, you can build up a remarkably accurate picture of each feature in this manner; an hour's work will give you details of feature size, and steepness of gradient. The only problem with this method is that the line from the first rod is likely to be fouled by the second, and so I use the following refinement: having located a feature, I break off the slider about 1ft (30cm) above the stop knot and tie a loop in the free end. A similar loop is tied in the end of the reel line, and the two loops joined with a firm tie of PVA. The float is then cast to the required position, left for a minute or two until the PVA has melted, at which time the free line is retrieved, leaving the marker in place. Isn't that clever? Obviously, however, only use this method if you have faith in your casting accuracy. Also, make sure that you can retrieve the floats after use – I use a special grapple made up of an in-line lead and large sea treble, which casts like a rocket.

Having found the features, which ones do we fish? There are no hard-and-fast answers to that, otherwise all those of us who love pit breaming would not experience so many blanks! However, reliable areas do seem to be gravel bars, especially those that exist in otherwise weedy areas and are

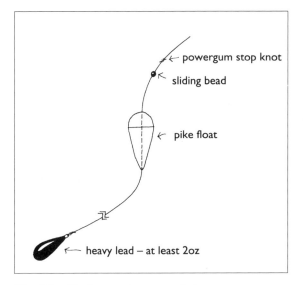

Fig. 15a. Rig for mapping a gravel pit.

themselves clear of all but light silkweed. The members of the now sadly defunct Queenford syndicate were of the opinion that the bream's dislike of thick weed would see them swimming over the top of it in the search for clear oases such as clean bars or plateaux, where we would hope to have our baits in readiness.

The other very reliable feature is the clean, apparently barren area of either mud or silt. This area more closely mirrors the situation in a reservoir, and big pit bream, once they arrive in such an area, will often hang around for days. Small gravel bars and humps, while reliable, rarely hold big bream for more than the odd night.

During the fishing session it is important to mark the swim in some way to ensure baiting and casting accuracy; when fishing bars, a miscast of only a few yards could see you fishing in thick weed. For short to medium range, permanent markers can be introduced, as previously explained. You can go to the refinement of equipping the floats with beta lights or, even better, starlights, though the latter would have to be changed daily; this is easy if you have a boat but a nuisance if you haven't. Having said that, as long as your casting accuracy is reliable, it shouldn't prove too much of a problem.

Should you want to avoid all that trouble, and the swim is a bit too far out for a beta light, use bulbous floats painted pure white; you can see these very well at night with a torch for recasting accuracy.

The correct direction of cast can be reproduced easily, either by using an illuminated swim marker, or by focusing on a known horizon feature. However, distances can be misleading in the dark, so it is a good idea to mark the line in daylight at the correct spot, so that at night you know when you have cast the correct distance. A foolproof method is to tie a small stop knot into the line at the tip ring after a cast in daylight, and before taking in the slack. Then when casting at night, allow the travelling line to run out loosely over your finger, and as soon as you feel the little knot pass your finger, check the rig in flight; it should alight in the right place.

Baits and Groundbaiting Techniques

Despite all the high tech advances in baits over recent years, it seems that giant bream are still just as content with maggots, worms, bread and sweetcorn as they ever were, and almost all the double-figure fish I know of were caught on these traditional offerings. The bait *par excellence* is undoubtedly large lobs, either fished on their own or in cocktails; lobworm together with bread flake has taken many fish, as has a combination of lobworm and corn. For fishing over light silkweed or soft silt, air-injecting the tail has proved deadly.

Among the other baits, obviously maggots and casters are excellent, and the famous cocktail of maggots and flake, one of Alan Wilson's favourites, has long since proved its worth. Big bream will also take boilies, as will all large cyprinids, and several fish have been taken this way. I myself have no experience of this method of fishing for them, although I have used soft, flavoured pastes which for a while were very successful at TC pit. All my flavoured TC pastes took only tench, but anglers such as Alan Smith and Cliff Dean took several nice bream on pastes. Obviously, there is plenty of room here for further experimentation.

Groundbaiting is a vitally important part of big bream fishing, and it is very difficult to determine the correct approach in a pit holding a small head of big fish. Very large shoals of fish will clear mounds of cereal feed, but in a gravel pit my normal approach will be a modest amount of cereal as a carrier plus plenty of particles to keep the fish foraging. These days, my cereal feed is invariably ordinary bread crumbs sweetened with pure molasses, which bream certainly like. The particle content can be maggots, pinkies, squatts, casters, rice, corn, pearl barley, stewed wheat and so on, though the one particle I no longer use is hemp; of all specimen fish, big bream are the only ones I have found which do not apparently touch hemp. I would choose casters as the particle content every time, fishing an air injected lob/caster cocktail over the top. My normal quantity of feed for a night at Queenford was a bucket of cereal containing two pints of casters and two tins of corn, plus perhaps a dozen chopped lobs.

The main drawback to using maggots and casters in the feed – apart from cost – is the one of nuisance fish, especially perch. One facet of pit bream behaviour that seems universally common is their preference for night feeding, with first light being particularly good. The trouble is that perch are avid dawn feeders too, and the last thing you want is to be pestered by hordes of tiny perch while waiting for your first bite from a double-figure bream. For this reason, a compromise particle such as corn or rice may be found preferable in a practical fishing situation.

Fishing Techniques

Of all big fish, specimen bream are among the most nocturnal, and angling techniques inevitably revolve around legering, coupled with audible bite indicators to cope with the long hours of waiting that will certainly be involved. The two rigs that have found most favour amongst big bream anglers are either the long-tail running paternoster (*see* Fig. 15b), or the short-tail fixed paternoster (*see* Fig. 15c). I favour the latter for the following reason: although there can be a lot of waiting for the bream to find your bait, when they do, they feed quite confidently, and

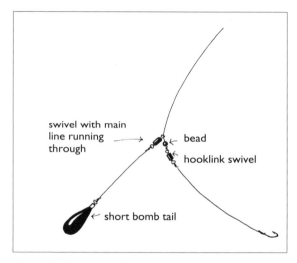

swivel with main line running through

bead

hooklink swivel

short bomb tail

Fig. 15b. Bream rig: long-tail running paternoster.

then with long tails there is the very real risk of them being deep hooked – I have witnessed several stillwater bream being very deeply hooked to this rig. With my short-tail fixed version, the 6in (15cm) hooklink, while giving bream enough rope to hang themselves, prevents deep hooking absolutely and a fish only has to move a little way for the rig to act as a bolt arrangement. The bream then swims against the resistance, giving a positive bite, but it is generally only lip-hooked, or at worst, hooked at the back of the mouth.

Obviously there are schools of thought for each method, both with very valid reasons for their choice. Derek Quirk, for instance, who enjoyed great success at Queenford, stated that he stopped using running paternosters because he wished to avoid the bites being drop-backs, which does happen often with short-tail fixed rigs. Derek felt that drop-backs could prove difficult to hit and he wanted to remove the possibility of missing bites. Perfectly logical and well thought out; obviously Derek was confident in the rig he selected. Using a heavy lead in his arrangement, every bite took the bobbins upwards, no matter in which direction the bream swam after taking the bait. I can see the sound logic behind Derek's argument, but the fact remains that every bream I caught on my short-tail arrangement gave just

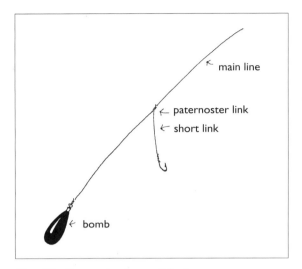

Fig. 15c. Bream rig: short-tail fixed paternoster.

Tony Miles' stillwater indicator.

as positive an indication, although they did all start as drop-backs as the lead shifted. Personally, I like to see an initial drop-back when breaming. The bobbin can go up for a variety of reasons including small nuisance fish, wind or weed drift, and also because of line bites, the bane of the big bream angler's life, and it is often very difficult to distinguish between all these indications. If the bobbin drops back, however, the lead must have moved, and only a big fish will do this.

Another rig that found favour at Queenford was an extension on the air-injected lob principle, but with the lobs hanging just off the bottom from a buoyant rig rather than being themselves buoyant (*see* Fig. 15d). This was widely used, although I was never entirely happy with it as I felt it could make foul-hooking more likely. Looking at the captures using the rig, it would appear that my fears were groundless, although at least one huge fish was returned unweighed after it was found to be foul-hooked. Nevertheless, I still say that foul-hooking with this rig is theoretically of higher probability than with more traditional rigs.

Another common approach in recent years to big bream fishing has been with double hook rigs, which allow different baits or variable presentations; for instance, one tail could be short with a lob and corn cocktail, while the other could be longer with an air-injected lob. The permutations are endless. There is one school of thought which considers the use of double hooks as totally pointless, since a fish seeing one bait is bound to see the other, no advantage being therefore gained from the second hook. Where the style of fishing involves frequent casting, I would go along with this argument; for big pit bream, however, there can literally be hours between indications. One of the problems with this is the jerky bite, which you know has come from a small perch and which you ignore. But all anglers must then sit and wonder whether the worm is still on the end of the hook, and using two hooks, both lobworm-baited, allows for more relaxed fishing in that respect; at least you will have had to ignore *two* separate indications before worrying about checking your terminal rig!

Where serious thought *does* have to be given to the wisdom of double hook rigs is in heavy weed, as the spare hook when playing a fish is a potential snag point. For this reason, although I did use double hooks at Queenford, I only did so because I was using very short hooklinks. I would never have contemplated using double, long-flowing traces in a weedy water, as that would have invited snagging.

As far as attaching the hooklinks to the main line is concerned, I have been through all the permutations of swivels, rig tubes and so on, and now use the simple rig shown to me by Alan Wilson many years ago. At the appropriate intervals on the main line I tie stand-off loops, and then attach the hooklinks by the matchman's loop-to-loop arrangement. Sliding a short length of rigid Drennan fine bore tubing over the two loops ensures a neat and tangle-free finish, and one in which changing the hooklength is possible in seconds. For my big bream double hook rig, see Fig. 15e.

Line Bites and Striking Techniques

Perhaps the most vital lesson for the would-be captor of double-figure bream from gravel pits is not to be in too great a hurry to strike. This is because, of all fish, big bream are most prone to giving successions of line bites before they commence feeding in earnest. Ignore a bream brushing your line and it will not spook, but continue to feed; strike and miss, or worse still, strike and prick a bream, and the swim can be wrecked for the night. For this reason, I recommend not sitting directly over your rods for this style of fishing. Once a big bream picks up your bait, he intends to eat it, and rarely will he drop it. My normal technique is to allow the bobbin to rise to the butt, or the butt indicator to fall away, and for the reel to start back-winding, before I attempt to strike. By sitting a few yards from the rods, any line bite will show itself for what it is before you get to the rod to strike. I cannot stress how important this is: premature striking of bream bites, a high proportion of which will be liners, is a sure way to failure.

In Conclusion

Catching very big bream from gravel pits is undoubtedly one of the most challenging tasks facing the all-round specimen hunter, and the sense of satisfaction when success finally comes is hard to express. So, when you finally land the fish of your dreams, treat it with the respect it deserves. Big bream are delicate creatures, and do not take kindly to being crammed into inadequate keepnets, or placed in sacks in 9in (23cm) of

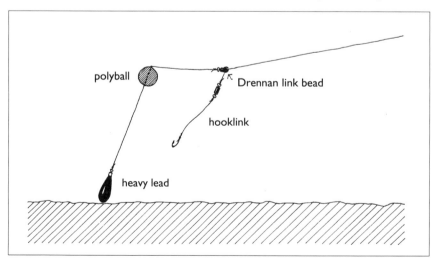

Fig. 15d Bream rig: an extension of the air-injected lob principle, with the lobs just hanging off the bottom from a buoyant rig.

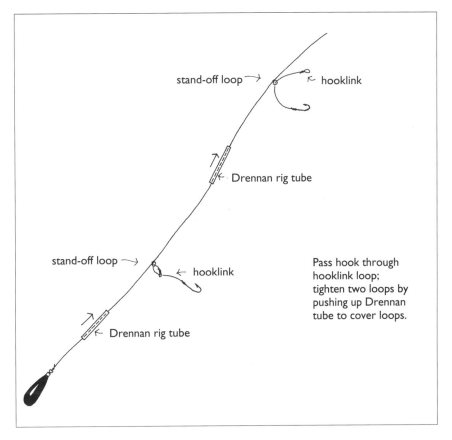

Fig. 15e Bream rig: double hook rig.

stand-off loop → hooklink

← Drennan rig tube

stand-off loop → ← hooklink

Pass hook through hooklink loop; tighten two loops by pushing up Drennan tube to cover loops.

← Drennan rig tube

water during the heat of the day. If you are retaining a night-caught fish for a photograph, do so in a properly positioned, capacious carp sack in deep water, or use a receptacle designed for the job, such as the Queenford retention system marketed by Bob Church. Like all specimen fish, double-figure bream are too precious to be lost by careless or thoughtless handling.

The author with a 9lb 8oz gravel-pit bream, a fish that had never been caught before, and was one of only six bream known to be in the 15-acre pit.

7 CHUB

Chub are contrary fish in many ways. Notorious for their catholic tastes, they have something of a reputation as a greedy fish, being quite willing to engulf huge baits presented on the crudest of tackle. And yet they can be painfully shy, 'spooking' at the merest hint of an angler's silhouette on the skyline, shadow on the water or careless approach to a swim. It is my belief that fishing for chub on a small river teaches anglers more about the skills of fishing than any other approach in the sport.

Chub are also all-year-round fish, being avid feeders in both summer and winter, and responding happily to a variety of baits and techniques; you can catch chub with a bait nailed hard on the bottom, trotted at mid-depth or floated across the surface. These qualities make chub our most reliable quarry – though catching big specimens can never be described as 'easy'. I find them fascinating, and if I had to fish for just one species for the rest of my life it would be the chub.

Contributors here are Peter Stone, an expert on both river and stillwater chub, and one of the pioneers of gravel-pit chub fishing with deadbaits; and Stewart Allum, a member of the 'Chub Study Group' since its formation over twenty-one years ago, and who boasts an enviable record of both river and stillwater fish.

Chub are our most obliging coarse fish.

SUMMER CHUB

To locate river chub successfully, two thoughts should be uppermost in your mind: cover and food. Chub are not fish that spend time roaming the river in search of food, preferring instead to occupy a favourite lie and wait for an easy meal to be swept down to them by the current. If this comfortable position happens to coincide with

some form of shelter or cover, so much the better, and chub are notorious for occupying the snaggiest swims on the river.

They can be found in a variety of waterways, being a tenacious fish that will exist quite happily in slow-moving water or in the pacey headwaters or side-streams of a major river. Let us consider chub location on small rivers and streams, since the same basic principles can be applied to finding chub swims on bigger rivers. Location of slow-water chub, is a little bit more complicated – more of this later.

Locating Chub

Flood Rafts and Overhanging Trees

Chub are synonymous with this type of swim, and even the tiniest, most insignificant-looking bush can harbour large numbers of chub *if the current is to their liking*. The biggest raft on the river doesn't necessarily provide a home to the largest shoal of chub, but you can bet that wherever a lively, smooth current runs under a bush or tree there will probably be a chub or two in residence. Watch chub in these swims, and you will discover that they do not sit patiently in one spot: rather they will establish a 'circuit' under the canopy of cover, exploring the outer branches, the root structure of the tree and mid-raft areas regularly. Only a severe flood or sub-zero temperatures will dampen their activity, when they will frequently retire to the densest part of the cover.

Rushes, Reeds and 'Onions'

Chub enjoy the cover offered by these plants, and if they happen to be growing in the middle of the river, so much the better. Chub like to lie in wait in the quiet water behind rushbeds, occasionally moving sideways to intercept passing food items.

Depressions in the River Bed

Depressions make excellent chub swims, providing both cover and a highly effective food trap. A depression doesn't have to be dramatic in order to attract chub, and I have caught them in 'holes' which are no more than 1ft (30cm) deeper than the surrounding area. Generally speaking though, the deeper the depression, the more likely it is to hold chub.

Undercuts

Anglers who have never swum or dived in rivers probably don't appreciate quite how undercut many of our river banks can be. Some undercuts, particularly on the outside of bends or where the root structure of a bankside tree has collapsed, can extend for several feet into the bankside. Evidence of this phenomenon can be found if you cast a bait into a seemingly barren piece of river. You get a bite and yet can't understand why.

Where were the chub? Tucked away under the bank is the most likely explanation.

Creases

A 'crease' is an area where a slow current meets a faster one. With a little practice you can spot these areas, particularly on bends, and you will observe that the area where the two currents meet is marked by a distinctive 'crease' on the surface. You might be tempted to wonder why bends in the river are such prolific fish-producing areas: the answer is that they possess creases, with the slacker water as the inside of the bend and the force of the current pushed to the outside.

Bends are not the only cause of creases; shelving river beds and obstructions which divert the flow cause them, and the area immediately below a bend is also a reliable crease area, with the current meandering its way back across the river in a long diagonal line from a point below the outside of the bend.

Creases are significant because they are giant food traps for chub. Food items are swept along the pacey section, and the chub simply have to lie in the slower water, occasionally moving across the current to pick off passing morsels.

Narrow Runs between Rushbeds

This type of swim is worthy of special attention because chub know that the river is funnelled into a long narrow run with an evenly paced current, and that it represents a giant food conveyor belt. Groundbait the head of the run, and the chub will obligingly move upstream, making this a classic swim for multiple catches.

Streamer Weed

Long, shallow sections of the river are often choked with streamer weed or *Ranunculus* to give it its scientific name. At a first glance the river may appear devoid of fish, but study the runs between the 'mares' tails' of weed carefully and you will undoubtedly spot chub. Their black-tipped tails and large white lips are an immediate give-away, and baits trundled down the runs between the weedbeds or rolled underneath the waving fronds, will be greedily gobbled up.

Weir Pools

Weir pools are interesting and mysterious places which combine foaming white water with steadily flowing runs, deep slack areas and back eddies. Frequently filled with snags, depth changes and all manner of chub-holding spots, they are worthy of exploration on any stretch of river that is characterized by them.

Baits

The list of baits that can be used to catch chub is almost endless. Their voracious appetite and willingness to consume all manner of food items – from pieces of banana to live frogs – has earned them an unparalleled reputation for being greedy. And when you sit on a shoal of chub in a feeding mood it seems impossible to over-feed them. Basically, however, chub baits can be divided into four categories: naturals, standards, particles and artificials.

Natural Baits

Chub are great opportunist feeders, with the instinctive compulsion to consume just about any potential food source that moves or falls into the water. The following list represents some of my favourite naturals:

Slugs

These can be collected at the bankside on the morning of your fishing trip; the big black variety appear to be the best. Hook them lightly through the back or through the tail on a size 4 or 6 hook. The great thing about the slug is that being such a 'meaty' creature, it possesses plenty of casting weight, and is dense enough to freeline.

Lobworms

Lobworms are a terrific bait: summer, winter, flood, freeze-up or drought, they are always reliable. They work well fished as large singles on a size 6 or 8, but even better, in my opinion, in large bunches on a size 4 or 6. Freelined or legered, they work equally effectively.

Prawns

I suppose that prawns are a natural bait, although they could hardly be classed as a 'naturally occurring' creature on our river systems. Nevertheless, peeled prawns from the supermarket are engulfed with relish by chub. Freelined, legered or float fished, they require no pre-baiting and provoke instant takes. Try fishing a single peeled prawn on a size 8 or a double prawn on a 4 or a 6.

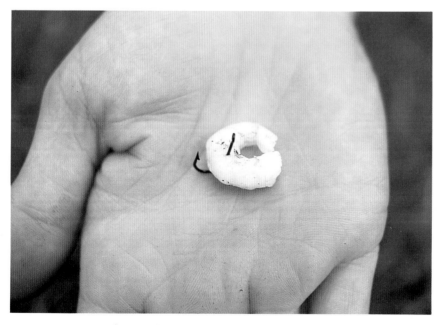

A peeled prawn, mounted properly and ready to be chomped by a hungry chub.

Standard Baits

Luncheon Meat

This is another superb chub bait, but one which has seen a great deal of use over the years. My favourite brand is 'Bacon Grill' which I mount in cubes on a size 6 for unpressured fisheries. In places where chub have become wary of meat, their resultant behaviour is typically fast, virtually unhittable knocks, and pulls on the rod tip. If this situation develops, try tearing chunks of meat off the block leaving plenty of rough edges, or make cylindrical baits using an apple corer.

Cheese Paste

This is my favourite chub bait above all others. Less popular than luncheon meat, it has nonetheless worked well on every chub stretch that I have tried it on, particularly those that have been 'hammered' on meat. Cheese paste is excellent when used in slightly coloured water and after dark, and I never go chub fishing without it. The size of the bait that you can use is totally flexible, and I mould it into an egg-shaped lump appropriate to the size of the hook. Anything from a size 2 to a size 12 will work, but remember to leave the hookpoint proud of the paste for instant penetration of the chub's tough mouth. I make cheese paste by blending together frozen Danish pastry mix, mature cheddar and Danish blue cheese in equal quantities. To replace the 'cheesy aroma' lost by adding the pastry mix, I 'pep up' the bait with synthetic cheese flavour. I also add a teaspoon of *red* powdered carp dye to the mix, because it is my experience that red paste outfishes yellow by at least two to one.

Bread

Bread is probably the most famous chub bait of them all. Flake or crust both work well, mounted on a variety of hooks from size 2 through to 10. Crust is a superb winter offering when fished 1 or 2in (2 to 5cm) off the bottom, and because it is buoyant it can be manipulated into swims where it would be impossible to present other, denser baits, simply by using the current to 'drift' it into place.

As a surface offering in the summer, crust makes for great and truly exciting fishing using simple freeline tactics. I have also found that bread takes flavours very well, and I rarely use it in its 'plain' form these days.

Maggots and Casters

These catch more specimen chub every season than any other popular bait. This is rather because of their more widespread use than any superiority, but their effectiveness cannot be ignored. When fed into the swim at regular intervals, maggots and casters have the potential to drive chub into a feeding frenzy. Float fished on both stick and waggler methods, or used in conjunction with a swimfeeder, a double maggot or caster on a strong size 16 hook they will be greedily accepted by shoal fish.

Boilies

The use of boilies as a chub bait is nowhere near as advanced as it ought to be. The chub's willingness to respond to new food sources and a wealth of flavours makes them probably more prone to accepting boilies instantly than carp. So far my experiments with boilies for chub in a range of sizes between ¼ and ¾in (6 and 18mm) have been very successful. Nor is there any need to be over-sophisticated, and the brightly coloured range of Richworth Shelf-Life boilies is tailormade for chub. 'Tutti-Frutti', 'Strawberry' and 'Banana' have been devoured with relish, while the results so far on 'Salmon Supreme' indicate that it might turn out to be the pick of the bunch. Hair-rigging as a catching method can be abandoned for the time being, too, because a side-hooked boilie, nicked lightly through the skin on a big hook, is very effective indeed.

Particle Baits

Hemp

This bait is a chub attractor *par excellence*: nothing can drive them into a feeding frenzy like hemp, not even maggots and casters. The problem with hemp is that it is very difficult to use on the hook, so I tend to use a bed of it in conjunction with a scattering of my chosen hookbait which is usually either sweetcorn, mini-boilies, maple peas or tares.

Sweetcorn

Sweetcorn is a devastating chub bait either fished over hemp or fed into the swim exclusively. Chub will tolerate large quantities of corn, unlike barbel, a species that tends to spook if too much corn is introduced. If chub become wary of standard yellow corn, a switch to a red or orange variety from the 'Pescaviva' range will produce bites again. My favourite chub flavours include: sardine, strawberry, cheese, banana, yoghurt and tutti-frutti.

Maple Peas, Tares

These are used as a hookbait when fishing over hemp. For instructions regarding their preparation, *see* the end of Chapter 3.

Chum Mixer

This simple bait takes the particle principle and moves it into a new dimension – to the surface. Flavoured, dyed mixers are absolute killers for summer chub on shallow, clean rivers.

Artificials

My experience of spinning or plug fishing for chub is rather limited, but I have caught them on artificials, including large, bushy dry flies. Any medium-sized floating plug is worth a try for chub, along with medium-sized blade spinners in silver, gold or perch patterns. The new range of Berkley Powerworms, distributed in the UK by Gold Label Tackle, look absolutely perfect for chub fishing, and I would expect chub to eat them straight off the bottom as well as on the retrieve. In addition to their lively wriggling action, 'Powerworms' are 'scented', being impregnated with a strong flavour which the chub appear to find very attractive.

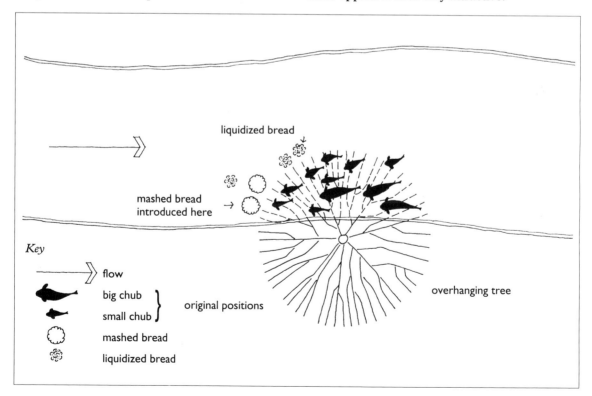

Fig. 16 *Tactical groundbaiting. Mashed and liquidized bread 1.*

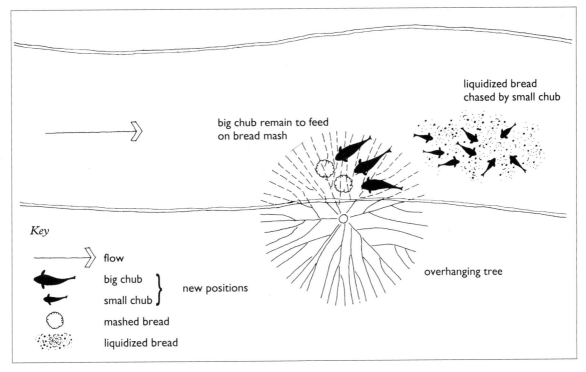

Fig. 17 *Tactical groundbaiting. Mashed and liquidized bread 2.*

Chub Groundbaits

I rarely use any other type of groundbait for chub than bread, either in mashed or liquidized form. Mashed bread is made by pulping up stale loaves of bread in water. On impact, some of it will sink while the bulk of it will shatter into bite-sized particles which drift downstream. Introduce a couple of balls of mashed bread into a number of winter chub swims at the beginning of a session, and follow it up by fishing each of them in rotation. Bites are often instantaneous following this 'priming' tactic.

Liquidized bread can be made by putting one-day-old loaves into a food processor. The resulting fine breadcrumbs will hold together simply by squeezing them in your hand; there is no need to add any water. Liquidized bread will shatter on impact into thousands of tiny particles which will drift for considerable distances downstream and as such it is an excellent long-range groundbait.

The differing properties of mashed and liquidized bread can be used to good effect by combining both types of feed in a single swim. The mashed bread, being heavier, will sink more quickly, leaving a loose carpet of bait on the river bed; the liquidized bread, when fed into the same area, will drift further, taking smaller, more active shoal chub with it. This leaves the specimen fish in the swim free to enjoy the carpet of mash, and increases their vulnerability to a hookbait since they no longer have the protection in numbers that they may have enjoyed previously.

Tackle

The chub fisher's needs are relatively simple. For small stream fishing in summer, an 11 or 12ft Avon rod with a crisp but through action will suffice for both float and leger work. For winter quivertipping and feeder fishing on larger rivers, a feeder rod is ideal. The type I use is an 11–12ft medium feeder rod with progressive action, and a range of tips between 1½ and 2½ oz. For very long-range work and heavy feeder fishing on a big river, a heavy feeder rod is the answer. Once again, a progressive action is desirable, but this time the rod should be at least 12ft long, and 13ft is better for picking up a lot of line quickly on the strike. Finally, if you intend to do a lot of float fishing for chub, a 13ft stepped-up match rod is essential. Without hesitation I would recommend the Shimano Ultegra match rod, but if your budget is limited, choose a good rod with a hollow tip 'through' rather than a spliced tip 'fast' action.

My favourite chub reel for small- to medium-sized river work is the Shimano Stradic 2000. It is a front drag model with the most precise slipping clutch I have yet to encounter on a standard production fixed spool reel. Couple this with lightness, balance, a superb spool design and line lay mechanism for smooth, accurate casting, and you have the perfect precision reel for small river work.

For feeder fishing I am equally biased in my recommendations: the Shimano G.T.M. or Symetre with their excellent clutches and unique fighting drag mechanisms are unsurpassed in their field.

For float fishing, unless you are able to afford the additional luxury of a centre pin, a straightforward match reel which will hold at least 107 yards (100m) of 4lb line is ideal. Try to choose the lightest and most balanced reel you can afford.

As far as line is concerned, my favourite is Berkley Trilene XL. It is limp, possesses virtually no memory, casts like a dream and feels soft to the touch. For float work, spools of 2lb and 4lb breaking strain will be carried, while for general leger and feeder work I make sure that spare spools containing 4lb, 6lb and 8lb line are a permanent feature in my rucksack.

Rigs and Tactics for Summer Chub

To enjoy the very best of summer chub fishing, mobility is essential. Summer chubbing is all about stalking; casting baits to fish that are vulnerable to an approach, and 'priming' swims in advance ready for a return (this time with a rod) after a brief rest period.

If you did nothing more than creep about the river bank casting with natural hookbaits to chub that show themselves in clear water, you would undoubtedly catch plenty of big fish. Slugs, lobworms and prawns are ideally suited to this approach, and simple freelining or basic legering rigs are perfect for presenting them. The only limitations on your catches will be imposed by your own ability, or lack of it, to approach swims quietly, making good use of bankside cover and presenting baits to chub without alarming them. Wherever possible I like to 'trundle' baits into position by making a cast above the chubs' position and allowing the current to drift the bait downstream to the waiting fish; depending on the flow, it may or may not be necessary to use weight on the line. In many cases a simple freelined bait will work perfectly, but occasionally a small amount of weight might need to be added.

The ideal summer chub fishing rig will be as flexible as possible, allowing a rapid change between freeline and simple leger tactics to cope with the conditions encountered from swim to swim. My simple freeline/leger rig is shown in Fig. 18. To switch from a freeline to a leger, simply mould the appropriate amount of Fox 'Supaweight' putty around the sliding rubber float stop. To revert to freelining, remove the putty and replace it in its airtight tub, ready for future use. Simple? Maybe, but it is highly effective, and is virtually the only rig I use for my summer chub fishing.

Now to discuss legering for summer chub. Some of the swims that you encounter may not contain visible chub, but your instincts tell you that they are present. The answer to this situation is to scatter some loose offerings into the swim, then return perhaps half an hour later with leger tackle. On major rivers, where stalking is not particularly viable, this approach is the standard method I would use for catching summer and autumn fish. Luncheon meat, cheese paste and bread are ideally suited to this method. Typical swims to try include beneath overhanging trees, on bends, glides, runs between weedbeds and depressions in the river bed. It is also an approach that pays dividends

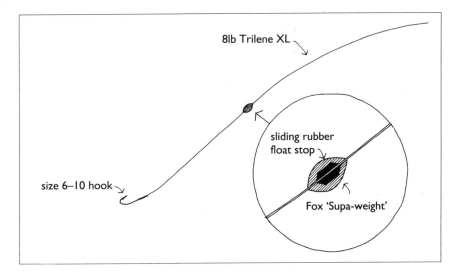

Fig. 18 *Simple freeline/ leger rig for summer chub.*

8lb Trilene XL

sliding rubber
float stop

size 6–10 hook

Fox 'Supa-weight'

at night, since chub will often feed well into darkness on warm summer evenings. Incidentally, night fishing is often the answer to tempting 'uncatchable' chub that are known to reside in totally inaccessible areas. After dark, fish like this will often leave their daytime sanctuary in order to search for food in the relatively open water nearby. By pre-baiting these areas just before dusk, the chances are that you will get a chance to do battle with that 'elusive' specimen by introducing a hookbait just after dark.

Simple leger rigs work well for this style of fishing, and on small rivers I use the simple free-line/leger tackle; larger rivers and pacier currents demand the use of Arlesey bombs fished either on a running or fixed paternoster basis. Whichever you choose, remember to use only just enough weight to cast the required distance and hold bottom (in order to minimize resistance from the tackle).

The particle or mass bait approach is ideal for producing large numbers of fish from a single prolific swim. On small rivers I would pre-bait

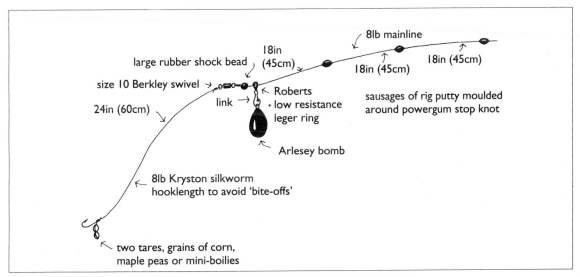

8lb mainline

18in
(45cm)

large rubber shock bead

18in (45cm)

18in (45cm)

size 10 Berkley swivel

Roberts
low resistance
leger ring

link

sausages of rig putty moulded
around powergum stop knot

24in (60cm)

Arlesey bomb

8lb Kryston silkworm
hooklength to avoid 'bite-offs'

two tares, grains of corn,
maple peas or mini-boilies

Fig. 19 *Summer chub particle fishing leger rig.*

The author with a 4lb-plus summer chub from the Dorset Stour.

with hempseed, using a bait dropper to deposit a pint or so of bait onto a clean gravel run, near to cover or a suspected chub-holding area. By extracting a fish or two and topping up the bait supply in between regular visits, surprisingly large catches can be made. Standard leger rigs with side-hooked or hair-rigged particle hookbaits will catch plenty of chub, but you will be faced with the inevitable problem of line bites. These are caused by the feverish feeding of the chub as they twist, turn and 'flash' over the hemp in an effort to get at the magical seeds, brushing into your line in the process. Line bites can be surprisingly aggressive, and false strikes are bound to be made unless you can avoid them. By placing two or three powergum stop knots up the line and behind the leger, thin sausages of Fox 'Supa-weight' can be added to nail as much line as possible to the bottom (*see* Fig. 19). Like this, you can be assured that when

the tip bends round, a chub is responsible. Note also that a braided hooklength is vital to the rig in order to avoid 'bite-offs', a genuine danger with particle fishing.

Larger rivers are synonymous with swimfeeder tactics and the regular introduction of maggots, casters and hemp. Casters and hemp is a particularly deadly combination and is designed to get a shoal of chub into a feeding frenzy. The basic rules for feeder fishing include:

a.   Pick a likely looking area and stick to it.

b.   Use a heavy enough swimfeeder to hold bottom without rolling for considerable distances.

c.   Keep your rod tip elevated so that water pressure on your main line is minimal, enabling the use of feeders well balanced to suit the flow.

d.   Don't turn your back on your rod!

e.   Make regular casts, perhaps every five or ten minutes, whether you are getting bites or not. The feeder technique will work in a wide variety of swims, but it is virtually unbeatable for far bank feeder fishing, particularly when overhanging trees are present.

f.   Cast to the same area, every time.

Finally, one of the deadliest summer chub tactics of them all, particularly on shallow, clear rivers, is freelined chum mixer or bread crust. I like to flavour and dye mixers to make them more attractive to chub and once chub have a taste for flavoured dog biscuits, big catches are on the cards.

As regards additives, my favourite colour is red, and 'Scopex', salmon and strawberry top the list. Begin by scattering mixers or crusts at regular intervals into the head of a long run. If chub are present, they should soon begin to display an interest and by careful, patient feeding you should be able to work a shoal into a feeding frenzy. Follow up the loosefeed with a simple freelined single or double mixer on a size 8 or 6 hook respectively, or a chunk of crust on a size 6. Remember to grease your line thoroughly so as to enjoy exceptional bait control; failure to do this will result in the line bellying in the current, causing the bait to drag unnaturally across the surface of the river. Chub are suspicious fish, and baits which do not behave in a totally natural way will

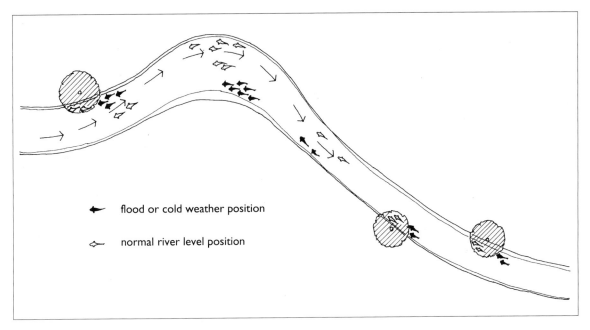

Fig. 20 *Effects of floods and very cold weather on chub location.*

be refused. Finally, do not be tempted to strike too soon: allow the chub to turn down with the bait before responding with a sweeping upward strike.

WINTER CHUB

I have never been a fan of fishing for chub during spate conditions, preferring instead to target winter barbel when the river is running high with dirty water. But in cold conditions I can think of nothing else I would rather fish for with the exception of pike, since chub are quite happy to carry on feeding, albeit at a reduced rate, even in severe freezing weather. The effect of both flood and cold on the location of chub is similar, however – and I would add that if you are prepared to target chub during a flood, despite the fact that you will probably only get one bite, it is likely to be from a big fish. Quite why this is so I don't know, but my records indicate that big chub seem more willing to feed in excessive floodwater than do averaged-size fish.

Cold or dirty water will push chub into slacker water, although they will rarely if ever move far from their favourite haunts, seeking instead the

The author's father with a big winter chub caught in freezing conditions.

nearest place that offers them a moderate and constant current in which to brave out the conditions. The diagram above shows the effect of excessive frosts and floods on chub, and how in a typical short stretch of river they will respond. Truly slack water will sometimes harbour fish, but a gentle constant flow is better in my opinion, while back eddies are a waste of time. Large smelly baits work best in a flood – luncheon meat, cheese paste and of course, lobworms being the most reliable.

In cold water it is tempting to switch to small baits on tiny hooks, but I have found that the best course of action is to do completely the opposite. My favourite bait in sub-zero temperatures is a huge chunk of bread crust or flake fished on a size 4 hook; this bait has worked for me on countless occasions, even in ridiculously low temperatures.

Rigs and Tactics for Winter Chub

Fishing for chub in winter is essentially no different to summer chubbing. On small rivers and streams, mobility and stealth remain the keys to success; on big rivers, feeder and leger tactics still work very well, although you will probably

need to increase the size of your legers (to cope with the increased flow) and reduce the size of feeders (to cut back on the amount of feed introduced). Indeed, as far as major rivers are concerned there is little more to add, other than to say that you should concentrate your efforts on swims that offer evenly paced currents rather than boily, unpredictable ones. Also, just because you are using a smaller feeder doesn't mean to say that you will get away with less weight; thus you may need to purchase some clip-on feeder weights or ski leads to ensure that your tackle holds its position in the increased flow. Remember also to cast regularly, probably at fifteen-minute intervals.

When legering for winter chub my particular favourite baits are cheese paste, bread crust, bread flake, luncheon meat and lobworms, and I find it pays dividends to pre-bait swims with bread groundbait and a scattering of the chosen hookbait. Generally speaking, I pre-bait roughly six swims at the start of the session, fishing each in rotation and topping up the groundbait between visits. Invariably I will carry both mashed and liquidized bread with me, unless I

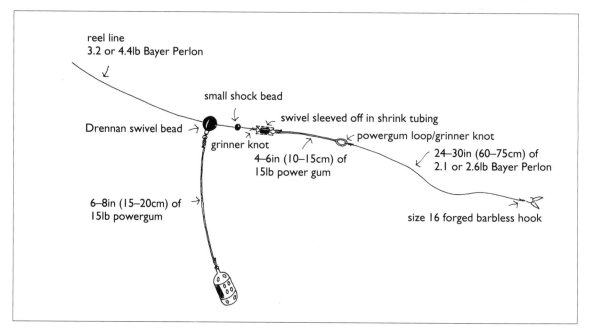

Fig. 21 Mini-feeder rig for winter fishing.

am fishing a big river when bread mash, due to its greater density, is better in the stronger flow.

The liquidized bread is ideal for regular introduction into long runs and glides, its tiny particles drifting a long way downstream and attracting chub from considerable distances. A couple of handfuls of heavier mash placed just below the head of the run will keep them occupied when they arrive. Mashed bread should also be fed into swims where the groundbait needs to sink quickly, such as flood rafts, and alongside rushbeds.

If a swim has a big head of chub, the danger is that the specimen-sized fish will be spooked long before you finish hauling out the smaller, greedier chub. Now is the time to use the specific chub groundbaiting tactics (*see* Fig. 16) to isolate the bigger fish in the swim and make them more susceptible to a hookbait.

Simple link legers or fixed paternosters can be used to present baits into winter chub swims, and unless the flow is excessive, I use swanshot as casting/leger weights in preference to Arlesey bombs. The use of SSG shot is preferable, since greater precision is possible by adding and removing single shots. The more balanced your leger tackle is with the flow the better, the result being much

bolder bites. When winter chubbing I will invariably use a quivertip rod, the tip itself being painted white for maximum visibility. An isotope attachment will be fitted too, to cope with after-dark fishing, which is very worthwhile indeed for winter chub. As regards my winter chub rigs, I now use a leger set-up that was designed after a protracted campaign on deep, slow river stretches, which revealed the inadequacies of traditional chub leger set-ups (more of this later).

As far as bait placement is concerned, the section dealing with chub location should tell you all that you need to know. Suffice it to say that in mild weather and with reasonable water conditions, chub will be quite active, and baits that are used to search the swim by bumping them across the current before allowing them to rest for a short period, will produce plenty of chub. Sometimes the chub will be lying in the main flow, more frequently they will be on the edge of creases; during cold weather and high water levels you will need to seek them out in steadier water and in the sheltered areas behind rafts, beneath overhanging bushes and in rushbeds. At all times you should place baits near to, or underneath cover, because regardless of the conditions, chub will always favour areas like these.

A 4lb 14oz chub caught on a cold winter's day.

Given decent river conditions, winter is the time to enjoy float fishing for chub. The early frosts and floods will have scoured away much of the weed in the river and by choosing a long, steady glide, you should be able to trot a float over considerable distances. Maggots and casters are the obvious baits to use, both as loosefeed and on the hook, and stickfloats and balsas for close-range trotting and waggler floats for distance work will catch plenty of chub. In open water I usually fish with 2lb line straight through to the hook, while in snaggy swims 3lb test will provide extra security.

In gentle currents, light shotting patterns will enable you to catch chub both on the bottom and 'on the drop' in case the chub move up in the water to intercept your loose feed.

In deep, pacey water a balsa float, with a bulk shotting pattern will help to present the bait at an acceptable speed to the chub; it will also help to prevent your hookbait being dragged unnaturally through the swim by the force of the water. Alternatively, a large 'chubber'-style float with bulk shotting is ideal for presenting bigger hookbaits like luncheon meat and bread flake. By feeding mashed bread into the head of a long run it is quite possible to enjoy a few hours trotting in a decent swim with the expectation of regular sport.

Remember, too, that a floating line will pay dividends when it comes to mending the line across awkward currents. However, in very windy conditions, with an awkward downstream gale, attempting to fish with floats fixed top and bottom to the line is invariably a waste of time. Backshotting, by placing a small shot such as a no 6 above the float might help, but in severe conditions even this won't work. The waggler is the answer, even for close range work, but you will need to sink the line to prevent the wind from dragging the float through the swim faster than

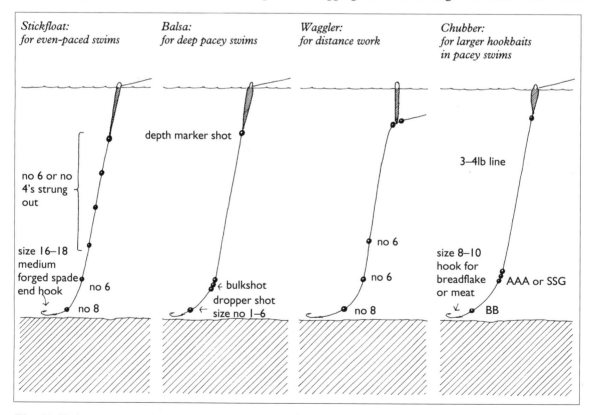

Fig. 22 *Chub float rigs for rivers.*

the pace of the current. Nowadays I always carry a small bottle containing diluted washing up liquid which can be applied to the line with a small piece of sponge. By simply winding the line through the sponge, which should be thoroughly soaked in the solution, you will find that it will sink very quickly indeed and allow the float to run through the swim at a natural pace.

SLOW-WATER CHUB

So far we have analysed chub fishing in traditional style on classic chub rivers that are characterized by bends, glides, shallows and a host of fish-holding features. Chub populations in such places invariably comprise a healthy number of fish of varying sizes. However, if you want the opportunity to catch bigger-than-average fish, slow-water chub offer exciting prospects. Take my local river, the Great Ouse, for example: I could take you to some fabulous-looking chub stretches that will provide hectic chub sport and where you could catch numbers of chub – invariably, among the 2lb and 3lb fish, you would eventually, over a season, catch a few 'fours' and possibly a 'five'. But if I took you to one of the stretches that run for the last mile or so above one of the Ouse's many weirs, the chances are that two or three bites in a session would be average, and five or six would be exceptional. The chub caught, though, would invariably be a 4lb fish, and a 'five' would be a distinct possibility.

Slow-water chub are a modern-day phenomenon, the result of man's intervention in the natural state of our rivers. Dredging, abstraction and the installation of weir pools has led to the development of long straight stretches of river that move, at best, at a slow walking pace. There is probably a stretch like this near to you, and as long as you have conviction, it could provide you with some exciting chub fishing. Chub populations on these stretches are almost always low and only a handful of swims in a mile of river will contain fish. It's my belief that slow-water chub are fish that have opted for a state of 'semi-retirement', free to live out quiet, untroubled lives away from the intense competition that shoal chub have to contend with. Chub on these stretches frequently inhabit swims on their own, or more usually in pairs, and occasionally in small groups of four or five.

When I first encountered slow-water chub I quickly realized that my whole approach to chub fishing would have to change fundamentally. Location became extremely critical (as it always is) and it simply wasn't good enough just to pick a couple of likely-looking areas and fish them. The chub invariably had their pick of the swims and locating favoured areas was a painstaking process at times. I could fish a dozen flood rafts (the most obvious-looking swims) and find chub in perhaps two of them. I learned too, that even in a good swim, bait placement was critical: inches made an enormous difference, and a bait that fell a foot short of the overhanging cover would be ignored.

To complicate matters still further, I was not used to sitting in a good chub swim for more than twenty minutes without a bite. Now I was having to wait for long periods, sometimes up to an hour, and I found that it was fatal to move a bait unless it had been in position for at least fifteen minutes. Certainly I learned the value of pre-baiting, of priming a number of swims with regular introductions of small amounts of mashed bread and a scattering of my chosen hookbait because the longer a swim was 'rested', it would seem, the more likely it was to produce almost instantly.

I also learned valuable lessons about feeding periods and seasonal factors. Rarely would these stretches produce fish before December, and on many winter days bites would be concentrated in the last hour of daylight and an hour after dark. On exceptional days, when it was mild, overcast and the river was carrying just a tinge of colour, bites could be expected at almost any time, but sessions like this were, and are to this day, very rare indeed.

Finally I learned a vast amount about the relationship between rigs and baits, valuable lessons that have stood me in good stead ever since and caused me to change my end tackle fundamentally. More of this presently; in the meantime, let us investigate further the subject of location. Overhanging trees and flood rafts will always be reliable chub-holding features, but of all the bushes and trees that I have fished, I have no doubt that long, unbroken rows of hawthorn bushes are the best. Quite why this is so I am not sure – perhaps it is the continuous canopy of cover, perhaps they are prone to undercutting around their root structure. Even so, a bait must be presented within an inch or two (2–5cm) of the overhanging branches or in a tiny gap between them if it is to provoke a bite. If you can cast accurately, these swims yield multiple catches of 4lb-plus fish. All the other chub-holding features I mentioned earlier are worthwhile too, but bear in mind that slow-water fisheries are usually not over-blessed with visible features. Seeking out depressions in the river bed can pay dividends, but with slow currents, depressions rarely betray themselves by causing the water to boil on the surface. Your best hope of locating them is to float fish the stretch, not with the expectation of catching chub, but with the purpose of finding out what lies 'down below'.

Creases on slow-water fisheries are critical. But once again, with a slow current the variations in flow tend to be very subtle, and it takes a great deal of effort to identify these areas. Perhaps the quickest way is to visit the river when it is in flood, when crease areas become more pronounced.

Invariably though, to get the most from the fishery, you will have to search it almost foot by foot, and not to do so can cost you fish, because on many occasions I have experienced bites in seemingly open, featureless areas. Following the capture of a fish, I've often been prompted to investigate the area in detail, discovering in the process a subtle feature whose presence I hadn't previously suspected.

During my years fishing for slow-water chub I have learned a very valuable lesson with regard to baits. I used to believe that bait choice was vital, and even though I still do, it is for different reasons – I always believed that you should select one bait in preference to another because the chub might prefer it, and to a certain extent, if fish have been subject to heavy angling pressure, this might be true, but as a general rule I now

know that this is nonsense. Provided that the bait is presented in the right place without alarming the chub, they will eat it. What really counts is the ability of a particular bait to assist presentation. What do I mean by this? Imagine a flood raft on the near bank. It is a large raft, and while a cast to the outermost branches can be made, getting a bait into the heart of the cover appears to be impossible. A dense bait such as luncheon meat or cheese paste would be useless, because its weight would sink the rig too quickly without a current to help it drift into a more favourable position. However, even with a gentle flow behind it, a large piece of crust could be cast out, held on a tight line and its buoyancy would help it to drift right underneath the raft.

Similarly, imagine a clump of rushes on the far bank – the ideal place to put a bait would probably be immediately behind the cover. Crust might be a poor choice because its buoyancy would prevent it from settling into position quickly enough, at least on light leger tackle, that is. But with a dense bait like cheese paste, a light, sensitive rig could be used because the weight of the bait would sink the tackle quickly and help to hold it in position. Once I understood this my catches were transformed. Note, too, the fact of leger weights and inappropriately balanced tackle leading to missed bites: if the leger weight being used is too heavy for the job it will be rejected by slow-water chub. Remember that these are fish which never have to compete, that is why they can sit and observe a hookbait for twenty minutes without picking it up; and why, if they detect too much resistance in the rig, all that the angler will see is a small tweak on the rod tip and then no further movement. Balance the tackle properly, though, and the bites are classic, slow pulls and virtually unmissable.

The first problem that I experienced on these stretches was when I used bread crust as a hookbait. Using traditional leger rigs, if I was fishing against the far bank it was quite often necessary to use 3 or 4 swanshot, not in order to hold bottom, but simply to reach the required distance. In truth, on many occasions the flow was only strong enough to warrant the use of 2 SSG to

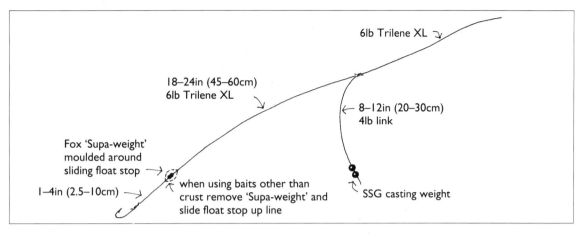

6lb Trilene XL

18–24in (45–60cm)
6lb Trilene XL

8–12in (20–30cm)
4lb link

Fox 'Supa-weight'
moulded around
sliding float stop →

1–4in (2.5–10cm) →

when using baits other than
crust remove 'Supa-weight' and
slide float stop up line

SSG casting weight

Fig. 23 *Chub paternoster.*

hold bottom. Now the problem with traditional crust-fishing rigs is that they involve placing all the weight within a couple of inches of the hook in order to keep the buoyant bait fairly close to the bottom. This I found invited failure, because the chub would pick up the bait, feel the immediate resistance of two or even three times the amount of weight necessary to hold the crust down, and reject it. The answer was to split up the weight loading. Fox 'Supa-weight' putty is used to anchor the crust in place. A small sliding float stop is employed to give the putty something to 'bite onto' without the need for knots and so on that weaken the line; I always use just enough putty to sink the crust and no more. The casting weights are located further up the line on a paternoster link (*see* Fig. 23).

The effect that this rig has achieved has been dramatic, to say the least. Every bite now is a good, confident pull, and what is more, if a change to a different bait such as flake, meat or cheese paste is required, I simply remove the putty and slide the small stop up the hooklink. This rig is now the standard set-up I use for about 90 per cent of my chub fishing – simple to tie, flexible and absolutely deadly.

The other valuable lesson I have learned when slow-water chubbing is the importance of upstream legering. This simple style enables a superbly balanced set-up to be achieved, the only danger with it being that bites can become almost too confident, with deep-hooking a realistic danger. In this situation, a shortened hooklink is the answer.

Conclusion

Slow-water chubbing is a fascinating and absorbing pursuit, and despite the fact that it can be painstakingly difficult at times, the rewards in the form of numerous 4lb- and 5lb-plus chub can be tremendous. Many valuable lessons will be learned in the course of a campaign, and success will be hard-earned. 'Crack it' though, and you can look back with the satisfaction that you have caught and outwitted ultra-wary chub in demanding conditions. This is a feeling that Peter Stone, the stillwater chub expert, knows only too well because the chub in stillwaters are, if anything, even more difficult than slow-water fish. I have no doubt about this, being gripped as I write by the early stages of stillwater chub 'fever'!

MY APPROACH TO
STILLWATER CHUB   by Peter Stone

My interest in stillwater chub goes back over thirty years to when I gained access to a small gravel pit close to my home. The chub were not large; a three-pounder was a good fish which I had no trouble catching on either legered cheese paste on a no 8 hook or a single maggot on a no 18 hook attached to a 1½lb b.s. bottom. Later, Geoff Barnes and I caught great numbers of fish between 4lb and 5lb 7oz on legered luncheon meat, mostly after dark. A love affair with big stillwater chub was by then firmly established, an affair which has not faded with the years.

In the late 1970s my attention turned to another gravel pit where pike anglers were reporting fast, unhittable runs when fishing mackerel and herrings. These runs I knew were caused by big chub suspicious of the wire traces, a problem I first recognized in the 1950s in rivers, and one which I managed to overcome by mounting deadbaits (bleak and gudgeon) on no 6 or 4 singles attached to nylon. To prevent 'bite-offs' meant striking immediately the rod top moved, and great concentration was required – but lazy anglers catch very few fish.

During the last twenty years chub have shown in ever-increasing numbers in gravel pits. Many different methods and baits catch them; casters fished on the drop under a float is probably the deadliest, live minnows fished under a float at various depths, maggots fished with a block-end feeder, and various baits on leger rigs, are just a few of the methods which have proved successful.

As always, the most important factor is location: as the late Dick Walker once said, you cannot catch a fish that isn't there. Features to look for are gravel bars, ledges, and bulrushes, but there is another feature which is guaranteed to catch chub: pipes through which water flows, either naturally or artificially. At all the pits I fish where there is a pipe or pipes, chub are always present at some time of the day or night. Another point to remember is that during the hours of darkness chub frequent the margins, often into no more than inches of water. Walk round a gravel pit at dawn and it is a fair bet that chub will be seen in the margins somewhere. So when fishing at night *never* ignore the margins. Margin fishing has its problems, however, and one in particular, which is that big chub can hear the slightest sound; absolute quietness is therefore essential.

One gravel pit I fish is situated close to houses. A very keen youngster lives here and when he sees my car he comes over for a chat. Normally he is quiet in his approach, but on one occasion I was horrified when well into darkness I heard the scrunching of gravel. I very rarely get annoyed with anyone, but on that occasion I gave him a serious ticking-off, for any big chub in the vicinity would have departed the area and not returned for several hours. Dick Walker maintained that for every pound a chub weighed it would take an hour for it to recover after being scared – thus, a five-pounder would take five hours – and I reckon he was about right.

Most of my big stillwater chub have been caught in the margins during darkness. Two of my six pounders were taken in just 2ft (60cm) of water less than 4ft (1.2m) from the bank. In that particular situation I did not wish my rods to be silhouetted against the sky so I laid them on the ground, making sure the line could run freely. My indicator was a piece of silver paper slipped over the line just above the rod handle – the sound of silver paper moving over gravel is very, very exciting!

The type of indicator I use depends on the situation at the time. If fishing, say, two rod lengths out from the bank in water more than 6ft (1.8m) deep, I use Delkim indicators and Terry Eustace swingers. When fishing the margins I use a simple cork bobbin with a betalite glued into the side positioned just past the reel. This enables me to slip the line into the grip without getting off my seat which may spook a chub close in. I like cork bobbins, their only drawback being that you cannot allow your eyes to wander elsewhere: complete concentration is necessary throughout the session. When fishing the margins I sit as far away from the water as possible with only the rod top past the water's edge.

My favourite method is deadbaiting, and my five biggest stillwater chub – four six-pounders (one a repeat capture) and one of 7¼lb – fell to sprats and sardines. This method is still largely misunderstood by many anglers, however. The biggest problem when deadbaiting is avoiding bite-offs caused when the bait is swallowed and the hooklink bitten through by the chub's pharyngeal (throat) teeth. The obvious answer is to use wire, but a bait attached to wire, no matter

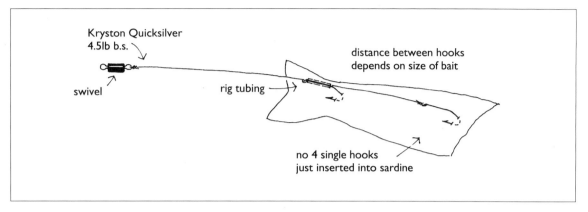

Kryston Quicksilver
4.5lb b.s.

swivel

distance between hooks
depends on size of bait

rig tubing

no 4 single hooks
just inserted into sardine

Fig. 24 *Peter Stone's deadbait rig for chub.*

how thin it is, results in a very fast run which is invariably missed because the bait has not been swallowed. Why stillwater chub in particular dislike the feel of wire is strange; recent experience has shown that chub in rivers are now far less frightened of it. Initially I used string, then 20lb b.s. Dacron, but despite its thickness this was still bitten through, as the following tale relates.

Geoff Barnes and I were fishing close together, our sardines no more than 20ft (6m) from the bank. A strong sideways wind was causing problems by blowing strands of floating weed against our lines, causing the bobbins to jerk upwards. 'Drat the weed!' exclaimed Geoff, as for the umpteenth time his bobbin jerked. With resistance (or rather lack of it) important every time weed fouled the line, it meant lifting the rod and striking it off, an irritating exercise with chub close in. Before Geoff could lift the rod, however, his line went slack, so he tightened, only to find his line fluttering in the wind. The Dacron was bitten through. A chub had swallowed a whole sardine without moving! I now use 45lb b.s. Kryston Quicksilver which, although not 100 per cent, is more resilient than Dacron.

Most times I use half sardines (the tail half), whole sprats or mackerel tails. For all three the rig consists of two no 4 or 6 hooks (*see* Fig. 24). When a chub picks up a deadbait it swallows it without moving very far, if at all. Immediately the indicator moves I lift the rod and *gently* tighten to the fish; invariably 'knocks' will be felt (as the chub swallows the bait), and I strike immediately.

Another fine bait is whitebait, lip-hooked on a no 6 hook. Bleak and gudgeon are also excellent, and are also lip-hooked.

Many of my big stillwater chub have fallen to legered luncheon meat. When Geoff and I first used luncheon meat I was puzzled as to why he always hit more bites than me. I never mind anyone – and certainly not a mate – catching more fish than me, but I do want to know *why*. One night matters came to a head when I missed seventeen bites. Then I hooked a fish of 4¾lb. On the next cast I hooked another, and at the same time I heard Geoff strike. Mine weighed 5lb 1oz, Geoff's 5lb 7oz, and shortly after Geoff caught one of 4lb 3oz – but these were his only two bites.

Despite catching two good fish I was concerned about missing seventeen bites. On our next trip I noticed Geoff was using much smaller pieces than me; also his tail was much longer, about 2ft (60cm). Smaller pieces of meat, longer tails, was that the answer? On subsequent trips my bite/hooking ratio increased dramatically, and I was wholly convinced that it was using smaller pieces of meat which made the difference. However, now I am sure that it was the increase in the length of tail. Big chub are not fools, and although you might think that the tail always lands in a straight line, this is not always so. The bottom of this particular pit was hard, and I believe my short tail resulted in the chub feeling the lead before they had got the meat properly between their lips, whereas the longer tail enabled them to take more line unhindered. That is my theory, and whenever I use meat or paste I make sure the tail is not less than 2ft (60cm). Until recently I used unflavoured meat but I now flavour mine with 'Wicked', obtainable from K/B Tropicals; however, any 'fishy' flavour is worth trying. As regards loosefeeding, I introduce a couple of dozen samples at the beginning, and a few more after each bite or indication.

At all times resistance must be kept to a minimum, and I prefer shots or a bomb on a sliding link in preference to a bomb straight on the line. The link is stopped by a swivel, a small ring or a Drennan leger stop. Bites usually consist of the bobbin/indicator going straight up, dropping back or continually jerking. The first two can be struck with confidence, but the latter requires some thought. If between the jerks the indicator either lifts or drops back a little I strike; but you should always do what you consider best at the time.

These then are some of the baits and techniques which I have found successful: and may your rods bend, and the line sing in the wind, not once, but many times.

STILLWATER CHUB   by Stewart Allum

During the early 1980s, inspired by the successes of Peter Stone and others who had recently captured an amazing string of 7lb-plus giants from the Oxford pits, my friends and I naturally assumed that the key to success with big stillwater chub lay in the use of deadbaits. Our own results at that time were, however, less conclusive and led me to consider other methods more suited to the conditions under which we were fishing.

Whilst I accept that deadbaiting is a particularly effective method for capturing chub after dark when they patrol the margins by sense of smell, it isn't always practical. On our waters night fishing was banned, so we had to apply our

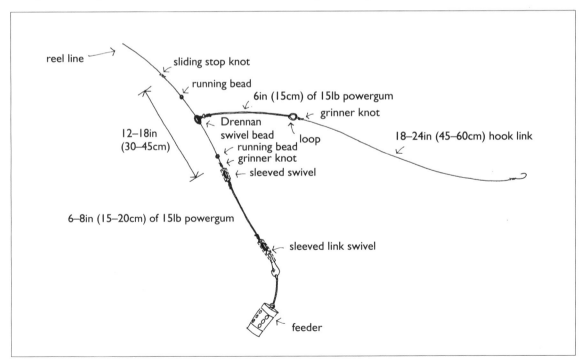

Fig. 25 *Anti-tangle feeder rig (helicopter rig). This type of rig can be used for both autumn and winter fishing with various line strengths if so desired; it is particularly effective for distance casting.*

methods during daylight, in competition with other anglers using all manner of baits. It quickly became apparent that whilst deadbaits scored well in cold, unsettled weather, during calmer, settled spells far more large chub were caught by anglers using light float tackle and maggots.

We had overlooked a fundamental rule of chub behaviour. Chub are a voracious, competitive species. During unsettled conditions they are generally less active and therefore respond best to large, static bottom-fished baits. Once conditions stabilize, however, they become much more aggressive, hunting in packs often right up near the surface in search of the most abundant food supply. During recent sessions I have adapted my techniques to suit these varying conditions and have since enjoyed consistent success with still-water chub. I tend to concentrate on the winter months, as these fish usually reach peak condition towards the end of the season. They are also more readily caught on anglers' baits at this time, when natural food is in short supply.

During dry, calm settled conditions, irrespective of light values or temperatures, the float seems to outscore all other daylight methods. On arrival at a water, however, I will normally introduce several handfuls of groundbait laced with mashed bread and maggots. This helps to hold chub in a swim and establish a baited area ready for the dusk period, when I usually switch to a legered bait.

Although my swim may be anything up to 20ft (6m) deep, I expect to catch the chub at depths anywhere between 2 and 10ft (0.6 and 3m), depending on how much activity and aggression I can induce by regular loosefeeding with maggots. By 'regular' I mean literally half a pouchful every minute until the fish are feeding strongly, whereupon I will either increase or reduce the amount of feed as conditions dictate.

Choice of tackle is important for these powerful fish. I use a light, through-actioned 13ft match rod, combined with a closed-face reel for ease of tackle control and repeated casting during periods of intense activity. A strong, supple, low-visibility line is essential when fishing near the surface in clear water, my own preference being Bayer Perlon. Bites can be swift and violent, with the chub

sometimes hooking themselves when in an aggressive mood; for this reason I always hold the rod, and am still occasionally broken 'on the bite' before I have had a chance to react. Lines must be durable enough to withstand the stress of frequent casting, tackle alterations and playing large fish repeatedly. Fine diameter pre-stretched brands should therefore be avoided.

The best hooks are strong, forged, eyed patterns in sizes 14, 16 and 18. The choice of an eyed hook enables me to use a grinner knot, which guarantees almost 100 per cent knot strength. The hook should always be tied direct to the main line, thus eliminating any risk imposed by intermediate knots. I normally use a line of about 2½lb breaking strain, which is fine enough for delicate presentation, yet strong enough to cope with most eventualities, including the occasional double-figure carp. Chub usually patrol close to the bank, so there is seldom any need for long casting. What matters is that the hookbait arrives amongst the loose feed accurately and with minimal disturbance.

Choice of float is therefore crucial, and the best I have used are Drennan Crystalight loaded wagglers. These are tough and durable, and being made of transparent plastic, they have a low visibility factor, which is an important consideration when fishing near the surface. Partially self-cocking, they come already loaded with an aerodynamic casting weight. On the aforementioned tackle, the 2BB version can be cast accurately over 40yds (36m), even against strong head- or side-winds. A choice of interchangeable coloured tips is available to accommodate varying light conditions. On large waters where there is always an element of surface glare, a black tip is usually best.

The float is set to slide with the bulk shot near the surface. I normally allow some 6 to 12in (15 to 30cm) between these and the sliding stop knot (see Fig. 26); this allows the line to travel better on the strike, unimpeded by the weight of the float. The use of a silicone sliding float adaptor also helps by 'folding' the float over on the strike, reducing resistance further. Because I want the hookbait (usually maggots or a pinch of bread

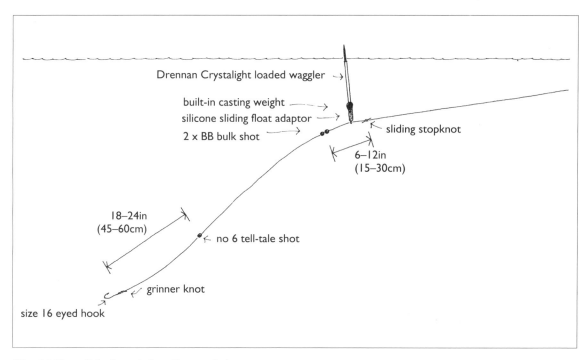

Fig. 26 *Crystalight float rig for stillwater chub.*

Drennan Crystalight loaded waggler

built-in casting weight

silicone sliding float adaptor

2 x BB bulk shot

sliding stopknot

6–12in
(15–30cm)

18–24in
(45–60cm)

no 6 tell-tale shot

grinner knot

size 16 eyed hook

Stewart Allum with a 4lb 10oz stillwater chub caught on float-fished maggots.

flake) to sink slowly, the only other shot on the line is a no 6 set 18 to 24in (45 to 60cm) from the hook.

My usual tactic is to cast just beyond the baited area, fire out some maggots, then wind the float back quickly so that the hookbait sinks amongst the loosefeed. Bites are often instantaneous and fast reactions are needed to hit them, since a suspicious chub can inhale and eject the bait within a split second.

Occasionally, particularly during bright, calm conditions, bites can become very shy and difficult to hit on the slider. Last season I partially overcame this problem by using one of the new-style 20ft match rods currently being produced, with a float fished top-and-bottom method beneath the rod tip. Whilst this enabled me to hit more bites and coped well enough with fish which obligingly stayed more or less in front of me during the fight, I lost several big chub which took off on long runs to either side of me. Once a fish was more than, say, 25yds (22.5m) away in a side-strain situation, I had very little control over its movements. Furthermore, any attempt to increase pressure usually resulted in the hook pulling out, due to the excessive torque generated by these long rods, which tend to be rather stiff in their middle sections. For consistent results then, I would advise sticking to the more forgiving 13ft models, which allow more power and control to be applied during a prolonged fight.

As darkness approaches, or during windy, unsettled spells, the leger comes into its own. I normally use an 11ft through-actioned rod of about 1lb test curve, a fixed spool reel and 5 or 6lb b.s. line. Bites can be shy and slow to develop, so I use a free-running link leger and an optonic bite alarm. Bite indicators should be as light as possible, a 'squeezy' bottle top being quite suitable, set to hang about 12in (30cm) below the rod. Hooks should again be strong barbless eyed in sizes 6 or 8 depending on the bait used. Bread flake is an excellent choice, particularly when flavoured with a sweet essence such as 'Scopex' or caramel, though cheese, luncheon meat, lobworms and deadbaits will all catch their share of chub. As long casting is unnecessary, a ¼oz Arlesey bomb on a running link stopped about 24in (60cm) from the hook, is perfectly adequate (see Fig. 27).

Finally, remember that populations of chub in stillwaters are seldom self-sustaining, so please treat them carefully. The chub in my local fishery were stocked ten years ago; they have experienced many recaptures, yet continue to pack on weight and exhibit few signs of damage, a testimony to sensible club rules which include a keepnet ban and the strict use of barbless hooks only. I mention these facts for the consideration of those seeking or intending to stock chub in stillwaters. Treated with care and respect, the hardy chub will live long and give consistent sport for many seasons.

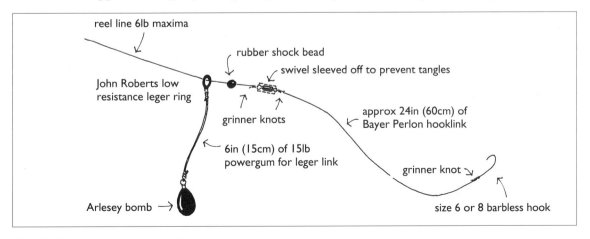

Fig. 27 *Simple running leger for stillwater chub.*

8 DACE AND GRAYLING
by Bill Rushmer

DACE

As a float angler, I recognize dace as a very important species. They allow me to tune up my reflexes and feeding patterns to the extent that I once described the species as the 'skill builder'. This description is far from the whole truth, yet it has a certain amount of validity.

I spend many evenings fishing for dace on local sections of the tidal Thames. This is a major river with good access and a large head of dace, making it an ideal practice venue. On the right day, with a low tide, the session can produce significant bags of dace in excess of 40lb. However, as I am using these sessions to build up my skills, it is important that I master those skills that are relevant for the particular task I have in mind. Thus, as most of my flowing water species such as chub and barbel are caught using centre pin tactics, it is important that I practise regularly with the pin.

Centre Pins

I use these because I believe they give me the edge over other specialists. Certainly better, smoother presentation is obtained, and a bait can be easily slowed down without any hindrances or jerks that are so common with other reels. I am convinced that the pin allows me to search out a swim and present the bait in a more acceptable manner than any other reel.

I originally used ariels, and in particular the old wide drum models, and was given my first ariel by my grandfather over thirty years ago. I have used this reel regularly ever since, though more recently have started to use the new 4½in (11cm) centre pin marketed by Ryobi. To my great surprise I found this reel to be more free-running than my ariels, and have changed over to it for much of my fishing. It is great to see that English craftsmanship is not dead.

To assist smoothness, I use only 50yds (45m) of line on the spool to avoid line bedding problems. The line is also run off in reverse so that it leaves the top of the drum; this means that less line is exposed to any cross-wind, and more direct line control is possible. Naturally the line has to be recovered by winding in the opposite direction, but with practice this becomes second nature.

I also take the handles off my centre pins as it improves balance and gives one less obstacle for line to tangle on. I would advise any reader seriously wanting to use a pin to remove the handles and reverse the line; and if you can not get on with it you can always put the handles back and fish more traditionally.

Stickfloat Tactics

Normally I use a Harrison spliced-tip 13ft match rod for this work, but recently I have been practising with the 15ft version. Certainly these sessions have improved my competence with a longer rod. Both rods are used with handle-less centre pins loaded with 50yds (45m) of 2lb b.s. line. When using maggots the terminal tackle is a conventional stickfloat shotted shirt-bottom style with no 6 or 8 shot. The hook is a fine wire no 16 or 18 tied to 18 inches (45cm) of 1.5 or 1lb trace.

Hemp and Berry

Without doubt, my favourite method of dace fishing is using elderberry on the hook, with mixed hemp and berry feed. This is largely confined to the autumn, when I can pick the berries off the trees and use them fresh on the hook. Elderberries are much larger than hempseed and consequently are fished on a larger hook; I find a size 14 hook is ideal. Not only does the berry appear to produce the better dace, it also attracts some interesting specimens of other species. In a short session after work I have used berry to catch large bags of dace, but have also had good double-figure carp, barbel to over 8lb, roach to 1½lb and chub to well over 4lb – not bad for bonus fish in an after-work session on a free section of the Thames! And very cheap as regards bait, too!

Waggler Tactics

Waggler tactics can also be perfected fishing for dace on the Thames. Basically, by constant light feeding with maggots the dace can be brought up fairly high in the water – this is somewhat similar to the 'spray' or 'mag and wag' tactics used by many leading match anglers for carp, and has the obvious advantage that it is far easier to catch fish shallow than to bring them up from the depths. I used fairly robust yet stable reversed balsawood wagglers for most of this work, the float locked in position by the bulk shot, with just a no 8 shot down the line. The great stability of the rig allows the float to be partly retrieved if a bite is missed, and to be quickly fishing again without recasting.

A few hours' dace fishing on the waggler can yield some remarkable results. It also serves to tighten up the reflexes and improve tackle control, both of which are really essential when fishing for specimen tench and bream with waggler tactics.

Carp Warning

If you are dace fishing on the Thames do not forget to carry a back-lead. These are essential, as carp are often hooked whilst dace fishing and can easily be lost by passing boats cutting the line. When boats are about, slide a back-lead on the main line to sink it to the bottom. This is far more effective than sinking the rod top, as the lead slides down the line taking it to the bottom, which is normally a far greater distance than the rod's length. This trick has enabled me to land many Thames carp that were accidentally hooked whilst dace fishing.

Specimen Dace

Most of my bigger dace – and grayling – have come from rich southern chalk streams such as the Test, the Itchen, the Kennet and the Hampshire Avon. Unlike the biggest grayling they tend not to be found in the uppermost sections of these rivers where it is too high up and cold for them to spawn. However, I have taken large grayling and specimen dace from the same swim on some sections of the Test.

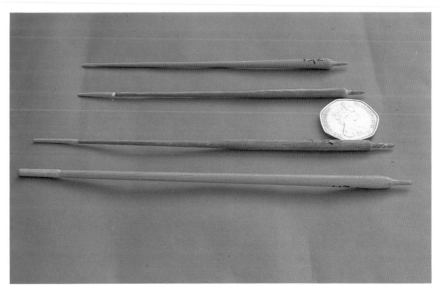

Home-made wagglers used by Bill Rushmer for dace fishing.

Most of my big dace, and the grayling, have come by trotting the swim with a wire-stemmed stickfloat. I have gradually changed over to these for much of my fast-water trotting for dace and grayling because they are such stable floats and are so easily cast. Generally on these trout streams it is better to move to the fish rather than trying to pull the fish into the swim with extensive baiting.

What is surprising is that I have taken so many big dace very close to the bank on these chalk streams, most of them caught virtually under the bank downstream from where I have been standing. When fishing this close in, line can be relatively shallow and very easily disturbed, and in these circumstances I am obliged to use special tactics which we call 'mowing the lawn'.

Mowing the Lawn

This is a technique which is also called 'grass cutting', where the float is run so close to the bank that it virtually touches, or 'cuts' the bankside grass. The float needs to be small, and I use very small, stickfloat-shaped balsas made by a specialist float-maker which are ideal for this job. Most of my big dace, including two over a pound, were taken using these tactics with the small float. I fished a swim of just under 3ft (90cm) deep with one of these floats with four no 8 shot grouped at 2ft (60cm) deep with two other no 8 shot evenly

placed over the remaining 1ft (30cm). I set the float slightly over-depth, holding back with my centre pin so that the float was working through the swim touching the bankside grass. The bait was two maggots on a size 18 hook. I caught big dace steadily, with the best a fraction over 1lb 1oz. Fish, and particularly big dace, seem to succumb to this method every time. Perhaps they think no angler would be daft enough to fish in that close.

GRAYLING

Grayling seem to have a limited distribution. They are not present in every river, and when they are, they appear to be found mostly in its upper reaches, sharing their environment with trout. I am fortunate in that I have gained access to the upper reaches of many top southern chalk streams which in the past were the exclusive domain of the trout angler; in these rich alkaline waters the grayling can certainly grow very big.

In the current economic climate it appears that many of the more exclusive southern chalk streams are having to look to the coarse angler for additional funds to survive, and an approach to owners can often result in, surprisingly, a positive reply, particularly if they feel they can trust you not

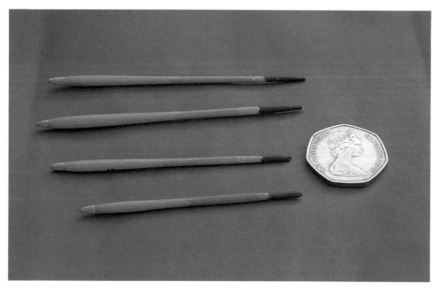

Home-made mini-balsas which Bill Rushmer uses for the technique known as 'mowing the lawn'.

Bill with a 2lb-plus Hampshire Avon grayling caught on a balsa and crowquill Avon.

to steal their trout. Most of the fisheries that I frequent would prosecute any angler stealing trout, and check regularly to make sure there are none hidden away in bags. And more than one top fishery has closed its doors to coarse anglers because some mindless idiot has stolen a few 'spotties'.

However, it is not often that a coarse angler is allowed onto a trout fishery until the trout closed season (which is our winter). For grayling this

could not be better, as they are great winter feeders, even in the coldest of conditions. Day tickets on these trout fisheries are not cheap, currently ranging from £7 to £15, although this extra expense is partly off-set by lower bait costs, as in practice very little bait is consumed.

I fish venues on the Test, Frome, Itchen, Kennet and Hampshire Avon for grayling; most of these are on sections of the upper river.

Tackle

As I am fishing the upper reaches of the river there is seldom the need to use long rods. The Upper Hampshire Avon where I fish regularly for specimen grayling is a typical example of a narrow stream; it is seldom more than 12ft (3.6m) wide, and generally I use an 11½ft Harrison spliced-tip float rod, which doubles up as a useful punt rod, for the majority of this work. The spliced tip acts as a brilliant shock absorber when a better specimen is hooked, and also prevents the risk of hooks being pulled out as a fish makes a sudden lunge under the rod tip.

Naturally these are excellent centre-pin trotting venues, and I use this rod with a 4½in (11cm) diameter pin loaded with about 2½lb b.s. line. Mobility is very important on these venues, as it is normal to travel to the fish rather than use a lot of bait to try to pull the fish into the swim, so my gear is very compact: it certainly *is* designed for mobility rather than comfort because other than my rod reel and landing net, it all fits neatly into my John Wilson waistcoat. Basically this consists of a tube full of floats, plummets, shots, weights, scales, trace line, bait and a small compact camera. At the end of the day, it is no use approaching this style of fishing armed with everything including the kitchen sink.

Watercraft

As most of my venues are fly fisheries they tend to be fast-flowing with extensive shallows and with well cut weedbeds. To help the trout fishermen with their extended fly lines, the bankside vegetation is generally cut back. Although both grayling and trout inhabit the shallows, in winter I find most of the better grayling are in sections with deeper water and steadier flows. These deeper sections are not that common, and long walks are often necessary to get from swim to swim.

It is also worth looking for deeper swims close to the bank. Grayling, and dace, appear to rest up in such swims, which are always worth a try because they can produce some remarkable results. Any weir pool is also worth looking at, as it tends to hold better specimens.

Tactics

When float fishing I try to walk downstream, stopping well in advance of any likely fish-holding area. Once in position I normally trot through for the first few casts with a worm fished at depth and not held back, a strategy which often brings instant success; however, great care must be taken in playing the fish to avoid spooking the shoal. Then I will start to feed in a few maggots, and in a little while change to maggots on the

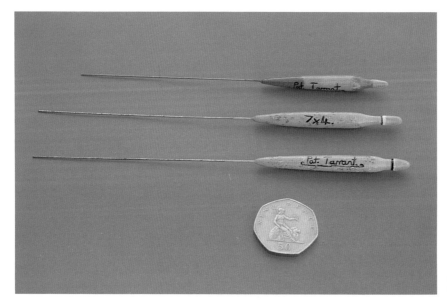

Bill Rushmer's home-made wire-stemmed stickfloat.

hook; this policy tends to prolong the life of the swim. On the chalk streams that I am fishing at present it is rare to take more than three big (2lb-plus) grayling from the same swim before the swim dies and a move has to be made. If the water has any colour it is always worth trying bread as an alternative to maggots, but on some waters trout can make this an impossible move.

As a rule, I do not put grayling in keepnets. Although they are good fighting fish, they appear to put everything they have into the fight, and die very easily if retained in this way. Most of my fish are gently unhooked in the landing net and allowed to return to the river without ever being out of the water.

Fly Tactics

Both grayling and dace can give terrific sport on fly, and certainly with grayling my records over the years give positive indication that the fly has often produced the better specimens. Although my two best grayling – at 3lb 1oz and 3lb 6oz – were both taken on bait, my average is much higher on fly. On the Upper Hampshire Avon I averaged 2lb 8oz on fly as against 2lb 3oz on bait. These figures show a significant difference, and justify my recommending fly fishing to any serious grayling hunter.

Certainly, I have had more 2lb-plus grayling than 12oz dace on fly. Perhaps it is the way I fish. Over the years I have put in a lot of time fly fishing for coarse fish, and during this time results have indicated that dace respond better to dry fly whilst grayling fall more readily to heavily weighted nymphs.

I am lucky in that my friend Lee Kitchen has turned into a professional fly tyer. Lee was a top-flight coarse angler who went over to trout fishing, but he still has his enormous knowledge of coarse fish, in particular of grayling and pike. Lee ties up many deadly patterns for grayling including the gold-bead gold-ribbed hare's ear, which is very effective. He is also tying a fly with a heavy metal under-body that sinks like stone and is proving to be my best-ever grayling fly.

Lee taught me to use very light tackle for grayling. I now use a 7½ft Shakespeare travel fly,

which is a five-piece A.F.T.M. no 4 rod. This is used with a small fly reel loaded with a DT 4F fly line. The traces are now always 2 or 3lb b.s. ultra-green maxima, which I believe is excellent leader material.

When fly fishing, I walk upstream so that I can cast upstream to the fish; with the fish looking upstream for food there is less chance of spooking it. When I see a fish or a likely spot I cast directly in front of it so that the nymph sinks right in front of its mouth. If the fly has been properly presented, a savage take usually follows and a great fight will be had on the light fly gear.

The golden rules are therefore to work upstream, and to use a light rod and line. The nymph should be heavy yet small – I seldom use a hook bigger than a size 12. A size 14 or 16 is about right for the waters that I fish.

Conclusion

Both grayling and dace are worthwhile species, and certainly worthy of the attention of an all-rounder. There is also the added pleasure of being able to use a whole range of tactics for these species. They tend to be the neglected species, but remember that, like pike, they 'thrive on neglect'.

Bill with a 3lb 1oz grayling.

9 ROACH
by John Bailey

When it comes to big fish I always feel that there are basic laws, or at the very least guidelines, and then variations upon a theme. The problem is, in my humble view, that most anglers tend simply to jump on the bandwagon and fish the accepted way without really exploring the variations. Carp fishing immediately springs to mind when we talk about this sort of approach, but roach fishing is no different really. Way back in the 1970s my friend and I helped the art of fishing to advance by legering for roach at night. In fact although it is effective, this sort of legering is not one of the most skilful art forms in the coarse fisherman's armoury. However, it does work, and it has become the base-line for most people wanting to catch big fish.

THE BASIC RULES

To my mind both still- and running waters can be grouped together at this preliminary stage because although the environments are different, the fish is still the same and displays pretty much the same characteristics.

I suppose the crucial factor is light: in many circumstances, big roach tend to feed best, or only, as the light begins to fail. Many years ago Richard Walker tried to analyse this characteristic more definitively with the use of a camera light meter, but I don't think this is really quite possible, nor is it particularly useful. An experienced roach man just knows when light values are low enough to start giving him a chance of catching. Quite simply, if the day is reasonably warm, or the weather has been long settled and the water has a certain type of tinge to it, then big roach will begin to feed just before dusk. If, on the other

hand, the weather is cruel and the water is very clear, then they might need a couple of hours of darkness before they feel tempted.

Current speed is another interesting subject and probably one that has never received quite enough attention. Can we talk about current speed in stillwater? Obviously yes – in my book *Roach, The Gentle Giants*, Tony Miles shows just how important current speed was in a reservoir when it came to finding the roach shoals. I have also come to believe that in a river big roach do enjoy some sort of current as well: I used to spend my entire life looking for slacks, but that was simply because these were easier to fish; and whilst a big roach will move out of the current and feed for a while in a slack, it is in the slow, steady, quite gentle current that a big fish probably feels most at ease.

To a lesser extent, depth is also significant. If the water is very clear and very cold, then deeper water does seem to attract fish, though shallower swims are often favoured, especially towards the end of the year when the fish are beginning to think about spawning. However, I must stress that these are basic and general guidelines, and not absolute laws engraved in stone!

Bottom make-up is important, and I have no doubts at all in stating that roach like to feed over a clear, gravel, sandy or stony bottom of some nature, they do not like to feed in areas of thick silkweed or mud, and you will find that roach on rivers and stillwaters will look out for patches of shiny clean bed when it comes to their feeding times. When the water is clear it is not too difficult to find these, and if you can get a boat out, or a canoe, so much the better.

There is intense controversy over the question of bait nowadays. Whilst this is probably justified

Classic roach baits – maggots, casters, bread, sweetcorn and lobworm.

when it comes to carp in a highly pressurized pool, I am not at all sure that it is very useful when discussing large, wild roach which have probably never seen a net in their lives. Bread, probably flake, must be the best roach bait there is, and maggots and casters follow on very close behind, especially when the water is clear and cold. Other baits have a place, worms in particular, but I cannot really think of any situation when bread, maggots and casters would not catch a fish, and so I see no point in trying to elaborate. What I will say is that the baits should be fresh – there is nothing worse than stale bread, rank maggots or smelly casters. Don't forget, big roach are finicky when it comes to this sort of thing.

I can be equally brief when it comes to terminal rigs. If you are fishing at long range on a reservoir then you might have to give the subject serious thought, but really, anything that will catch a bream will catch a roach. And as regards most roach swims which are close in, then there is no problem whatsoever: nearly all my big roach have fallen on the simplest possible running link legers or light fixed paternosters because, by and large, if a big roach feels confident and hungry and likes your bait, he will simply pick it up and trundle off and there will be no complications at all. Certainly I have never really found any. Hook sizes will vary: for flake my general purpose hook is a 10; for maggots I generally go to a size 14 or 16 if the weather is very cold; and I have caught big roach on sizes 18s and even 20s – although this is a very heart-in-the-mouth type of operation if you are playing a wallowing three-pounder at 40yds (35m) range.

Really, none of this is too difficult: if you can find a water where big roach exist, then you will catch them if you show any degree of patience and dedication at all. I must have landed over 400 roach of 2lb-plus in my lifetime; I haven't caught many of late so I doubt whether I'm up to 500, but I suspect I will get there in the end – and yet I don't really regard myself as a magnificent roach angler. Anybody could have caught those fish if they had put in the numbers of hours that I have over the years. What pride I do have in my roach-fishing history is that I have become more and more open-minded when it comes to variations of the art, and it is these I would like to discuss.

TROTTING

Before the roach specialist appeared in the early 1970s, most big roach fell to anglers trotting their baits downstream. They were masters at this, men like Captain Parker, Gerry Swanton and the dear departed Owen Wentworth, who caught big roach long before the legering technique took over. In fact, these three men between them have probably seen more big roach pull a float down than all the rest of us put together.

There are a great many things I like about trotting: first and most obviously, you cover a lot of ground and therefore stand a good chance of running into fish, rather than waiting for them to come into view. This can be important, and certainly when fish stocks are low, I like to trot vast stretches of the river. I will start at the upstream boundary and just keep moving down until I see some indication on the float or in the water and then I will dig in and stay a bit. Alternatively, in the Wentworth mould, you can really build up a swim with vast amounts of groundbait – providing the fish are there in sufficient numbers, as they used to be on the Wessex rivers just after the war.

Ideally, I like fairly settled conditions for trotting, but this is not strictly necessary, and I can remember taking roach from gin-clear water at midday when there was ice in the margins. So, really, you can trot for roach in any conceivable weather conditions with some hope of success. Obviously, the colder and clearer the water the more likely a small bait is to succeed.

We get back to baits again, and certainly if the water is warm and coloured, a big piece of flake is almost bound to succeed. The clearer the water becomes, however, the more likely a maggot or a caster is to come into its own. This is really common sense, and no great intelligence is needed.

What I like about trotting is that it is a physical art – and an art form of the highest order. The truly great trotter can control his float at 30 or even 40 yards (25 or 35m) range, even in a wind or unpredictable currents, checking it, moving it subtly left or right, letting it go, always aware of a bite, always working to tempt one. Some men are better than others: perhaps it is practice, perhaps it is simply inborn. Good eyesight helps, but above all what is needed is a feeling for the river, a vision of the water as a three-dimensional entity. This is when roach fishing really gets interesting, and I cannot think of a more precious achievement than a 3lb roach on the float at 30 yards (25m) range. I have come near it myself but not quite succeeded, and it is one of my last remaining roaching ambitions!

VISIBLE FISHING

By far the most exciting way of catching roach is in the summer when the water is crystal clear and you can walk along the bank, looking for the fish.

However, the weather conditions really have to be on your side for this, and you need crystal-clear water and bright sunlight – yes, bright sunlight! You see, you don't have to catch roach in the gloom of a December night! I walk slowly and methodically along the river bank using polaroids, making use of all cover and really studying every single piece of water until I find fish. Once the fish are found, you have to consider your approach.

Generally I will watch them for a good few minutes just to get the feel of them; once I know they are not spooked I will begin to introduce the merest few samples of bait to gauge their reaction – perhaps that will be half-a-dozen maggots or a couple of pinches of bread flake. Watch to see if any of the fish show interest, or even alarm. If it is the latter, rest them and then try them with another bait, or if using bread, a small piece. If fish begin to show interest, keep at it gently and gradually, working up the flow, waiting until every fish in the shoal is busy foraging.

It should then be possible to separate the fish a bit so that you can begin to concentrate on one fish in particular. This is where the game becomes really exciting and tense. You may have to throw half-a-dozen maggots or so into one part of the swim to attract the smaller fish away, and then perhaps one piece of flake closer in, near your feet, to keep the one big fish interested.

Once you have the fish that you want feeding reasonably confidently, then you go out to try and catch him! I tend to use a 12 or 13ft rod as this gives me that little bit more control. Wherever possible I won't use a float or even a shot, but simply freeline a piece of flake on a size 10 or 8 hook, depending upon how keenly the fish is feeding. It is then simply a case of making your hookbait fall as naturally as a free offering in front of the fish. I say 'simply', but this may take a bit of practice, and not a little patience, and the fish will be very easily spooked in such conditions.

But, believe me, there is nothing more exciting than seeing a very big fish moving up to your bait and then engulfing it...!

THE VAST STILLWATERS

For decades now I have been fascinated by the glamour and mystery of the huge stillwaters: the rumour of colossal fish resident in waters like Abberton, Ardleigh, Grafham, Lomond, Tring, Wilstone and all the rest has kept me on my toes for twenty years or so. Indeed, on one or two of these waters I have had some quite notable successes – but never the flux of four-pounders that I was told to expect in Lomond.

Obviously, all the traditional big water specialist methods work for roach, although I do think that for roach specifically, you do have to think of fishing a little bit tighter and a little bit lighter. As I have already said, Tony Miles taught me just how important current speed is on these large waters. In fact, I don't often really set out on one swim on large waters, but move about, until I find a good undertow and begin to get the odd bite or two; when this happens I will dig in and bait up, but not before. I know this is a very unconventional approach for a large water where most people think of sitting in one swim for hours and even weeks, but I simply have neither the time nor the inclination for this war of attrition; and I like to keep everything light and mobile, and I don't think my results suffer at all by comparison.

I have meant this to be a lightweight discussion. I have not gone into vast detail with water temperatures or bait recipes – but then neither did maestros like Wentworth, and they caught plenty of roach. In fact, I feel that a lot of modern developments are leading us far away from the truth, and the man who succeeds constantly will be the one who knows the ways and the habits of fish rather than some complicated theory or another. Perhaps in some branches of the sport you have to ally the two skills, though thankfully I don't think this is necessary yet in roach fishing, where often the simplest approach is the most successful.

10 PERCH

It would be a very blinkered angler indeed who could not marvel at the splendid beauty of a big perch. The perch is a bold, striking fish in every sense of the word, with dashingly handsome with looks to match its roguish behaviour. Anglers have described it as possessing bristling defiance, a characteristic it displays both in and out of the water when it raises its distinctive, spiked dorsal fin. After years spent in abeyance after the devastating effects of perch disease, perch are now enjoying a new surge of life, and many of our lakes and rivers contain healthy stocks of them.

BIG PERCH FROM SMALL RIVERS

There can be no doubt that if you want to catch a truly gigantic perch, stillwaters offer better prospects than rivers. But there is something about river perching that stillwaters cannot compete with. The river is a vibrant place, always moving, changing and never standing still, possessing a character of its own that lakes and ponds do not offer. I love small river fishing; there is always new hope around every bend, and approaching a new swim offers exciting fresh prospects. As a realistic target, a 3lb-plus river perch is quite achievable and two-pounders are within every angler's reach.

Location

Perch are traditionally associated with deep, slack holes, and although there is some truth in this, I have found that seeking perch out in truly slack areas is more reliable in winter than in summer. During the warmer months then, my favourite perch swims are where faster and steadier waters meet or evenly paced runs which are

John Watson unhooks a perch on a day that is perfect for perch fishing.

populated with rushes, reeds, cabbages, lilies or overhanging trees. Perch rely on ambush, using cover to pillage shoals of minnows and small fry, and their renowned dislike of bright sunlight and these predatory instincts should tell you that swims with ambushing potential and cover will make the best perch lies on the river.

Summer perch prefer to feed at dawn, and to a lesser extent at dusk. In periods of very low light, just before dawn in fact, one of the most reliable places to find them is in very shallow water where they will spend the first hour of daylight decimating the minnow shoals. At times like this, a simple freelined minnow or lobworm can yield spectacular perch catches. Later in the day you will need to seek them out in their natural haunts, and the brighter the day, the deeper into cover they will retreat. A classic perch area is a deep slack which borders faster, more turbulent water; the perch like to lie in wait, near to the fast water, ready to take advantage of its confusing currents to sneak up on prey fish. Thus a simple float-fished lobworm drifted around the slack or trotted along the edge of the flow, is likely to produce a decent bag of fish.

Steady glides and runs will also hold perch, but you can rest assured that they will never be far from cover; overhanging trees, rushbeds, lily pads and cabbages provide perch with essential shelter and excellent camouflage in the dappled green water of such places. In the first and last two hours of daylight a bait presented close to this cover will produce bites, but unless the weather is overcast and dull, it is likely that you will have to take increasing risks with tackle to present it closer and closer to the cover in order to provoke takes.

As summer mellows into autumn, and then into the early stages of winter, perch are more often found in the steadier, deeper areas of the river. Stretches found immediately above weir pools, where the last mile or so slows dramatically before tumbling over the weir sill, are very reliable late autumn-winter perch areas. The perch's preference will be for even-paced runs with a depth of 4ft (1.2m) or more, moving no faster than a slow walking pace. In times of flood, true slacks, cuttings and tributaries will hold large numbers of perch, but with the river at normal winter level it is my belief that they prefer a gentle flow across their backs.

Prime areas include marginal rush and reedbeds and the area immediately behind or underneath overhanging trees. Bends can be good, too, especially if the bank is undercut; in this sort of swim, with the river at normal level, the perch will often be found lying near to, or inside the undercut, which is invariably on the outside of the bend. As water levels rise, they will move across the river, into the slacker water on the inside of the bend.

Baits

Fortunately the perch's tastes are very simple, and the list of baits that will catch them is very short. Maggots and lobworms are perhaps the most convenient and reliable, the maggots being used as a loosefeed attractor with lobworms as hookbait. Live and dead fish will also catch perch, although I have largely given up using them because of the pike problem. In a really 'hot' perch swim I might be tempted to trot a minnow, but a wire trace is essential to avoid the risk of 'bite-offs' by pike, and perch *do not* like the feel of wire traces. In practice, lobworms produce perch of an average size, quite comparable to those caught on minnows and even gudgeon, a fact which tends to make using the latter somewhat unnecessary.

Occasionally perch will refuse a whole lobworm, and yet gratefully accept the tail end of a lob or a bunch of redworms on a smaller hook; nevertheless lobworms really are *the* river perch bait.

Tackle

For float fishing, a normal match rod is perfectly adequate for perch. Wherever possible I prefer to use a slightly 'beefed-up' match rod, with a little more backbone than standard. A rod that will cope with 3 to 4lb reel lines is ideal, and my favourite is the Ultegra 'Fast Action' 13ft model by Shimano. This is a truly superb rod with a very fast tip action but with a soft and forgiving fish-playing capability, and its 'spineless' construction means that there are no flat spots, a feature which drastically reduces perch losses. Whichever float rod you choose, make sure that it is soft enough on the tip section not to tear the hooks out of the perch's bony mouth; perch also have a soft membrane in their mouth, so choosing a rod with a forgiving action is doubly important.

The same can be said of leger rods, and despite the fact that quivertip rods are not generally popular with perch anglers, I use them a great deal on rivers. A medium feeder rod between 11 and 12ft long, with a through but crisp action is ideal and it should be complimented by a range of quivertips between 1 and 2 oz.

As far as reels are concerned, a standard match reel will suffice, even for leger work. I am able to couple the Shimano Stradic 2000 reel with my light/medium Twin Power feeder rod; this reel has a truly superb slipping clutch, though to be fair, although a reel like this might be essential for chub, it is a luxury for perch.

I load my reels with 3, 4 and 6lb Berkley Trilene XL, an 'extra limp' mono which is soft to the touch and possesses very little memory. Since I prefer to fish straight through for perch, a soft, reliable line is essential.

Hooks should be carried in sizes 6 to 12 to cope with whole lobs, bunches of reds and lobworm sections; my favourite pattern is the 'Jack Hilton' by Partridge.

A few Arlesey bombs, a selection of split shot and some balsa and crowquill Avon floats complete my small-river perch-fishing needs, although a good pair of artery forceps and a disgorger are both essential accessories since perch are notorious for gorging baits.

Rigs, Methods and Tactics

My favourite technique for locating river perch involves the use of the quivertip rod. A simple, light fixed paternoster is cast into likely looking perch 'holes' and is manipulated so that it thoroughly explores the swim. The bait will be a single, large, lively lobworm and if perch are around, bites won't be too long in coming. A soft quivertip to minimize resistance to taking perch is necessary, particularly if you want to continue using quivertip tackle throughout the session. However, I will usually change to the float after experiencing a bite or two, but it is important to use a soft tip since the first perch from a new swim will frequently be the biggest. For fishing far bank swims, or underneath overhanging cover, I will stay with the quivertip, experimenting with the number of swanshot or the size of the Arlesey bomb on the paternoster link so as to be continually balancing the tackle with the changing flow rate found in different swims. A properly balanced perch paternoster will hold bottom, but only *just* and should be capable of being dislodged by simply drawing on the line in front of the reel.

Perch bites will usually consist of a series of preliminary 'jabs' on the tip before it pulls smoothly round. This is the signal to strike, responding with a positive and smooth sweeping

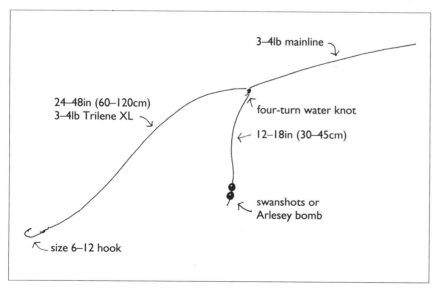

24–48in (60–120cm)
3–4lb Trilene XL

3–4lb mainline

four-turn water knot

12–18in (30–45cm)

swanshots or
Arlesey bomb

size 6–12 hook

Fig. 28 *River perch paternoster.*

action. Should the jabs persist without developing into smooth pulls, there is undoubtedly a problem with your set-up, namely:

1. The quivertip is not safe enough, or
2. The paternoster hooklength is too short, or
3. The leger weight is too heavy.

As a guide, I usually start with a 3ft (90cm) hooklength and an 18in (45cm) paternoster, using just enough weight to hold bottom.

For fishing against far bank cover you cannot beat upstream legering, a truly deadly method for converting perch bites into hooked fish. The rod should be positioned to point at the bait, and is elevated, with the tip pointing upwards. This helps to keep as much line off the water as possible, which in turn allows the use of lighter leger weights to hold bottom. If it is very windy, point the rod parallel to the bank, facing downstream at roughly 90° to the bait. The tip should be positioned low to the water to avoid buffeting by the wind.

Cast the bait out, allowing it to settle in the desired spot. The soft quivertip should have a healthy bend in it, since the greater the deflection on the tip, the more positive the bite indication. Takes will consist of a short jab before the tip straightens as the perch moves toward the angler with the bait. A smooth, sweeping strike should be made at this point, and at extreme range you might find it necessary to wind at the same time in order to recover excess slack line. This is a devastating method – master it, and you will miss very few bites.

Wherever possible, I like to float fish for river perch. Having located the fish by casting around with the quivertip, a switch to the float is in order so as to search the swim methodically.

My favourite float tackle consists of a balsa and crowquill Avon float with a shot capacity somewhere between 3BB and 5AAA, fished 'straight through' on 3 or 4lb line. For a big lobworm or

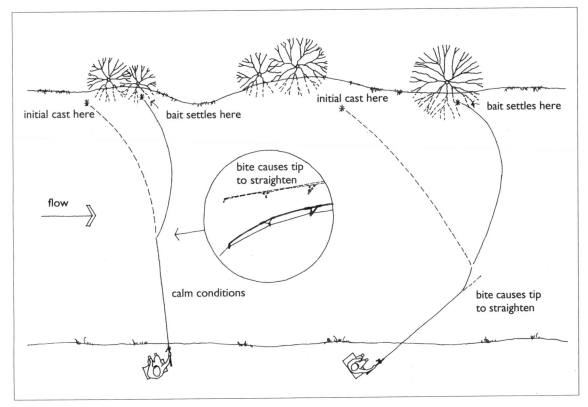

Fig. 29 *Position of rod in upstream quivertipping.*

double lob hookbait, I will tie on a size 6 Hilton, while smaller lobs will be fished on a size 8 or 10. Sections of worm or bunches of reds are ideally suited to a size 12.

Float tackle like this can be fished in three styles, namely trotted, 'stret-pegged' and laid on. The balsa and crowquill lends itself to all three styles, and provides stability, good visibility and sensitive bite registration thanks to its unique design. It is a float that lends itself to bulk shotting, and to presenting a bait slowly at a level somewhere between half the depth of the swim and dragging bottom.

The beauty of float fishing for perch is that, provided the float is shotted correctly (dotted down to the sight tip), it provides minimum resistance to a biting fish. Bites tend to consist of a series of dips before the float simply 'sails away'; a strike should be made at the moment the tip disappears or when a positive 'run' develops, to avoid deep hooking fish.

I usually begin by trotting the float through the swim approximately 6 to 12in (15 to 30cm) off the bottom; this is especially deadly if you can run the float as close to any available cover as possible. If bites dry up using this method, as they inevitably will, a switch to 'laid on' baits in likely areas should produce another fish or two. To achieve this, the float is pushed over depth, 1ft (30cm) at a time, until it lies comfortably at half cock. Bites will cause the float to bob, tip up, run and (hopefully) disappear. As a general rule, the closer you place the bait to cover, the better. This is a truly exciting method, too, with bold, almost unmissable bites being your reward nearly every time.

Finally, a change to stret-pegged float fishing, which involves moving the bait downstream at regular intervals, will help you to make that final inch-by-inch search of the swim. Again the float is fished over-depth, but with a little less line on the bottom than with the 'laying-on' technique.

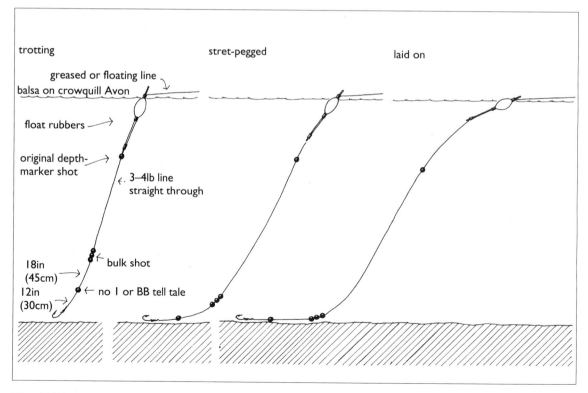

Fig. 30 *River perch float rigs.*

John Watson with a mind-blowing 4lb 10oz perch.

By periodically lifting the float and releasing a few coils of line, the tackle can be bumped a few feet downstream before tightening up and bringing it to rest again. Bites will usually consist of jabs and positive pulls under, and can come either on the move or stationary, so it pays to be on guard at all times.

The beauty of small river perching, is that it is essentially a mobile and active pastime. If bites dry up in one swim, you can move downstream to another, unfettered by heaps of tackle (which discourages mobility in my opinion). And as every good river perch angler knows, there is always hope around the next bend.

BIG PERCH FROM
SMALL PONDS   by Steve Burke

Almost all of you will know the whereabouts of a number of small ponds, many of which are full of stunted fish. Some are overstocked modern-style carp venues, others are centuries-old farm ponds. Few specialist anglers bother with these waters, believing them incapable of producing big fish of any species. However, it is just this sort of habitat that can produce monster perch. Firstly,

there is food galore in the form of innumerable stunted roach or rudd. Secondly, nobody fishes these ponds for perch, which thrive on neglect the same as any other predator.

Of course, not all such waters hold the species, but even the odd perch means that the venue could be worth a try. For instance, one pond I have fished contains almost no perch at all, but it has nevertheless yielded specimens to 4lb10oz! Others are full of stunted stripies, but sometimes contain just a handful of giants which have grown fat on a diet of their smaller brethren.

The very small number of big perch coupled with a plentiful food supply means that such specimens can be extremely hard to catch. This is especially so in summer when fry are very abundant, and thus most of my perching takes place in the winter, with the last couple of months of the season being particularly productive unless it is very cold.

Location
As ever, location is the first step and any ambush points such as weedbeds, changes of depth or sunken trees are good places to start. Sometimes you will have to fish within inches of the feature to stand any chance of catching, particularly in

bright conditions – in fact, years of specializing in perch has convinced me that light intensity is the key to locating the specimen fish. Perch have exceptional eyesight and feed hardest when they can put this to maximum use. This is not, as you might expect, in bright light, but in dim conditions when their poorer-sighted prey are then at a disadvantage. At these times, such as dawn and dusk or in overcast weather, big perch will leave their murky sanctuaries and go hunting; it is then that they can be caught from shallow open water.

But what if your pond is featureless? Once again, light intensity can be your guide. Here deep water, especially if it is shaded, is likely to be the best bet in bright conditions, whilst in poor light the shallows will usually be preferred. There are exceptions of course, but I have found that such waters invariably respond best in dim light. Indeed, in the pond mentioned earlier, it is very rare to get a run before late afternoon. The same was true on the farm reservoir from which I had my first three-pounder way back in 1982, and there have been many more examples since.

Baits and Groundbaits

Whilst it always pays to offer the perch a choice when you first start to fish, I have found that on most overstocked ponds the perch prefer live- and deadbaits. One of the main alternatives is lobworm, and although I have had 4lb gravel-pit tench on both whole and half lobs, in ponds I have often found small perch to be a nuisance on worms – and all fish a nuisance on maggots and casters! After all, the perch in these ponds have grown big by eating smaller fish, so what could be more natural than a live- or deadbait? Finally, most overstocked waters are relatively well coloured, and I have found that whilst lures are very productive for perch on clearwater venues, they are almost a complete waste of time in murky water.

Freshwater deadbaits are certainly productive, especially perch and roach, but static seabaits don't seem to be liked by the larger perch at all. Don't be afraid to use big baits, as perch have huge mouths and a three-pounder can easily manage a 6oz roach. However, such large offerings can present hooking problems, and therefore I often use half baits, particularly as these have the added advantage of creating a scent trail.

Livebaits tend to be whatever I can catch from the water, gudgeon being my favourite as they seem to work forever and constantly dive for the bottom. On the other hand, rudd can be a hand-

The author with a stillwater perch of 2lb 10oz caught on a lobworm.

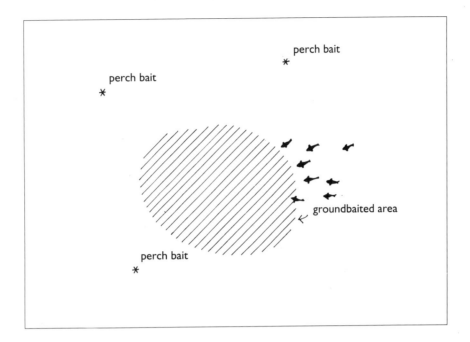

Fig. 31 *Positioning of perch baits in relation to groundbaited area.*

perch bait

perch bait

groundbaited area

perch bait

ful and tend to tangle many rigs, limiting the choice of presentation.

Invariably I will use groundbait, both to colour the water and to attract small fish to catch as bait; these tiddlers are then constantly active in the swim, which in turn brings in the perch. Angling colleague Archie Braddock has also shown that certain flavourings attract the perch themselves, although which ones are most effective seems to depend on water temperature, with curry being the best in the winter. One important point is that I always fish my baits a yard or two *away* from the groundbait, and not in it; rather than charging into a shoal, a solitary perch picks off the stragglers, and thus a bait isolated from the main group stands a better chance of being taken (*see* Fig. 31).

Tackle and Rigs

Whereas small perch are easy to catch, specimens are a different matter altogether, and the right gear is essential for success. Runs from big perch are rare enough anyway, and so it is foolhardy to take chances. For instance, because perch have a very thin membrane behind their lips, a rod with a soft tip is absolutely vital to avoid tearing the hook out if it lodges in this membrane. In fact I couldn't find exactly what I wanted for this, and have therefore designed a rod especially for big perch and roach, and this will shortly be on sale.

In my area I can use three rods, one of which is initially set up to catch baits on float-fished maggot. Later in the session I will replace the hooklength with a 4lb Silkworm trace and either a worm or a deadbait, or possibly take off a shot and fish a free-roving livebait. Float fishing has two particular advantages: firstly, if the bait is twitched back, any takes can be detected immediately; and secondly, there is minimal resistance, which is absolutely vital when perching.

The other rods might be set up to fish livebaits on sunken float paternosters, which I have modified from low resistance rigs invented by Vic Bellars and Colin Dyson. As you can see, by sliding the float stop down the paternoster link, I can quickly change from a Bellars to a Dyson set-up, the latter being used for rudd livebaits to minimize tangling. However, this rig is less versatile because the hooklength has to be kept short, and also in shallow water baits can more easily reach the bottom, which you may not want. Both rigs are fished lightly clipped up in conjunction with

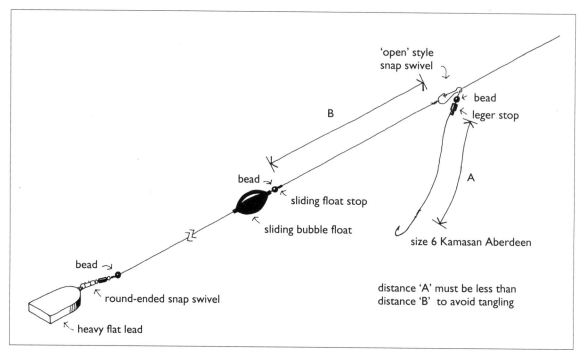

Fig. 32 *Modified Colin Dyson rig.*

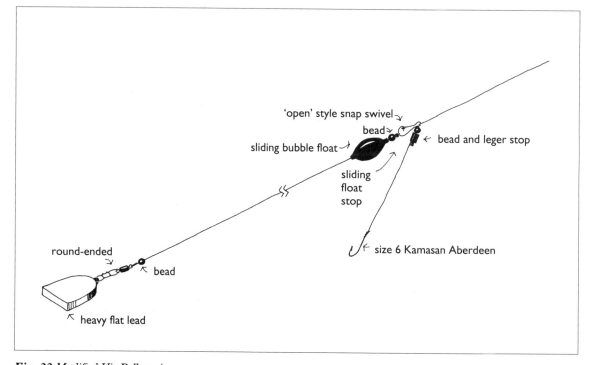

Fig. 33 *Modified Vic Bellars rig.*

drop-off alarms, and by varying the tension of the line I can quickly change the working depth, slackening off leading to the float and bait rising, and vice versa. By incorporating a snap swivel, the links can quickly be replaced by others of different lengths, including short versions to make running legers. The most important point with these rigs is that the lead must be heavy enough to stay put when a perch takes. This creates *less* resistance because the indicator moves rather than the lead.

My conscience allows me only to liphook livebaits, although this undoubtedly costs me fish. The hook is therefore a single, usually a size 6 Kamasan Aberdeen, which is relatively fine in the wire and has a small barb. Finally, please *do not* use barbless hooks in such large sizes because these can penetrate too deeply, and as perch have their hearts near their throats, can kill them.

Conclusion

I hope the foregoing will convince you that, although by no means easy fishing, small overstocked ponds can produce big perch. In fact I will stick my neck out and predict that, providing we don't suffer another outbreak of perch disease, such a water will produce a record within a few years. I hope it will be to my rod – but it could be to yours!

STILLWATER PERCH   by Stewart Allum

Ten years ago, few specialist anglers would have considered big perch a sporting proposition. In many parts of the country the species had been all but wiped out by disease during the 1970s and reports of even 2lb fish were exceedingly rare. However, the last decade has seen this beautiful fish make a striking recovery, to the extent where the perch specialist now stands a better chance than ever before of catching a 3lb or even 4lb specimen from dozens of waters throughout Britain.

In recent seasons I have concentrated on large stillwaters such as sand and gravel pits, achieving consistent sport with fish to over 3lb on the methods I shall now describe.

Summer Fishing

During summer, perch are not localized and tend to keep on the move, hunting the shoals of small fry around the margins. It may therefore be necessary to spend some time locating them. If the water is clear, a good pair of polaroid sunglasses will help you to locate those deeper areas adjacent to marginal weedbeds, snags or lily beds so often frequented by perch. Look out for areas where there is a marginal shelf a few feet out leading off into deeper water. Perch will patrol along the edge of this shelf, waiting to pounce on any unsuspecting fry which stray too far from the weeds; at certain times, particularly late afternoon, you might even see them attacking the little fish in the margins, scattering them in all directions. In this situation I may use a small bar spinner such as a Mepps or an Abu Reflex retrieved slowly just below the surface, as the opportunities present themselves.

My favourite summer method, however, is float fishing. This technique comes into its own on warm, still evenings, when it is possible to work a shoal of perch into a feeding frenzy by loosefeeding maggots. Tackle is fairly straightforward, a lightweight 13ft float rod matched to a closed-face reel with 2½lb line straight through to a size 16 hook, baited with a cocktail of red and white maggots.

The float is a 1BB Drennan Crystalight loaded waggler fixed by a sliding stop knot at whatever depth the fish are feeding (*see* Fig. 34a). Action can be fast and furious, with fish boiling on the surface at each pouchful of maggots once they are feeding hard; two pints of bait can easily disappear during a short evening session. Hooks should be strong, forged, barbless, eyed patterns; these will not open out on the strike and usually gain a good purchase in the hard, bony mouth of a large perch. Remember to check the hookpoint after each capture, however, as today's chemically sharpened points can easily become blunted after contact with such unyielding surfaces.

If no large perch are forthcoming, change the small hook for a size 10 and a lobworm as bait, set to sink amongst the loosefeed. This can sometimes attract the largest fish in the shoal.

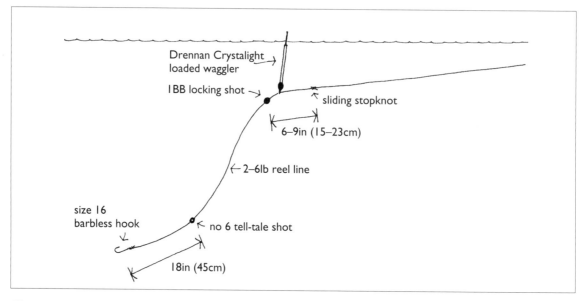

Drennan Crystalight loaded waggler

IBB locking shot

sliding stopknot

6–9in (15–23cm)

2–6lb reel line

size 16 barbless hook

no 6 tell-tale shot

18in (45cm)

Fig. 34a *Crystalight float rig.*

Autumn Fishing

During the autumn months, perch move into deeper water where they generally remain until February or March, when their spawning urges encourage them back towards the shallows. Autumn is therefore by far the best time to seek out the bigger specimens on large, deep still-waters; at this time of year the adult fish become very hungry and aggressive as they pack on weight prior to spawning. Large numbers of these fish become concentrated in the deeper areas, often at depths of 20ft (6m) or more. The angler who has done his homework with the plummet earlier in the season and located a few likely hotspots within casting range of the bank, can therefore look forward to some tremendous sport once October arrives.

My own preference at this time of year is leg-ering, using either free-running link legers or swimfeeders, with lobworm as bait. The rod is a standard 11ft Avon of 1lb test curve, with a fixed spool reel and 6lb main line. This strength of line is necessary as a result of the stress imposed by regular casting of the loaded swimfeeder and striking upwards through deep water. Optonic bite alarms in conjunction with the lightest possible bite indicators should be used for bite

detection, as perch are extremely wary of the slightest resistance.

For feeder fishing, I prefer the open-ended variety on a running link *(see* Fig. 34b), filled with a mixture of breadcrumb, maizemeal, 'Ace' worm extract and dried blood, dyed red and laced with red and white maggots. This breaks up into a nice red cloud effect which perch find very attractive. The hooklength is a 24 to 30in (60 to 75cm) length of 5lb b.s. Bayer Perlon, and the hook a size 4 or 6 Drennan Starpoint barbless. Bait is a whole lobworm tipped with a single red maggot to keep it on the hook. If the bottom is covered in leaves or debris, the worm can be air-injected and popped up, as in Fig. 34c.

If a change to straightforward leger is required, I merely exchange the feeder for an Arlesey bomb. The rest of the rig remains unaltered *(see* Fig. 34).

I now use 'power-gum' links for all my feeder and swivel trace attachments. The 15lb strength doesn't tangle during casting, and provides that extra bit of cushioning whilst casting and striking, considerably reducing the risk of accidental breakages. When a run occurs, lift the rod steadily into the fish whilst pumping in any slack line, this is a far safer and more effective way of hitting

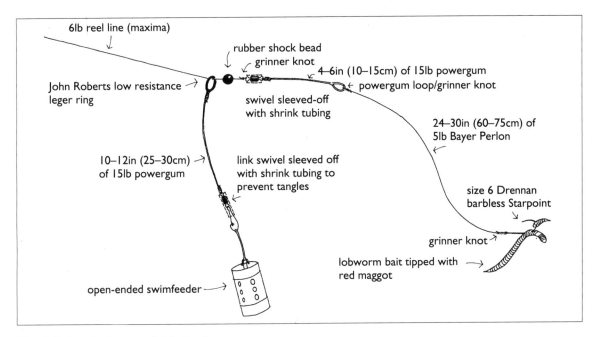

Fig. 34b *Standard open-ended feeder rig.*

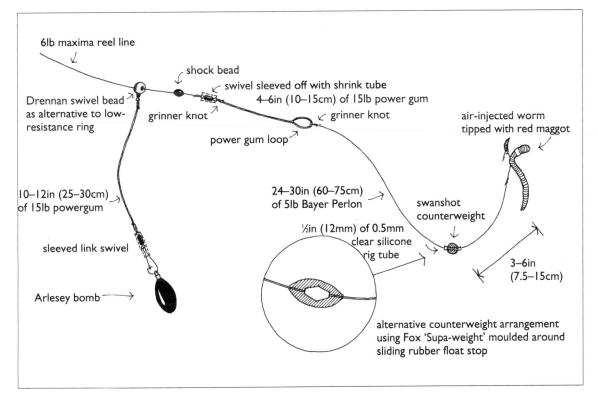

Fig. 34c *Air-injected worm on running leger.*

A big stillwater perch caught by Stewart Allum at the back end of the season. Note the condition of the fish as it gets ready to spawn.

bites when fishing in deep water. Striking wildly only imposes a sudden and unnecessary strain on the tackle, greatly increasing the risk of breakages.

Winter Fishing

Whilst the very depths of winter are generally too cold for consistent perch sport, during February and March the fish once again become active as they prepare for spawning. Unless conditions are particularly mild, I find that maggots tend to out-fish lobworms as bait, particularly when flavoured with curry. Perch seem to love this flavour, and I have taken some good catches in very cold weather using maggots flavoured with curry powder and a liquid enhancer such as 'Bio-trak' prior to fishing; approximately one tea-spoonful of dry powder and two teaspoonfuls of enhancer per pint is about right.

Whilst the fish might be willing to feed, they are generally less aggressive than during the autumn, so I tend to scale the tackle down a bit, using a lighter rod, 3 to 4lb reel line, and a mini feeder containing a dozen or so maggots, with a 2lb hooklength to a size 16 hook and double maggot. The float tackle remains similar to that used during summer, the only difference being that a slightly heavier float may be needed to combat any wind or surface drag.

Whilst deep lakes and pits produce large numbers of good perch in the 1½ to 3½lb class, they often lack the huge shoals of small fish such as gudgeon or bleak which enable perch to grow on to reach truly massive proportions. Some of the biggest specimens of recent years have come from small, overstocked ponds where perch are fewer in number yet are able to grow huge on the abundance of tiny prey fish. Fellow perch fisher Steve Burke has concentrated on such waters during the past few seasons, with some pretty spectacular results.

11 CARP

Carp have become the vogue fish of the nineties. The largest fish that swim in British stillwaters (with the possible exception of pike), carp have developed a cult status in recent years. It is an ironic development that up until as recently as twenty years ago, carp fishing was a minority pursuit considered to be the exclusive province of eccentrics. The cult status of the carp has also been accompanied by a cult status among carp anglers, a breed of fanatics who seem to relish their notoriety.

Whether you enjoy carp fishing or not, as an experienced or developing big fish angler you have a great deal to thank carp anglers for. Make no mistake, if it wasn't for the advances in carp fishing, modern fishing tackle and accessories wouldn't be anything like as sophisticated as they are today. It is carp anglers who have pushed back the barriers of rig, tackle and bait technology, and the spin-off benefits of being able to apply carp fishing ideas and methods to catching other species are enormous.

The author with one of the many 20lb-plus carp he has caught in the UK and abroad.

I would strongly recommend that you fish for carp, not to the exclusion of other species, but as an essential part of your specialist fishing education. More importantly though, the carp is a magnificent creature in every sense of the word, no sight in angling can set the pulse racing as the incredible ferocity of a carp run. And when you experience the sheer power of a big carp as it powers its way across the lake, you will understand the adrenalin-pumping attraction of the species.

My personal experience of carp fishing is widespread. I have fished for them in the UK and abroad on a variety of waters from small to large, and have caught them on a multitude of tackle set-ups from 'traditional' to 'advanced'. My favourite type of carp fishing, however, is on small to medium-sized waters, where the fishing takes on a more intimate, intensified nature.

Fishing for carp on big waters presents a whole different set of challenges, where tackle and technique enjoy a status equal to their location; big water carp experts are made from special stuff indeed. One such angler is Dave Thorpe, an expert all-round carp angler of some twenty-five years' standing who shares his hard-earned knowledge of big water carping in this book.

CARP BAITS: BOILIES

The serious carp angler is constantly concocting new recipes, blending ingredients and testing new flavours in a bid to create the ultimate carp bait. 'Playing around with bait' is his constant pre-occupation – and in fact is almost as much fun as the fishing itself! Natural, standard and particle baits and their application have already been covered in some depth, so we will now look at boilies in more detail.

It is easy to go 'over the top' when it comes to talking about baits. The H.N.V. (High Nutritional Value) theory is a case in point, proposing that carp are able to recognize the superiority of one bait over another in terms of its nutritional value either by conscious or subconscious means. Personally I don't believe it, though many anglers do. The theory may have been valid in the early days of boilies when very few anglers used them, but nowadays with so many boilies entering our waters, how does a carp differentiate the food value of one boiled bait from another? 'Purists' would argue that exclusive 'labels' can be created to aid the carp in their recognition; these comprise distinctive attractors (flavours and so on) which give the boilie its 'exclusive' tag.

I recognize the validity of the 'label' theory, but surely carp eat boilies because they like the taste of them. A good attractor still operates on this basic principle, and the fact of the matter remains that it is the taste flavour of the boilie that makes the carp pick it up in the first place. However, when carp develop a taste for a particular 'boilie', they will keep coming back for more, and in my opinion we should therefore direct our concerns to the overall palatability, digestibility and sheer taste experience that a carp enjoys when it picks up a bait. For this reason blends of ingredients can contribute significantly to the quality of a finished bait – it is not just about flavours, and that is why palatants, extracts and oils should play a major part in the construction of a good boilie. Rod Hutchinson expresses this concept very succinctly when he talks about the Chinese meal 'just-one-more-taste syndrome' which causes human beings to eat a lot of food and still feel hungry, and maintains that the same principle can be applied to carp baits.

Base Mixes
Base mixes provide the food value in the bait and are the bulk ingredient. A cheap base mix comprising simple products such as semolina and soya flour is merely just a carrier for the attractors (flavours, oils and so on), but a good base mix will be blended from various ingredients and will contribute to the overall taste and palatability of the bait in its own right. Milk proteins, bird-foods, fishmeals, animal proteins and of course semolina and soya flour are commonly used products. Even a 'fishmeal' base mix will not contain purely fish meals – if it did, it wouldn't roll. Thus all base mixes use blends of ingredients for their different properties, and the best among

them will roll well, taste good and will be highly digestible. There are various types of base mix sold to carp anglers:

Milk Proteins

Milk proteins are currently suffering from a downturn in popularity in favour of birdfoods and fishmeals. They are still the number one choice for winter carp anglers, however, and most manufacturers make an H.N.V. or 'cold water' mix. High in protein and easy to roll, but as a general rule not as digestible as birdfoods and fishmeals.

Birdfoods

Birdfoods are available in red and yellow mixes. All birdfood base mixes contain blends of birdfood ingredients, and these are further combined with milk protein ingredients to make them easier to roll. Red birdfoods tend to be spicier and more bitter to the taste than yellow birdfoods. They are also highly digestible; traditionally more difficult to roll than milk proteins; good food value; and of good texture.

Fishmeals

Fishmeals are the vogue bait of more recent years. They certainly have addictive qualities, and their high digestibility has led to their use in mass baiting campaigns. Like any other bait, fishmeals will 'blow' after protracted use, but there are so many individual types of fishmeal around that complex blends of ingredients have tended to extend the life of the bait. They are highly digestible; difficult to roll unless blended with other ingredients; fairly buoyant (useful for fishing over weed); rich food value; strong natural taste.

'Bulk' Base Mixes

These are the 'carrier'-type mixes made from cheap bulk ingredients; their food value is principally carbohydrate, but they make a good base for effective attractors. They are of average digestibility; poor to average food value; they roll well, and are cheap (cost effective). It is easy to dismiss 'crap' baits as they are known, but the fact is that many carp have fallen to them.

Flavours

The flavours sold to carp anglers are synthetic imitations of naturally occurring smells and tastes. Highly concentrated, they are not often included at a level higher than 5ml per pound of base mix. The purpose of flavours is to attract carp, sending out pleasant 'eat me' type messages to the fish's chemo-reception hunger mechanism. Following ingestion, the flavour then plays a secondary role in helping to make the bait palatable and, it is hoped, pleasing to the carp from a taste point of view. Flavours play an absolutely vital role in the effectiveness of boilies: if it smells good and tastes good, the carp will eat lots of it!

A whole host of flavours and smells are known to be attractive to carp, and a fruity flavour may work well on a savoury base such as fishmeal; carp have wide-ranging tastes, and all sorts of weird combinations appear to find favour. Eventually you will develop a feel for such things, and a combination that sounds repulsive may prove to be highly successful.

Try to choose flavours which smell and taste like their description on the bottle, not something that is vaguely reminiscent of what they are meant to represent. The chances are that if it smells good to you, the carp will like it. There are basically five types of flavour: dairy, fruit, spice, savoury and sea-food. All five work well during the warmer months, though many leading carp anglers swear by the fruity and spicy attractors in the winter.

The two most commonly used chemical bases for flavours are propylene glycol and ethyl alcohol. The latter sort are highly favoured for winter use and short session work because they tend to have a greater 'leakage' factor when immersed in water, transmitting attractive smells to the carp at a faster rate than propylene glycol-based flavours. On the other hand, pg-based flavours are more popular for long session and all-round summer/autumn use.

Flavours can also be blended. For instance, combining a smooth dairy flavour with a harsher fruity one gives a much smoother, creamier back-note to the essential fruitiness of the attractor. Similarly in winter, blending a small amount of a spicy attractor with a fruit flavour appears to provide an extra 'something' which the carp approve of and enjoy.

In recent years 'essential oils' have suffered the 'slings and arrows of outrageous carp bait fortune'. In the late 1980s and early 1990s, they were *the* vogue attractors, and a wide range of essential oils were marketed; more recently, however, their popularity has declined – and rightly so, in my opinion; I never rated them highly as attractors in their own right. Like many other 'fashions' in carp fishing, they worked because they were used by a lot of anglers, and not because they were particularly good. Nowadays the most common use for essential oils is as a 'backnote' additive for a main flavour; since they are a highly concentrated natural product a few drops are easily detected in a bait, and indeed some of them, like garlic oil for instance, are so strong that one drop is almost too much. I generally only use essential oils in the winter now to add a spicy edge to the main flavour. The only ones I personally rate are 'Black Pepper' and 'Juniper Berry', both of which are sold by Nutrabaits.

Sweeteners

Sweeteners are an indispensable additive to 90 per cent of the boiled carp baits that I use. These are not sweeteners in terms of human palatability, and most baits will benefit from their inclusion unless the blend of ingredients and palatants used makes the bait sweet enough already. Sweeteners are just as important in savoury and fishy mixes as they are in fruity and dairy ones, their purpose being to improve the palatability of the bait; and they play a significant role in the overall taste experience. The simplest sweeteners are natural products, the most notable among them being good old table sugar and liquid molasses. Table sugar has its limitations, however, because the sheer amount of it required to sweeten the bait can lead to rolling problems. Liquid molasses is an excellent sweetener, but its natural, rich brown colour will 'colour' bright white, yellow, orange or red baits.

Man-made sweeteners produced specifically for the carp market are many times sweeter than sugar. They can be used purely to sweeten the bait or to 'smooth off' a slightly bitter-tasting mix. Available in both liquid and powdered form,

it is advisable to follow the manufacturer's instructions regarding inclusion rates, because a bait that is over sweetened tastes simply hideous and leaves an unpleasant after-taste.

Palatants

The term 'palatant' is the 'buzz' word in the world of carp baits, though even the hardened cynics have to admit that it provides an apt description for the function of these products. Palatants do not attract carp as such, but they play a vital role in improving the taste of the bait. In the early days they were known as 'flavour enhancers' and were based on 'monosodium glutamate' (msg), an additive which is widely used in the human and animal food industries. Nowadays they are more sophisticated, and are given additional ingredients to produce a spicy, fruity or dairy taste in their own right.

There can be no doubt that palatants are effective. In the animal food industry for example, they are smeared onto the teats of female pigs to improve the palatability of their milk to their offspring. Cattle feeds are sprayed with palatants to encourage beef animals to eat more and thus reach the slaughter house more quickly. The role of palatants in carp baits is exactly the same. I regard them as a standard ingredient because they have the potential to boost the carp's enjoyment of the bait to the extent where it simply has to eat the lot, including my hookbait!

Extracts

Extracts perform a similar role to palatants since they enhance the overall palatability of the bait. Being made from natural products, they play a key role in providing the carp with a good nutritional source – but their primary function is to add a further taste dimension to the mix. To this extent they differ from palatants which nowadays perform both roles, as a booster *and* additional taste. Do not undervalue the importance of extracts, however, and the contribution they can make to adding extra taste to an already good boilie. To be honest I would not rank extracts as being indispensable, but if I want to create a really high quality boiled bait, I always include them.

Vitamin and Mineral Supplements, Digestion Enhancers

There are also a number of products on the market that are designed to add key vitamins and minerals, essential to the carp's survival, to the bait. This principle has been extended still further by the development of enzyme additives which are intended to assist the carp in breaking down the bait and thereby gain higher nutritional benefit from it. The idea is that a bait which satisfies *all* of the carp's dietary needs will be irresistible to it.

On the face of it the only reason I can think of for including these products seems to stem from a genuine care and concern for the welfare of carp. If I genuinely believed that by adding these substances carp would be healthier, I would include them without hesitation. But I am not convinced. I would be the first to acknowledge that some anglers are highly irresponsible in their form of over-use of certain bait ingredients, notably oils, and that this is not doing the carp in some of our waters much good. The condition of these fish tells me all I need to know, and the scientific tests carried out on some of them appear to confirm this. But not enough is known about the carp's dietary requirements, and how to satisfy them with 'designer baits', to persuade me to spend money on vitamins, minerals and enzymes. Besides, these supposedly delicate compounds which we are advised to store in the fridge are then thrown into boiling water for three minutes... So, until the issue is resolved conclusively, it is surely better to let the carp sort out their own vitamin and mineral requirements.

Oils

The subject of oils, and specifically their over-use in carp baits, has recently been headline news in the angling press and one which is developing so quickly that I can only give you my opinion based on what I know at the moment. Oils, and notably fish oils, have been very popular in recent years. At first anglers were including them as a source of 'fats' when the nutritional value/balanced diet argument was widely accepted. However, anglers soon realized that carp are attracted to the smell and taste of oils.

In winter, oils are rarely used since water temperatures are seldom high enough for them to 'emulsify' (mix with the surrounding water); in this situation the result is a bait whose attractors (including the oil-based ones) tend to get 'locked in' due to the presence of the oil. In summer, though, oils are widely used. But not satisfied with putting perhaps 10ml of a good oil into a mix, anglers began to 'glug' baits – that is, they would soak both hookbaits and freebaits in a rich combination of their chosen flavours *and* oil. Inclusion rates in the mix went up, too, as high as 50 and 60ml per pound and even more. The result was rapid oil leakage, meaning instant attraction and big catches; but ultimately, it would seem, unhealthy carp.

So where does this leave us? Until someone proves categorically that using oils is bad for carp, I personally shall continue to use them in moderate doses. I have always limited my use of both fish and non-fish oils to a maximum of 5ml per egg in the base mix; I can only think of one occasion when I 'glugged' my freebait, and I won't be doing it again because the 'slick' was incredible! I shall continue to soak my hookbaits, however, in a mixture of oil and a further single ml of my chosen flavour. At the end of the day, the sensible use of oils will not cause a problem; let us just hope that the 'enthusiastic' among us amend their baits accordingly.

If you are unfamiliar with oils, there are many to choose from. Most anglers using a fishmeal base mix will combine it with a fish oil or a blend of fish oils. Non-fish-based oils are quite rare at the moment, though Dave Thorpe's 'Lump' and 'Lunker' Liquids are superb, in both purity and aroma; their new product 'Liquid Smoke' is also excellent. I use the 'exclusive oil' range extensively both in H.N.V. and birdfood mixes and as a 'soak' for hookbaits. Sesame seed oil, available cheaply from leading supermarkets, also makes a superb bait soak when mixed with a few millilitres of your chosen flavour.

Making Boilies

There are several tips which, if followed, will greatly shorten your boilie-making sessions and improve the quality of the finished product. The picture sequence shows you how to do it; note that it is very important to use precise measuring equipment. Study it, and follow the tips below, and soon you will be turning out perfect baits at high speed.

DO
- Wash your hands thoroughly in unscented soap.
- Use a clean, glass mixing bowl.
- Invest in a sausage gun and rolling table if you intend to make bait regularly.
- Make sure that the water you use is boiling whenever you immerse baits, not just hot.
- Wash your equipment thoroughly at the end of each session.
- Follow the manufacturer's instructions.
- Make sure that everything, including all the ingredients, are to hand before you start.
- Use fresh eggs.
- Mix everything thoroughly.
- Use proper measuring equipment (syringes and pipettes) for flavours and sweeteners.

DO NOT
- Smoke when you are making bait.
- Exceed recommended dosage levels.
- Use dirty equipment.
- Try to cut corners.
- Use a teaspoon to measure out flavours and sweeteners.

Conclusion
Bait-making is a science of sorts. Each ingredient you include in the recipe should be included for a particular reason, and by understanding the benefits of each type of ingredient, it is possible to produce baits of the highest quality that will perform specific functions.

So far, no one has managed to create a single, magical combination that is irresistible to carp. Long may it remain that way.

RIGS

The development of carp-fishing tackle and rig-making accessories over the past decade has been at a bewildering pace. My major concern regarding the information in this section was that it would quickly become out of date, but after considerable thought it is my belief that the rate of development has in fact slowed dramatically. New products and ideas will continue to appear regularly, but I believe we are now in a period of refinement and fine-tuning; the revolution is long since over.

How to make boilies.

1. The equipment you need: 16oz of base mix, oil, sweetener, flavour, palatant, mixing bowl, syringe, eggs, rolling table and bait gun.

2. Weigh out 16oz of base mix. Be absolutely precise.

3. Add the powdered ingredients to the base mix in a polythene bag. Powdered ingredients include palatant and extracts (optional).

4. Thoroughly mix the powder by blowing air into the bag and shaking vigorously.

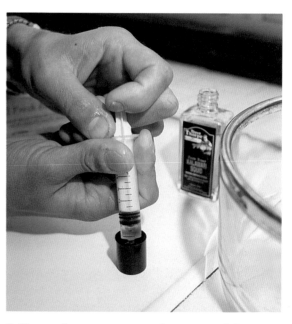

5. *Break the recommended number of eggs for a pound of base mix into a bowl and beat them thoroughly.*

6. *Use a syringe to measure out the recommended quantities of liquids (sweetener, oils, flavour) and add them to the eggs. Beat the eggs again thoroughly to disperse the liquids.*

7. *Add the powder to the eggs a little at a time, stirring the mix with a wooden spoon. Eventually you will need to work it with your hands to produce a stiff but pliable paste.*

8. *You can roll the paste into small boilie-sized round balls by hand if you don't possess a bait gun.*

9. A bait gun is faster. Push the mix into the gun and extrude it across the rolling table into long thin sausages.

11. You should end up with a number of round balls, ready for boiling.

10. Close the two halves of the roller together. Hold the base firmly and shuffle the top backwards and forwards vigorously.

12. Boil the baits, approximately twenty at a time, for one and a half to three minutes, depending on the hardness required. The longer you boil the baits the harder they will be.

13. The finished product. Allow them to dry and either use them within twenty-four hours or freeze them.

Understanding Rigs

Fifteen years have now elapsed since the two most significant developments in carp rig construction, the bolt rig and the hair rig, were introduced to anglers. Everything that has happened since then has been centred around improving the effectiveness of these two basic principles – if you understand them, adapting to the latest improvement is simply a matter of reading the specialist carp press or experimenting for yourself. This is not meant to be cynical, but the carp fishing press and the 'grapevine' are both now so acutely developed that there are no real secrets any more.

In the early days anglers freelined for carp using simple baits like bread (crust and flake), potatoes, and sausage meat. Ultra-lightweight indicators, usually coils of silver paper, were used to detect runs. At that time everyone's thinking was centred around avoiding resistance, but compared to modern styles it was an inefficient way of fishing. Purists may deny this, but their affection for bygone techniques is born out of nostalgia, not efficiency. I am not discounting their opinion altogether: as an angler who enjoys stalking carp, I openly acknowledge that in the pre-buzzer days your average carp angler must have possessed superior watercraft, and the pioneers of carp fishing can still teach modern anglers skills that are becoming rare these days. There can be no doubt though, that the development of the bolt rig led to the downfall of many carp that would not have been caught otherwise. Apart from the obvious difference that you can cast further with a very heavy lead, a greater number of takes were converted into fish on the bank. Imagine freelining on a windy day: runs would be difficult enough to detect, but drop-back takes, when the carp moves towards the angler, would be almost impossible to spot.

The Bolt Rig

Originally the bolt rig was developed when anglers began to experiment with particle hookbaits. It was found that side-hooked baits fished in conjunction with a very short hooklength (a few inches) and a heavy, fixed lead out, fished both freelined and traditional running leger styles. Carp would pick up the bait, feel the unnatural resistance and rather than spit the bait out, would bolt from the swim. This panic reaction produced a partially hooked fish every time, and was known originally as the 'shock rig'. As far as bite indication was concerned, anglers discovered that both runs and 'drop-backs' were easily detected due to the dramatic style of bites produced by a rig incorporating a heavy lead. Nowadays bolt rigs incorporate 'semi-fixed' as opposed to truly fixed leads; this means that the lead is fixed in a fishing situation, but will detach itself in the event of a 'crack-off' thus avoiding the dreadful problem of a carp picking up a lost rig and having to tow a heavy weight around the lake. Lead designs and attachment systems have certainly changed since the early days, but the basic principle remains the same; here are some of the modern lead designs and their advantages.

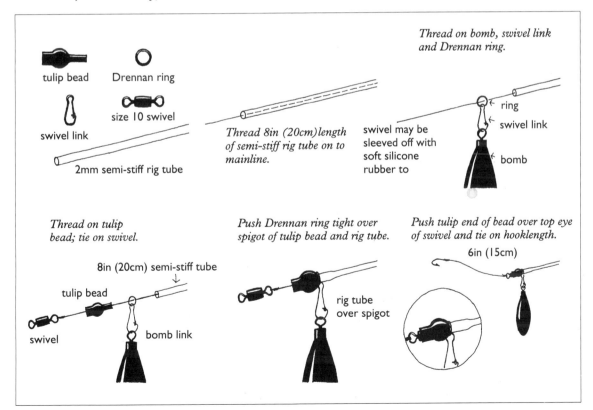

Fig. 35 Safe 'semi-fixed' bolt rig.

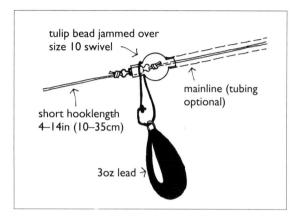

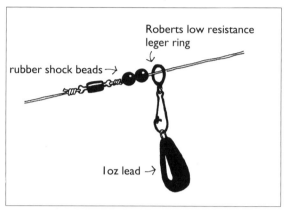

Fig. 36a *Lead attachment – modern semi-fixed bolt rig.*

Fig. 36b *Lead attachment – running leger rig for sensitivity.*

Traditional Arlesey Bomb

This lead was designed by the late Richard Walker, and was purpose built for casting. Its aerodynamic shape is perfect for distance work, and it is still the most popular leger in use by anglers today. Available in a range of sizes from ⅙oz upwards, it is my first choice for running-lead-style carp fishing. Despite the fact that the whole carp world has gone fixed lead crazy, I still use running leads for snag fishing and close range work.

Pear-shaped Bombs, 'Dumpy' Bombs

As rigs progressed, it was found that a dense, 'dumpy' lead with a low centre of gravity helped to enhance the bolt effect. Longer, more stream-lined legers have a tendency to 'rock' when carp pick up the bait, and even this small amount of free movement given to the carp before it encounters the full weight of the lead can lead to dropped takes. Pear- and round-shaped leads avoid this problem, and are now the standard choice of most anglers.

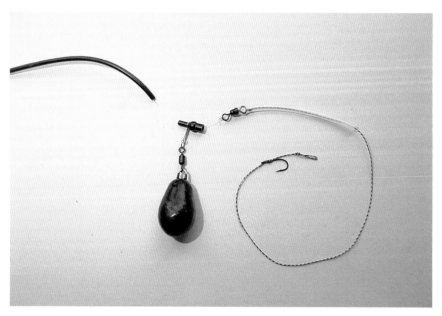

A modern semi-fixed bolt rig will fly apart under pressure so that carp don't suffer if the rig is lost.

In-line Leads

The concept of passing the line through the centre of a lead is not new, and modern in-line leads are a more refined version of drilled bullets or barred-style leads which are popular with lure fisherman. 'In-lines' have three major advantages, namely, they tangle less; they can be cast considerable distances; and they possess a low centre of gravity (thus enhancing the 'bolt' effect). 'In-line' leads are my standard choice for carp fishing, unless I am fishing a running-lead style.

Currently semi-fixed bolt rigs are the standard method of lead attachment for carp anglers, and this has lead in turn to the development of bite indicators specifically designed to be used in conjunction with them. Modern carp indicators are a long way removed from the days of silver paper. Heavy indicators may seem to lack sensitivity, but in fact for heavy lead-style fishing, they don't:

if a fish moves away with the bait, it has to move the heavy lead in order to produce any type of indication at all. This usually takes the form of a belting run (in which case the indicator serves very little purpose), or a slack line bite or a 'drop-back'. In this situation a heavy indicator gives improved bite registration, since the heavier the indicator, the more dramatic the bite registration, as tension is released from the line.

The latest generation of bite indicators incorporate a fixed arm, an adjustable weight loading and a bobbin, and can now accommodate the full range of carp legering styles. With the adjustable weight pushed toward the indicator head a correspondingly heavier 'loading' is achieved, while for sensitive, running-lead-style fishing the weight is pushed in the opposite direction, to produce a light, 'weightless' indicator that can even be tuned to exaggerate slight indications.

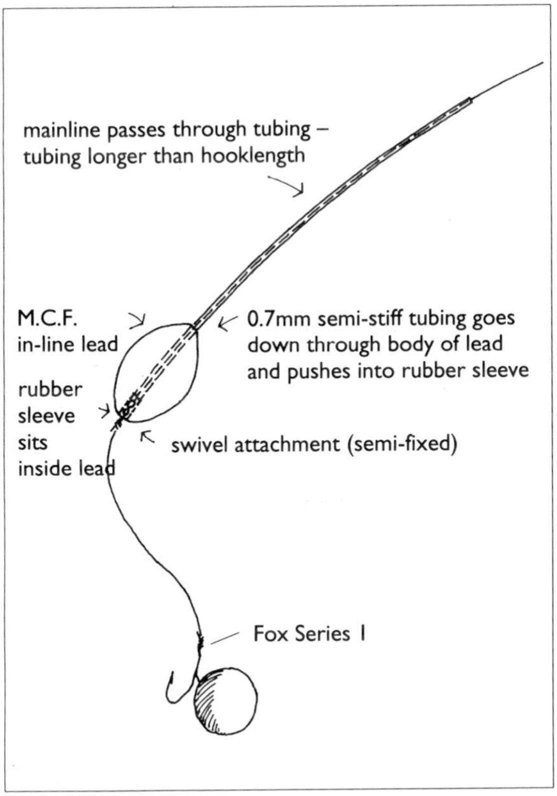

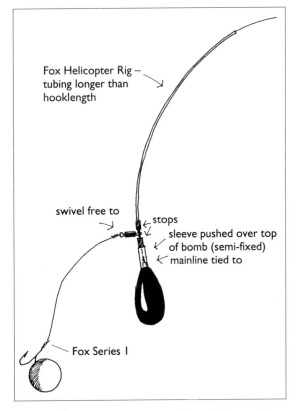

mainline passes through tubing – tubing longer than hooklength

M.C.F. in-line lead

rubber sleeve sits inside lead

0.7mm semi-stiff tubing goes down through body of lead and pushes into rubber sleeve

swivel attachment (semi-fixed)

Fox Series I

Fox Helicopter Rig – tubing longer than hooklength

swivel free to

stops
sleeve pushed over top of bomb (semi-fixed)
mainline tied to

Fox Series I

Fig. 37a *Avoiding tangles using tubing. In-line presentation.*

Fig. 37b *Avoiding tangles using tubing. Helicopter rig-style presentation.*

The most popular among them is the Fox 'Swinger' which also possesses a line gate to allow free passage of the line when the fish takes off on a screaming run. The gate is designed in such a way that the line pulls free when the rod is picked up, allowing a fast, clean strike.

The Hair Rig

The next development to take place in carp fishing rigs was the hair rig. Traditionally baits have always been mounted on a hook. Nowadays we take the hair rig for granted, but one of its co-inventors, Kevin Maddocks, highlighted just how profound the effects were on anglers' thinking of mounting the bait off the hook. To quote Kevin: 'When Lennie [Lennie Middleton] and myself invented the hair, we made an agreement to keep it a secret for as long as possible until we'd perfected its use. Anglers aren't stupid though, and the fabulous results we achieved with it, everywhere that we went, didn't go unnoticed. I remember one particular occasion when, under severe pressure from several anglers to reveal the secret, I told them that all I was prepared to say was that the bait was not mounted on the hook. You should have seen the looks on their faces! The whole concept was so alien to them that they simply couldn't work it out, and they certainly refused to believe me, preferring instead to think that I was using a secret bait...'

The story is fascinating, and one fact in particular is significant: that the rig was incredibly successful wherever it was used. Further discussion revealed that the catches made with the hair were so far and away better than the norm, on every venue that it was used, that only one conclusion was possible: that prior to the use of the hair, carp were picking up baits and ejecting them without anglers knowing, or were now accepting baits that had been refused with a side-hooked presentation.

Herein lies the crux of the effectiveness of the hair rig: that the amount of 'free play' that the hair gives the bait allows it to behave more naturally and moreover, that it makes the hook much more difficult to eject.

Initially the 'hair' was made from the finest materials available, which at the time was human hair, plucked from the co-inventors' heads! Kevin and Lennie were quick to realize that they were on a fast track to premature baldness, and soon substituted ultra-fine monofilament with a 1lb breaking strain. This gave the bait a great deal of free movement, a phenomenon that was improved by the use of 1in (2.5cm) long 'hairs' mounted off the bend of the hook. The development of modern hooklength materials such as first Dacron, and more latterly braided materials, led to the hair becoming an extension of the hooklength material as opposed to a separate piece of fine line. Experimentation with the

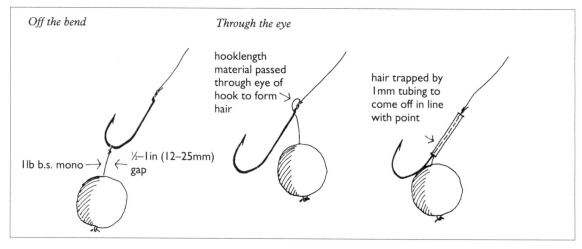

Off the bend *Through the eye*

hooklength material passed through eye of hook to form hair

hair trapped by 1mm tubing to come off in line with point

1lb b.s. mono → ← ½–1in (12–25mm) gap

Fig. 38 *Hair-rig styles development.*

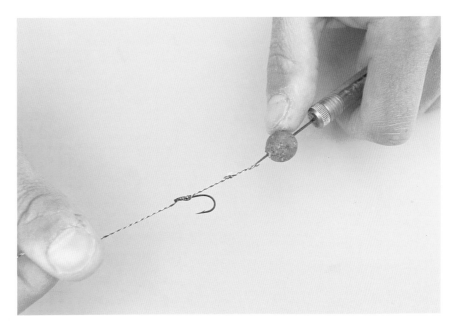

Boilies are mounted on the hair with the aid of a baiting needle.

position of the hair also began to take place, as carp began to wise up to boilies mounted 'off the bend'. Hairs which were passed through the eye of the hook, off the back of the shank, and in line with the point of the hook (the current 'vogue'), became commonplace. There were also experiments with the length of the hair and over the past decade or so this has generally become shorter and shorter. Currently many modern carp rigs incorporating hairs are merely a more refined version of side-hooking, with the boilie

mounted on a short hair which gives very little free movement.

Indeed, it would seem that the original concept of the hair, which was to increase the number of takes received, has been overshadowed by its ability to prevent the carp from ejecting the rig. This line of thinking is largely the result of the development of bait buoyancy to improve the number of takes enjoyed. At first anglers found that 'popped-up' buoyant baits which were tethered between one and several inches off the

How to make a helicopter rig.

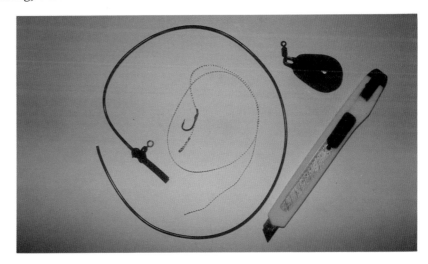

1. Here is the equipment that you'll need. Make up the hooklength using the 'knotless knot' sequence featured in the 'tackle' section of the book.

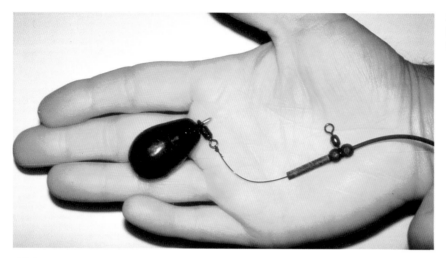

2. Thread your mainline through a Fox Helicopter rig. Now tie the bomb.

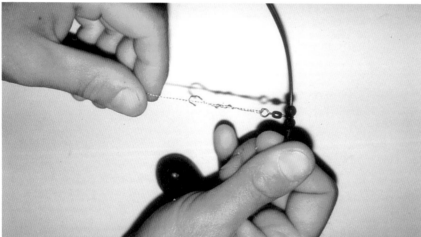

3. Tie the hooklength onto the swivel on the Helicopter rig. Make sure that it is free to revolve.

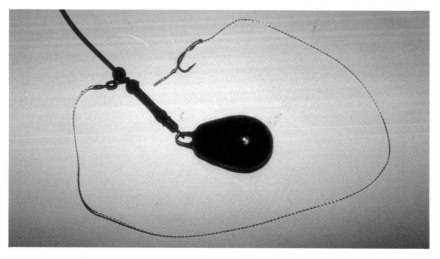

4. The finished rig.

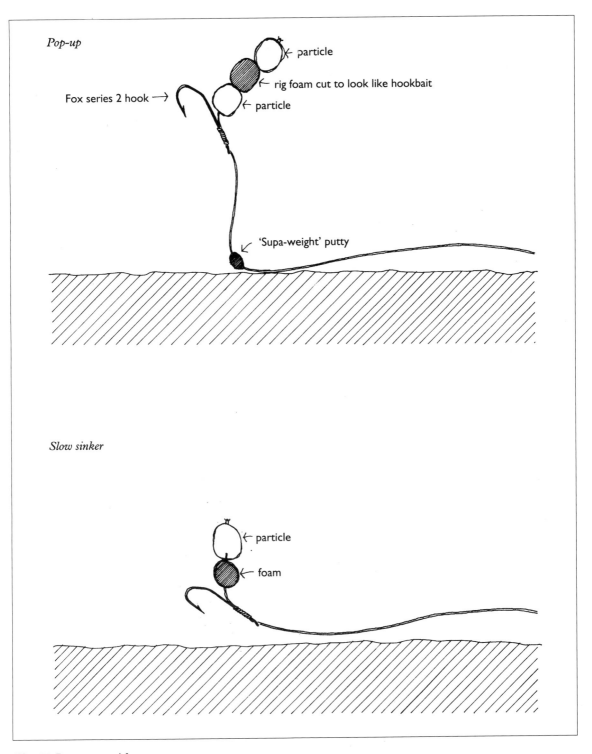

Fig. 39 *Buoyant particles.*

bottom encouraged a greater number of takes. However, eventually carp began to wise up to early pop-up presentations, and the refinement process began all over again. Initially this took the form of fine tuning the 'counterweight' (which holds down the pop-up), so that it was barely effective at all, the theory behind this being that if a carp aimed a suck at a general group of baits, the bait with the least resistance to lifting off the bottom would find its way into the carp's mouth first. It certainly works, too, and the 'critically balanced' pop-up, as it became known, is still popular today.

Experimentation with bait buoyancy continues, and the critically balanced hookbait is the latest development, a technique which involves microwaving hookbaits to achieve varying levels of buoyancy. The idea is to produce a bait so critically balanced that it is semi-buoyant until the weight of the hook is added, when it sinks very, very slowly. Not only does this type of presentation produce more takes (since it has all the advantages of the pop-up method but does not appear unnatural), but it is also ideal for presenting baits on top of weed and suchlike. However, if you prefer not to fiddle around with microwave cooking times, the answer is the 'woodpecker' rig: this uses a pop-up boilie and achieves the slow sinking effect by the addition of rig putty to the eye of the hook. Alternatively – and this is my favourite way of achieving this presentation – you can mount two boilies on a hair, one of them a pop-up and the other a normal sinking bait; by holding the rig underwater and squeezing air out of the pop-up it is possible to get it so that it sinks very slowly to rest on top of silt or weed. My personal best UK carp of 33lb fell to this deadly presentation.

The Bent Hook Rig

Anglers are constantly playing around with rigs and presentations to stay one step ahead of the carp; as the fish wise up to one particular style, the angler must switch to another to maintain any degree of success. The main dilemma of course, relates to the timing of the change, and judging when a rig has passed its particular peak of efficiency. Part of the problem is the almost universal use of extremely heavy 3 and 4oz leads to create the 'bolt' effect. (Remember what I concluded about the hair when it was introduced, that the vastly increased numbers of takes had to imply that carp were picking up hookbaits more often and finding them difficult to eject?) With a heavy lead, the angler rarely experiences any indication at all when a hookbait is tested and ejected, and of course it is impossible to detect a refused hookbait. It is my belief that carp test and eject rigs far more than we can begin to imagine, and this circumstance was certainly highlighted when the 'bent hook' was developed. Anglers in the Colne Valley guessed that instead of 'sucking and blowing' hookbaits, carp had learned to control their natural behaviour and were picking boilies up gently and backing off slowly with them to test for resistance; the moment the heavy lead was felt, the bait would be dropped. At first they were hitting minor indications, such as single 'bleeps' from the buzzer, but with only limited success. Eventually it was found that by bending the hook in a certain way it could be made to 'flip over' whenever it was drawn across the fish's lips. More importantly, this effect took place from whichever direction the hook was facing, and the point would dig into the carp's lower lip. The result was flying indicators again – and the latest wonder rig was born.

At first the carp scene went 'bent-hook crazy' – until it was discovered that bent hooks operated on a corkscrew principle during the fight and that as a consequence, untold damage was done to a fish's mouth. Carp anglers being carp anglers, however, soon found a way round the problem and developed the 'safe' bent hook; the most popular type now in use involves using a length of tubing to extend the shank of the hook, thus creating the necessary bend, but it will straighten out under pressure. The most effective example is the 'Line Aligner', which was invented by Jim Gibbinson. It is also possible to create the same effect by 'whipping' eyed hooks instead of tying them on and gluing the braid in front of the eye of the hook to create an angle (*see* photo sequence overleaf).

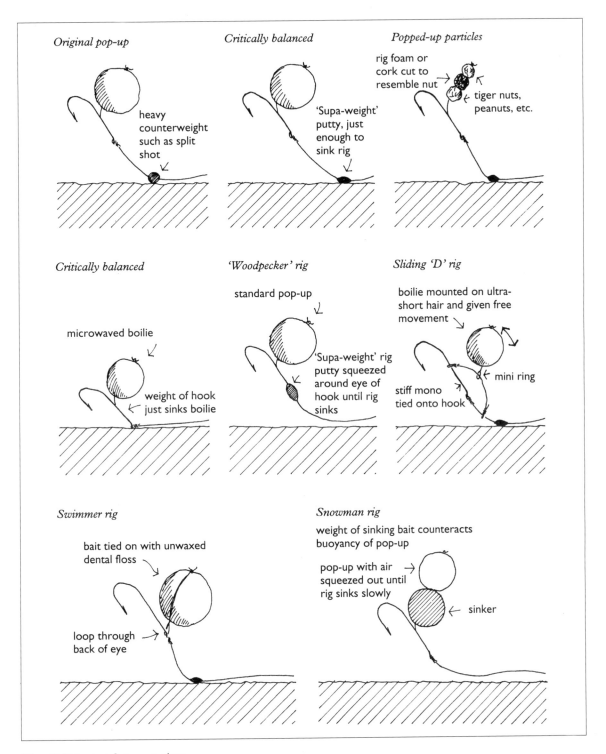

Fig. 40 *Pop-up style presentations.*

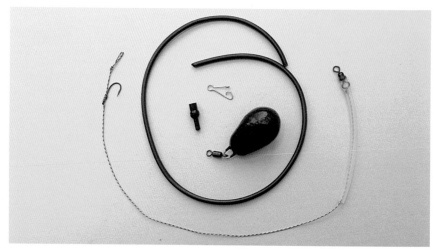

Making a basic semi-fixed bolt rig.

1. Here are the components you'll need. Hooklength (approximately 12in/30cm), swivel link, tulip bead, and an 18in/46cm length of 2.5mm semi-stiff rig tube.

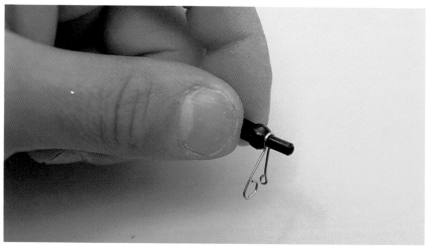

2. Fix the swivel link onto the spigot end of the tulip bead.

3. Thread the boom tube onto the mainline, followed by the tulip bead and tie on the hooklength. Attach the bomb to the swivel link.

4. *Now push the boom tube over the spigot of the tulip bead and the front of the tulip bead over the top eye of the hooklength swivel.*

The Stiff Link Rig

The latest phase in carp rigs has seen the introduction of the 'stiff link', which is about as far away from the original concept of the hair as it is possible to get. Using an extremely short hair and deliberately stiff hooklength material, the object of the exercise is to get the carp to mouth the bait, whereupon it finds the rig impossible to eject because of the stiffness of the hooklength material. Personally I think the carp will soon wise up to this one.

Full Circle

The constant juxtaposition between finesse and the creation of deliberate resistance has characterized rig development over the past few years, yet everything, it seems, goes full circle – although this is by no means a bad thing, since carp do not possess infinite memories. Just recently, for example, I have been doing well with some heavily pressured carp using a hair passed through the eye. This is a presentation that was used with the same carp five or six years ago, but

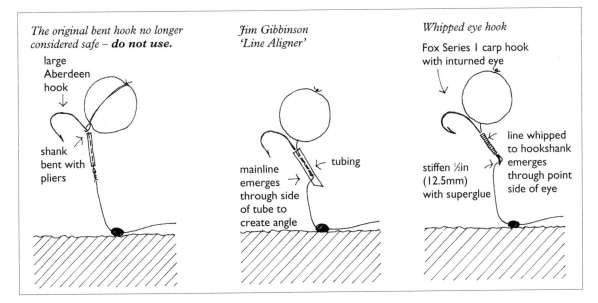

Fig. 41 *Bent hooks.*

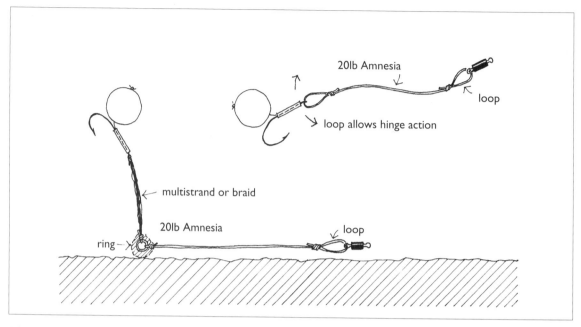

Fig. 42 *Stiff rigs.*

everyone these days is on stiff links and Line Aligners. The fish are beginning to wise up to these latest rigs, and yet they are falling to a presentation that 'blew' several years ago. Perhaps my next move should be to try ultra-fine hairs, 1in (2.5cm) long, mounted off the bend – now there's a novel idea!

Float Fishing Rigs

To my mind, float fishing is one of the most effective presentations for carp. Essentially a margin method, the use of floats in carp fishing these days is negligible, but I know no better way of putting a bait to carp that prefer near-bank areas. Floats offer a number of advantages, namely:

1.   They scare fish less because they make less disturbance.
2.   They provide instant bite registration.
3.   They provide warning that fish are in the area by wavering and bobbing if a carp comes close.
4.   They put the angler in immediate control as a result of this forewarning, which is especially important when snag fishing.
5.   They do not cause the fish to bolt in panic –

again, especially important when fishing near to snags.

After much experimentation, my favourite float set-up combines strength with sensitivity (*see* Fig. 43). Bites will cause the tip to disappear completely, since the weight of the 'Supa-weight' putty is enough to sink the float tip. Generally I will use side-hooked particles, lobworms or redworms with the rig, supergluing a sliver of cork onto the back of the shank to neutralize the weight of the hook; but there are occasions when a hair-rigged presentation is better, noticeably when boilies are the hookbait.

The Essentials of Rig Making

There are a few loose ends relating to areas of rig construction that have not been covered.

Preventing Tangles

Tangles are a by-product of the current popularity of alternative hooklength materials. Because nylon is relatively stiff by comparison, its tendency to tangle is much less pronounced than braids or multistrand. The most obvious way to overcome tangles is to use nylon hooklengths, some-

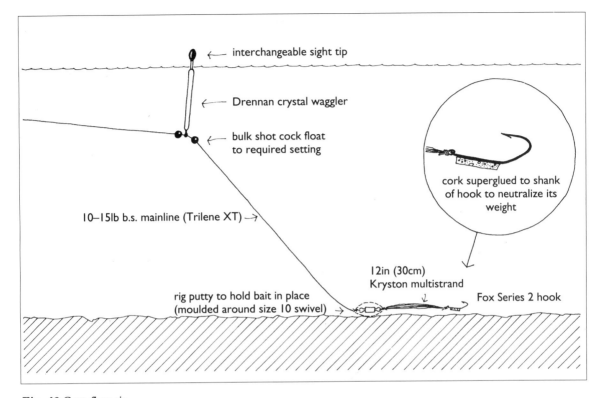

interchangeable sight tip

Drennan crystal waggler

bulk shot cock float to required setting

cork superglued to shank of hook to neutralize its weight

10–15lb b.s. mainline (Trilene XT) →

12in (30cm) Kryston multistrand

Fox Series 2 hook

rig putty to hold bait in place (moulded around size 10 swivel) →

Fig. 43 *Carp float rig.*

thing that I am very keen on; my favourite nylon hooklength material is Berkley Trilene XL, a soft, supple line with a very high wet knot strength. I usually use either 8lb b.s. XL in open water, or 10 to 12lb in snaggier areas.

If you prefer braided multistrand hooklengths, an alternative is to use tubing of some kind; my favourite variety is semi-stiff tube in 0.7mm diameter. It should be longer than your hooklength, and you thread it up your main line above the lead. Some anglers believe that exceptionally wary carp are afraid of the appearance of tubing, especially in clear water, and it is currently fashionable to use green or brown tube to imitate weed or twigs along with 'camou-coated' leads to blend in with the colour of the lake bed.

If you dislike the idea of using tubing but still want to use modern hooklength materials, the answer is to stiffen the top half of the hooklength, either temporarily or permanently. Kryston Advanced Angling Products produce a perma-

nent stiffener, 'No Tangle'; this takes the form of a gel-like substance which is rubbed into the hooklength prior to casting out. Its effect is to stiffen the leader until it comes into contact with water, whereupon the gel will dissolve and the hooklength becomes flexible again. Conservation-minded anglers will be pleased to learn that 'No Tangle' does not leave a residue and dissolves completely.

The tangling problem is particularly acute with Kryston multistrand, and its use is further complicated by the way it picks up all manner of bottom debris. Using 'neat' multistrand as a hooklength is fraught with difficulties, but at the same time anglers want to use it because it is the most superior hooklength material available for fine presentation. The solution is to make a combi-link, which involves knotting multistrand together with a length of less problematic material such as nylon or silkworm. The basic rule is to use one-third multistrand together with

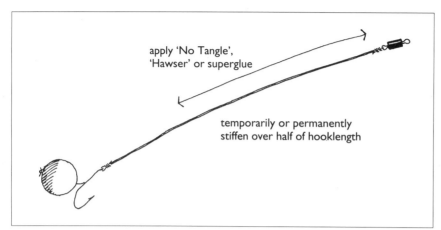

Fig. 44 Avoiding tangles without tubing.

apply 'No Tangle',
'Hawser' or superglue

temporarily or permanently
stiffen over half of hooklength

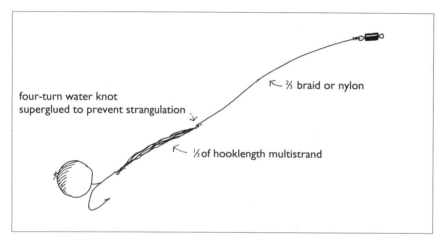

Fig. 45 Combi-link.

four-turn water knot
superglued to prevent strangulation

⅔ braid or nylon

⅓ of hooklength multistrand

two-thirds alternative material; this is the best combination to avoid tangles and yet still achieve a sensitive presentation.

Using the Right Knot

Tying the correct knot is absolutely essential if you want to learn how to use carp rigs effectively. Arguably this is the case with all styles of fishing, but it is even more essential with carp because their sheer power will exploit any weakness in your tackle. The photo sequences demonstrate how to tie various knots, and I would strongly advise that you study them carefully if you are unfamiliar with their construction. The development of multistrand and braids has highlighted the knot problem which has been constantly raised by anglers for a number of years.

Braids and suchlike are very intolerant of poor knots due to a concept known as 'strangulation' in which many knots – including the popular blood knot – will actually strangle, weaken and eventually destroy themselves under pressure. Braids are particularly prone to this, and carp anglers have had to become very 'knot conscious' as a result.

When tying knots, try to follow these basic guidelines:

1. When knotting to swivels, hooks and bomb eyes, pass the hooklength twice through the eye. This spreads the pressure exerted on the knot over a wider area and increases knot strength.

2. Always moisten knots before tightening to avoid friction damage and slide them together carefully, moistening further if necessary.

3   Test *every* knot before you cast out (John Roberts makes a superb knot tester which costs very little but is worth its weight in gold).

4   Finish the knot by adding a small amount of superglue to it. This doesn't increase its strength as such, but it does reduce strangulation.

My favourite knots are as follows:

The five turn grinner, for hooks, swivels; the four-turn water knot, for the combi-link; and the Mahin knot, for shock leaders. The latter was highlighted in this country by Jim Gibbinson, but was developed by a very talented Belgian angler, of the same name as his knot.

PVA String and PVA Bags

There can be no doubt that a tight group of free baits located close to your hookbait can some-times fool wary carp. This is especially the case in winter when the use of big carpets of free bait can be the 'kiss of death'. Regardless of the time of year, however, a tight group of baits will always appeal to carp, since it represents maximum food intake for minimum effort.

One of the latest trends in carp fishing is to use a PVA bag filled with trout pellets to surround a single boilie hookbait. Better still, in my opinion, is the use of a hookbait which resembles the free offerings. Trout pellets are impossible to mount either on the hook or on a hair because of their brittle nature, so the answer is to use a boilie hookbait that looks like a trout pellet. This can be achieved by using a fishmeal boilie mix with a fish flavour, and making it up into a stiff paste; instead of rolling this into small baits, extrude the mix from a sausage gun and chop it up into trout pellet-shaped pieces before boiling for a couple of minutes. The finished hookbait can then be mounted onto a hair. Indeed, when the fish have wised up to traditional round boilies, why not produce 'chop-up' freebies too, and use the PVA bag method to get them 'out there'?

The same tightly grouped effect can also be used to present traditional boilies. This method involves the use of PVA string, a dissolving cord which can be tied onto your hook. On contact with the water, the PVA stringer dissolves, leaving

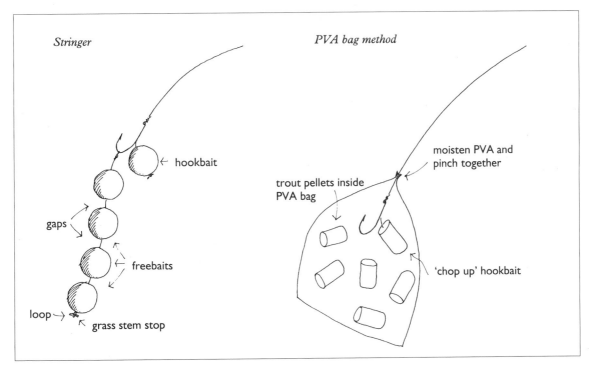

Fig. 46 Stringers and PVA bags.

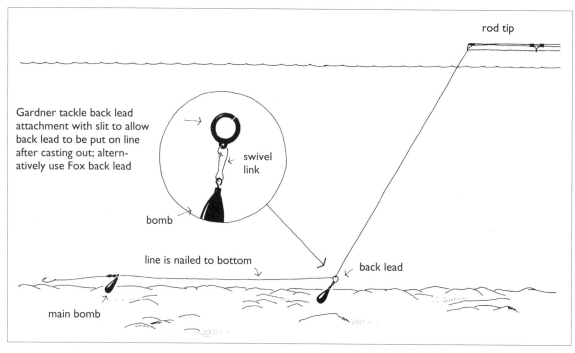

Gardner tackle back lead attachment with slit to allow back lead to be put on line after casting out; altern- atively use Fox back lead

swivel link

bomb

rod tip

line is nailed to bottom

back lead

main bomb

Fig. 47 *Back leading.*

your hookbait surrounded by a tight group of free baits. The best PVA to use in my opinion is Krys- ton 'Meltdown', which is fast-dissolving and leaves no residue. Remember though, when using 'stringers', to leave a gap between the top bait and the hook, and between all the individual baits so that the water can attack the PVA.

'Pinning Down'
'Pinning down' either the main line behind the lead or the hooklength itself is gaining increasing popularity in carp fishing as a growing number of anglers become concerned about the appearance of line and its effects on carp. This is especially the case in clear water, but even in coloured lakes it is possible that accidental contact with line and its unnatural 'feel' will cause the fish to spook.

For pinning the main line to the bottom most anglers use back leads and the best example of a commercially produced model is the Fox Inter- national back lead. Like them all, the Fox model is attached to the line after casting out, via a large attachment ring which can be opened out. While

fishing, the ring closes up again and will not fall off. This effect is created by placing a cut in one area of the nylon ring which can be opened up when forced apart by pressure from the angler's fingers. Once on the line, it closes together again. After attachment, the back lead is allowed to slide down the line rather like a cable car; when it reaches the desired area, a small amount of slack line is given until it pins itself to the bottom. This keeps the line behind the lead firmly pinned to the lake bottom and out of the carp's way.

The Fox model is particularly good because its flat bottom is ideal for keeping the back lead on top of weed and silt upon which it will rest gently. The large bore, low resistance ring also means that the angler is in direct contact with his terminal tackle, and indicators can be positioned as normal.

It is also possible to nail hooklengths to the bottom in either one or several places. The most obvious example of this is when a counterbalance is created for pop-ups. The best way I have found for this is to thread a small, sliding, rubber float stop on to the hooklength prior to attaching the

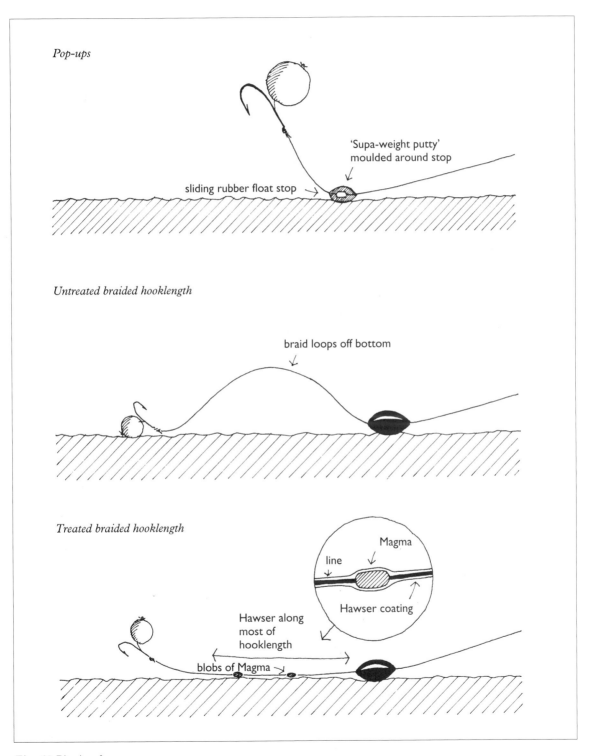

Fig. 48 *Pinning down.*

swivel; Fox 'Supa-weight' putty is then moulded around the stop until enough weight is in place to sink the pop-up very slowly. By pulling off and adding on tiny amounts of putty you can achieve a truly critically balanced hookbait. The advantage of a rubber float stop over a stop knot is that it slides easily under pressure (enabling a rapid change to the height of the 'pop-up'), but remains fixed in a fishing situation. Whether you prefer to use this method or a sliding stop knot, it is vital that you give the putty something to 'bite onto', to prevent it from falling off either during casting or retrieving.

Finally, anyone who has placed a braided hooklength in a fish tank will realize that after casting out, it does not sit in a perfectly straight line, conveniently hugging the bottom contours. Rather, untreated braid will rise in a loop off the bottom. Personally I don't mind this effect, since it gives the carp a small amount of resistance-free play before it encounters the weight of the lead. If you want to avoid it, however, small blobs of Kryston 'magma', a fast-drying liquid putty, can be applied at intervals along the hooklength to sink it. Combining this technique with stiffening the majority of the hooklength with 'hawser' will keep everything flat and taut.

The Use of Snag/Shock Leaders
The use of a much stronger length of line or leader material above hooklengths is becoming commonplace these days. There are two reasons for employing leaders, namely:
1. to absorb the 'shock' of a cast when comparatively light main lines (6 to 8lb b.s.) are used to gain extra distance;
2. to provide abrasion resistance and extra strength when fishing in the proximity of snags.

Most shock/snag leaders are used at a length approximately double the length of the rod – usually around 24ft (7.3m) – and are attached to the main line via a special knot (*see* photo sequence). The most popular materials are stiff, abrasion-resistant monos, for example, 20lb Amnesia, Berkley Big Game or XT, or a special material developed by Kryston known as 'Quicksilver'.

The main point to remember with leaders of this kind is that the knot, where they are connected to the main line, is likely to be bulky. This can cause problems when tubing is employed with the rig because low-diameter tubing will not pass over the leader knot. In this case I dispense with tubing altogether, and stiffen the majority of the hooklength with 'Hawser' to minimize tangles. Those of you who prefer to keep faith with tubing, please ensure that the tubing will pass over the leader knot easily should you be unfortunate enough to crack the rig off during a cast, or to experience a 'snap off' when playing a fish. Care must also be taken with in-line leads to ensure that the central bore on the lead is also large enough to pass over the knot.

The Mahin snag leader knot.

1. Here is the equipment you'll need: shock/snag leader, mainline, Kryston Hawser or superglue.

2. *Make a loop in the leader material and pass the end of the mainline through it.*

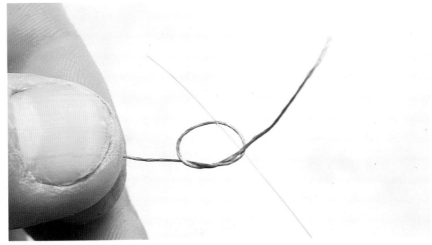

3. *Twist the mainline over the shock leader ten times, working away from the loop.*

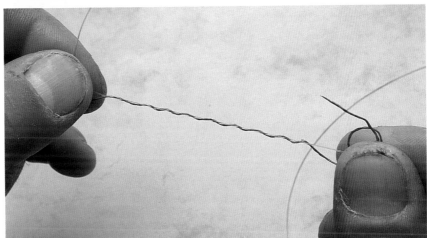

4. *Now twist back six times, going over the previous twists and working back towards the loop.*

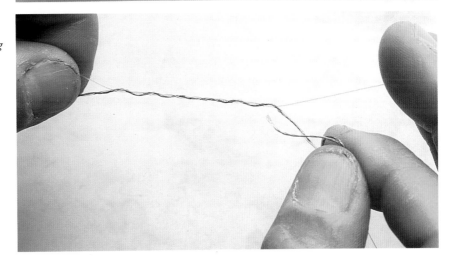

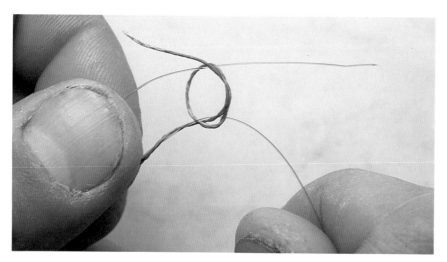

5. *Pass the free end back through the loop.*

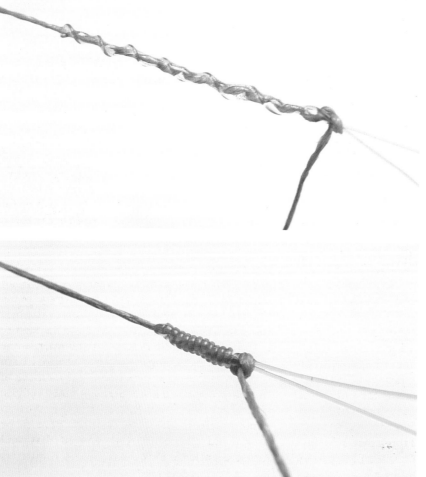

6. *Close the loop, but don't tighten it. Pull on the mainline, after thoroughly moistening all the coils with saliva.*

7. *Eventually the knot will butt together to form a neat, tapered finish with the tag ends facing back up the line to prevent fouling in the rod rings. Trim off the tag ends almost flush.*

8. *Now add Hawser rig resin to the knot and allow it to dry overnight. For hastily tied knots on the bank, you can finish off with superglue.*

Carp Rigs: In Conclusion

No doubt I will be plagued for the next few days by the things I have forgotten to include. However, serious anglers will keep up to date with rig developments by subscribing to the carp society and purchasing specialist carp magazines, thus continually increasing their knowledge.

An important aspect regarding carp rigs in general, is that the aforementioned process of refinement will continue. Remember though, that the carp's memory is a limited one, and that by revisiting previously learned techniques you might just achieve results that are every bit as good as the latest 'vogue'; there is a great deal to be said for 'being different' and not slavishly copying the latest trend. Remember that average anglers achieve mediocre results, and it is just as important to understand *how* and *why* a rig works, as it is to be able to tie it.

So what about carp rigs and the future? I consider that the next big breakthrough in carp fishing will be in bait, not rigs. For the foreseeable future, I can't envisage the development of anything that will have as profound an impact as the hair/bolt principle. Rather, I think that the refinement process will continue and that old ground will be revisited, but with the benefit of increased knowledge that will make previously tried and tested methods even more effective. It's a bit like a merry-go-round, really...

CARP FROM SMALL TO MEDIUM-SIZED WATERS

Although I would not consider myself a dedicated carp angler, I enjoy the challenge of fishing for carp. My favourite waters are invariably small to medium in size, usually ponds, estate lakes or gravel pits, 1 to 15 acres in size. Waters of this size possess an intimacy that is lost on vast gravel pits. They also possess character, to the point where it is more important to understand the mood of the water than it is to possess the best rigs and bait available. Another essential feature is the lack of angling pressure: I will tolerate the presence of a few anglers on the bank, but I am certainly not prepared to become a member of the 'carp circus' that frequents popular venues. Give me a quiet, intimate lake and I am very happy. Carp in this type of water have to be stalked and it is precisely this type of intense and intimate angler versus quarry at close quarters fishing that I enjoy most.

Approach and Location

I have never been in favour of fishing lakes 'blind'. Before I decide to begin a campaign on a new venue I will carry out certainly one, and if possible a number of visits both with and without plumbing tackle, firstly to assess the carp population, and secondly, to establish the areas that offer the best prospects.

The first visit will consist of a walk round the lake, during which I will be searching constantly for signs of carp. Spotting carp will undoubtedly be easier on a bright, warm day with little or no wind. Dusk can be good too, when the carp are likely to betray their presence by rolling or even jumping. A good pair of polarizing glasses is essential to get the most from the visit; the difference they make is remarkable, and with their help and a bit of practice, you will soon learn to pick out the blue purple shapes of carp either drifting around beneath the surface, cruising the shallows or lying up in weedbeds. The following is a basic guide to carp location on this type of venue, and the key features to look out for.

Lilypads

Lilypads constitute a prime area in which to spot carp because they simply cannot move through them without creating a disturbance. Sometimes they will be lying virtually motionless amongst the leaves, and by searching the gaps in the pads you will be able to identify them basking in the sun, especially on warm days; and carp pushing their way through the underwater jungle of roots and stems will give away their presence by causing the pads to quiver and sway.

Soft Weed

Carp are equally fond of soft, blanket-type weed, especially in those areas where it is so thick that it makes its way to the surface. This type of weed is usually choked with small food items, such as shrimps, corixa and hoglouse, and frequently carp will be found feeding in it. There may be gaps in the weed or 'holes', and by studying these for long enough the chances are that you will spot a carp or two as they drift across the clear area.

The Shallows

Carp will often cruise the shallows, especially on warm days. If there is some form of cover such as weedbeds or submerged trees, they will feel more secure in the shallower water, and are likely to spend considerable amounts of time in it.

Scum Patches

These are very reliable carp-holding areas. At the windward end of most lakes there will be a quiet little corner somewhere that has 'scummed over' with all manner of accumulated debris and surface algae. Watch these areas very carefully, and you could well notice the water bulging as carp either suck at the debris itself or move around just under the surface.

The Margins

In spite of the old angling adage 'never neglect the margins', most anglers do. The margins comprise the area that is no more than one rod length from the bank, and if there is a warm, stiff breeze blowing, groups of carp are quite likely to be feeding in shallow water very close to the downwind bank. Therefore you should approach marginal areas carefully, and wherever you find cover you are likely to find carp. If you look carefully at reed and rushbeds, for example, you may notice the stems knocking violently, or perhaps even spot a fish or two lying quietly right in the heart of the bed itself.

Overhanging Trees

Overhanging trees are another reliable carp-holding area, and it would be most unusual not to find carp near to trees which grow into or over the water. Trees of this kind have the added advantage of providing an excellent observation point if you climb them (see below).

On small to medium waters it is important to bear in mind that carp will probably be hyper-sensitive to your presence. Thus clumsy movements, skylining the bank, and failing to take advantage of marginal cover are grave misdemeanours that will be heavily punished in terms of the number of carp that reveal themselves. The best advice that I can pass on is that you should try to merge with the landscape, moving quietly and stealthily as if you were trying to creep up on the carp and surprise them. Provided you can do this, your initial visit should be rewarded by sightings of carp in a number of areas; but there are other tactics that can be employed to improve your prospects still further.

Climbing Trees

Climbing trees can make an enormous difference to what you see. From a vantage point high above the lake you will be able to spot cruising fish that are simply not visible from the bank, including carp that are cruising well out in the lake, and because you are well above the fish, you will be able to watch them for longer periods and gain a better impression not only of their size, but also of their habits. Studying carp behaviour provides fascinating information that may bring genuine benefits when it comes to actually fishing the lake on future visits. From a position above the water you may be able to identify holding areas and patrol routes as well as likely carp-holding features such as bars, plateaux and weedbeds.

Baiting Marginal Areas

On an initial visit I usually carry a bucket of hemp with me, and a selection of bright, visible baits such as sweetcorn, yellow boilies and bread flake. Bait several likely looking areas in the margins, carry out periodic visits to the same areas, and you just might see carp actually feeding on your bait. This tactic can be doubly useful since it will enable you to test the carp's reactions to various bait samples, thus providing invaluable information for future visits.

On all but the dourest of days, the introduction of Chum mixer into several areas of the lake is likely to be rewarded by at least some, if not most of the carp feeding on the surface. This tactic, above any other, will give you a better indication of the lake's population of carp, especially if the day in question is warm and sunny. I never carry out an exploratory visit without a large bag of Chum for company.

Choosing Swims

Following your first visit you should already have identified several potential fish-holding swims. All the areas mentioned – lilybeds, rushes, weedbeds, shallows, margins, overhanging trees and scum patches – make excellent swims. If you have spotted fish in some of them, so much the better. There are other areas, too that may offer prospects for sighting fish; these may be more restricted, but they will be productive nonetheless. On your second visit to the water you should carry plumbing tackle to explore some of the open areas of the lake, by systematically casting around, you will be looking for the following features:

Bars

These narrow, shallow areas are always worth exploring. Carp often use them as patrol routes, and they are susceptible to baits placed both on top and at the base of a bar where there are often rich silt deposits. Their other advantage is that they force fish to swim higher up in the water, and a bait placed on top of a bar is almost certain to come within a carp's line of vision at some point.

Plateaux

Similar to bars, a plateau is a large, irregular-shaped shallow area surrounded by deep water; it can be considered like a dining table since fish of many types, including carp, are fond of feeding on its surface. It is important that you use your plumbing tackle to map out the extent of a plateau, marking the extremities by lining them up with bankside features.

Clear Areas

By dragging a heavy lead around the lake you will undoubtedly encounter huge amounts of weed, especially during late summer and early autumn. Occasionally, however, you will encounter clear patches consisting of clean gravel, probably cleared by the feeding activities of waterbirds or even fish. The position of these areas should be noted very carefully for they can be very reliable swims indeed. You will know when you have found a clean patch because the rod tip will vibrate quickly as the heavy lead bounces across the gravel.

The author's personal best UK carp – 33lb 1oz caught from a medium-size lake.

Submerged Snags

Sunken trees and suchlike are a confounded nuisance as far as tackle losses are concerned, but they can always be counted on to attract fish. Thus fishing near to snags can be very productive, and as long as you establish a strategy for playing and landing the fish, they should present few problems and many opportunities.

Islands

Islands are very popular with carp. In character they are in fact marginal areas located well away from the bankside, and subject therefore to little human disturbance. If the island in question is populated with overhanging trees, so much the better, since those will provide additional cover and security for the carp. It is not often that you can cast close to an island, and in spite of the fact that the closer you get, the shallower it becomes, a bait placed within a couple of feet of its margin will be better than one that is dropped several feet short. Even better is a bait that can be 'bombed' actually between tree branches or underneath a canopy of cover.

Narrows

Peninsulas or points often cause the lake to become narrower and restricted areas like this make superb carp ambushing points, the patrolling fish being obliged to swim through the more limited space. Tactically, I would approach swims like these by staggering baits at varying distances and groundbaits in a line, so that fish passing through cannot miss the opportunity to feed. This sort of narrows rarely 'holds' fish as such, but provides an excellent opportunity to pick them off as they make their way around the water. If a big wind is pushing through the channel so much the better, since this almost guarantees that fish will pass over your bait as they follow the wind down the lake.

I have discussed the subject of location at great length because it is undoubtedly the single most important factor in carp fishing. Your first task is to find a lake which holds fish of the size that suits your ambition, the second is to locate the areas within that lake which offer the best chances of success. There are no short cuts, and the time you spend on essential preparation will be rewarded many times over on future visits.

Baits

An enormous amount has been written about carp baits. There are, without a doubt, a great number of baits that will work equally well on both small and large waters, but on small waters I believe that the opportunities to use natural and standard baits are much greater than on huge pits and reservoirs. This is primarily because the opportunities for stalking are so much greater on small to medium-sized waters; after all, you are never likely to be far from the fish. In the course of a season, I will use a wide selection of baits on waters of this type.

Stalking Baits

For stalking I like to use a mixture of particles, naturals and standards, and I will very seldom visit a water without hemp which will act as my principal groundbait. Over the top of the hemp I may choose to use a larger particle hookbait, the

most likely candidates being tiger nuts, peanuts, maple peas, sweet lupins and of course sweetcorn. Natural baits, and specifically lobworms and redworms, can be devastating stalking baits, and their great advantage is that they will never blow. Standard baits, too, such as luncheon meat, bread flake and crust, cheese and other pastes, will also be effective and should never be ignored, even on heavily fished waters. Last but not least we cannot afford to ignore surface baits, and I would never contemplate a visit to a carp lake in summer or autumn without taking both Chum mixers and bread crust.

Ambushing Baits

Baits for ambushing carp as they make their way from one area of the lake to another, should be capable of stopping a cruising fish in its tracks. In many cases a bright, obvious bait will be a favourite, perhaps a boilie made from a yellow birdfood base. Using hemp is also a good idea, since it is a bait with genuine holding power. Certainly for ambushing I wouldn't look beyond boilies and hemp, except of course to consider a natural bait which could be strategically placed to catch perhaps a single fish during a short session. Lobworms spring to mind, air-injected and fished somewhere between several inches and several feet off the bottom; and bread crust which might be an old-fashioned bait but it is the type of offering with the potential to arouse the interest of a passing carp.

Baits for Holding Areas

It is my experience that on most of the carp waters that I have ever fished, the carp display a marked preference for feeding in specific areas. You may be able to ambush or stalk the odd fish from areas all over the lake, but find the favoured feeding spots and a big 'hit' of fish is on the cards. Locating these hotspots is essential if you truly want to establish a bait as a 'going' food source. Regular introduction of your chosen bait into the area will increase the carp's awareness of it and willingness to eat it, but it is probably fair to say that if you place a half-decent bait into a feeding area it will be instantly accepted.

The sheer range of baits that I have used on carp waters is mind-blowing and I am not even a dedicated carp angler! Nowadays, boilies are most anglers' first choice, a bait which I use extensively but with the following provisos:

1. I always attempt to establish which bait has been used on the water in the past and in recent weeks. My first move is then to do the exact opposite. If everyone is using fishmeals I'll use birdfoods, while if a fruit flavour is 'murdering' them, I'll probably use a dairy or spice.

2. The same rule applies to boilie size. By choice I like to use ½in (12mm) or ⅝in (14mm) baits, but if other anglers are onto them I will go up to ¾in (18mm) or even ⅞in (20mm).

In an ideal world, and given the opportunity to fish the water for any period of time, I would try to establish a good, long-term bait. This would comprise a high quality base mix, palatants, attractors and extracts, all in all, the best combination of ingredients I can find to provide the carp with a highly digestible and enjoyable (from a taste point of view) boilie. Particles can also be used successfully in holding areas in fairly large quantities.

Peanuts are one of the most instant particle baits that I have ever used. However, they fill up carp quickly and I tend to treat them as boilies; a few pouchfuls around each hookbait are quite sufficient to get fish feeding. If a take occurs, the bait can be topped up between runs. Maple peas are another instant carp bait which can be used either in their own right or as a hookbait over a bed of hemp. You may find that tench and bream become a real problem, however, since both species love maples.

Tiger nuts are the long-term particle bait for carp; once sampled, they seem to draw carp like a magnet time and time again. It is my experience that whereas peanuts tend to 'blow' quickly, a similar sized tiger does not. They are useful as a hookbait, and as a groundbait over which to fish a boilie, and carry the additional advantage of being immune to 'nuisance' species.

Sweet lupins are a relatively new particle and instant as far as carp are concerned, although a major problem is that being bright they tend to blow quickly. I have found it best to use them sparingly, fished as a hookbait with a scattering of free offering over hemp.

CARP FROM BIG WATERS   by Dave Thorpe

To be confronted by a big gravel pit or reservoir for the first time can be a mind-blowing prospect and knowing how to get started is a dilemma that everyone on his initial venture onto a major stillwater has to resolve. Almost certainly the barrier is principally a psychological one: as we all know, the prospect of acres and acres of open water is daunting enough in the first place, but combine it with a low stock density of fish and the situation can seem very gloomy indeed. Thus to begin with, if you are thinking of tackling large stillwaters, you must be sure that you have the conviction to go through with it. Probably you were attracted to the water in the first place by the prospects of catching some very big fish. Low stock densities and the rich environment that is characteristic of most big gravel pits and reservoirs together mean specimen-sized carp; but you should also be aware that it will not be easy, and that you must be prepared to endure some inevitable blanks.

To begin with, visit the water as often as possible. Initially I would not take plumbing tackle, but would content myself with visiting the water and having a good look round. Talking to other anglers can help, particularly match and pleasure anglers, since they have no vested interest in keeping the presence of carp a secret; otherwise as we all know, carp men are inclined to be secretive and you might find yourself chasing 'red herrings'; after many years experience I have learned to consider the information given to me by other carp men with circumspection, even if I know them very well.

Location and Approach
So, you will visit the water regularly in decent conditions for spotting fish. Dusk can be good,

Dave Thorpe, captor of numerous big water carp both at home and abroad, with his Dutch record common carp of 49lb.

and very hot days with little or no wind will help you to spot fish because they will be cruising on the surface. Your first priority, simple as it sounds, should be to establish the presence of carp in the water; it is amazing how sighting a few fish can boost your confidence. You should also make use of initial visits to note any obvious fish-holding areas: these will include islands, weedbeds, and in clear water, visible bars and plateaux which will appear as light, sandy-coloured areas. Shallow bays can also be good, especially in warm weather, while points or peninsulas (to use the correct term) are ideal for intercepting travelling fish.

Before you explore the lake in more intimate detail, it is a good idea to divide the lake up into manageable 'chunks'. Try to visualize the water as a series of lakes, rather than as a single large sheet of water, and in this way you will make the task of exploring it all much easier. Choose an

area, ideally the one that looks the best, and visit it with plumbing tackle. In many instances the most likely place to start will be the north-east corner of the water, since this receives the effects of the prevailing winds in this country, south-westerlies – isn't it fortunate that a good south-westerly is the best carp fishing wind of them all, and that carp on big waters do actually tend to follow winds that blow from this direction? Thus, the north-east corner of the lake is a good start-ing out point.

Building Knowledge

You might expect that I would now recommend that you systematically plumb every inch of your chosen area, and I suppose that this would be the classical approach; but I can only talk about how I approach big waters myself and to be quite hon-est that is not what I do. Certainly I will carry out a cursory plumbing of the area so that any major features such as hidden bars, plateaux and sunken snags are quickly located, but it won't be long before I start fishing. I would begin by choosing a promising looking swim. Experienced carp anglers *know* what that is: it just *'feels'* right, and no amount of articles and diagrams are a substitute for experience. The swim that I decide to fish on this and future visits will be plumbed very carefully indeed; after all, having decided on an area, you want your hookbaits to be in the best possible place for a pick-up.

In the words of Peter Springate, he always tries to fish a swim that offers excellent prospects for observation when he is on a new water. This is a fair point, and one which leads me to the crux of big water carping as far as I'm concerned.

My initial visits will not be carried out with the serious expectation of catching carp. Sometimes I do catch, and it's a bonus when it happens, but what is more likely is that I shall have to content myself with watching the lake very carefully indeed. All the time I shall be looking for signs of fish, anything that gives away the presence and location of carp: rolling, leaping, bow-waving, cruising – it doesn't matter; what really counts is the opportunity to spot carp and note their position, and if they consistently or even sporadically show themselves in an area, this would be good for a visit on the next session. The procedure in a new swim is exactly the same: plumbing thoroughly, baiting, fishing and watching. Over a period of time you will build up a great deal of knowledge about the lake, and eventually perseverance should be rewarded with the capture of the odd fish.

Once this happens, the fishing will take on an exciting new dimension, and now you will be fishing with the serious expectation of catching carp. Captures, more sightings, and a working knowledge of an increasing number of swims will help you to choose a likely area given the conditions on the day in question. Eventually your knowledge of the carp's habits in the lake will enable you to choose the best swim regardless of the weather, and it shouldn't be long before you make serious inroads into a major part of the lake's carp population.

One of the most valuable lessons that you will learn is that on waters of this kind the carp become very predictable in their behaviour; even huge gravel pits with extremely low stock densities can be cracked if you understand how they behave. Thus, although you might be fishing in an 80-acre (32-hectare) lake with a head of only twenty carp, they will not be located as one in every fourth acre, it is more likely that the majority of the fish will be in a single small area. Twenty carp in less than an acre of water is not such a daunting prospect, and your only task is to locate that single area.

Carp Behaviour
The most important influence on carp movement is the wind, and as a basic principle you should never ignore the wind because carp on big waters will invariably follow it. In winter, a good south-westerly is the wind that you are looking for, since it will accompany mild, damp weather and low pressure. In summer, however, carp will follow other winds, too, in general, southerly and westerly based winds are the best, but in extremely hot weather a refreshing northerly or north-westerly wind might move them. North-easterly and easterly winds, regardless of the time of the year, are poor in my opinion. I don't expect the carp to follow them, and the only influence they will have over my choice of swims is to find a comfortable area to fish, and that might mean being protected from them, especially in winter. Even so, in the summer, particularly if a big 'positive' wind is blowing, I may well be tempted to fish into it.

The other big factor that influences carp behaviour is temperature. In summer the effects of cool or hot weather can be less dramatic than in winter, when prolonged cold weather can kill your prospects of sport. Surprisingly, however, a cold snap in winter can actually improve your chances of catching, and my own experience suggests that the early stages of a cold spell can induce feeding – though to be honest I would much prefer to be fishing in a big warm south-westerly. Even in summer, temperature changes will affect the behaviour of carp. In prolonged bright, hot weather they often become indifferent, choosing to cruise for long periods on the surface. In these conditions, unless you can tempt a fish on a floater, the best chances of a pick-up are either in the first or last few hours of daylight, whilst the hours of darkness are invariably worthwhile, too.

Carp behave differently on individual waters. Gravel pits, for instance, tend to fish better in bright warm weather than big reservoirs. But this is a generalization, and it is up to you to discover the feeding habits of the carp on your water and how they correspond to the weather. There will be preferred feeding periods, and the duration of these will vary; in winter they may be as brief as half-an-hour to an hour in the day, and not every carp in the lake will feed once in every twenty-four hours. In summer, however, every carp in the lake will probably feed every day through the feeding period(s) – and there can be two or even three – although this might vary according to the conditions. And, regardless of their duration, the feeding periods will probably correspond to approximate time zones: generally speaking, early to mid-morning, in the later afternoon to evening, and in the hours of darkness are the most reliable; the middle of the day is the least likely, although a well presented bait in the right place could just tempt a pick-up at any time – in summer, anyway.

Thus at any time of the year, carp will display a marked preference for feeding at certain times. However, this doesn't mean that you can casually arrive just before a feeding spell and fire out a load of bait, cast out your rig, and wind the specimen fish in – that would be too simple. In my experience you will have your best chances of a take if your free bait and rig have been in position for some time prior to the feeding period.

Tackle for Big Water Carp

As a general rule, I would use a long-range carp rod to cope with extreme distance, although the rod I use must be able to perform at a variety of ranges without causing fish losses. On a big water I might be fishing anywhere between 5ft (1.5m) and 140yds (130m) from the bank, and that means using a rod that will cast a 3oz or 3½oz lead to the horizon, but is forgiving enough to hook and play fish under the rod tip. Such a rod is a very rare piece of equipment indeed, but with modern technology they do exist. My personal choice is the Leslie's Insight International 12ft 2¾lb test curve model, and it is far superior to any other rod I've used; it might not be quite as good as their 2¼lb version at close range, but it is better than most other close-range rods I've tried, and at distance it is superb. I am told that the Shimano 3lb Diaflash is a superb multi-range rod, too. Never choose a rod with a fast taper, poker-stiff middle/tip action because it will cost you fish in the long run.

As far as reels are concerned, I tend to rely on distance reels, which in my case are the Daiwa SS3000s with a baitrunner conversion. The wide, open spool is perfect for distance work, and they will operate at close range, too. There are alternatives available, the most notable of these being the Shimano Biomaster Special GT7000. The spools on my big reels will be loaded with line strengths appropriate to the distance I am fishing, everything from 8lb Berkley Trilene XT with a shock leader, through to 17lb Berkley Trimax for snag work. As a general rule I will use 12lb Berkley Trimax because of its general strength, castability and abrasion-resistant qualities. If snag or shock leaders are necessary I will use 20lb Amnesia which is extremely tough, very slippery and altogether reliable whether you are fishing next to a sunken tree, over gravel bars or adjacent to thick weedbeds.

For bite indicators, I use the tension arm variety. The effect of these virtually spring-loaded indicators is to exaggerate even the shyest bite, especially drop-backs, the most common form of bite at extreme distance. The make I prefer is the new improved 'Wanger' (by Dennis McFetrich), which has a small, neat head and the choice of two quivers.

I must confess that I am very particular when it comes to rigs, and my current set-up is the result of years of refinement and experimentation. It is an in-line set-up that is virtually tangle-proof, and one that will operate at a variety of ranges. The basic principle is that the line runs down through a length of 0.7mm semi-stiff tubing which is slightly longer than the hooklength. The tubing passes through the body of the lead which will either be the long streamlined variety for distance, or the dumpier pear-shaped version for short range fishing. The dumpy lead compensates for a slight lack of resistance in the set-up at short-range, thus maximizing the bolt effect.

After passing through the lead, the tubing is pushed into a rubber sleeve which also houses a connecting link which joins the main line to the hooklength. After tying the hooklength on, the special connector, which replaces a swivel, sits inside the sleeve which, in turn, sits up inside the lead. In practice it has been found that this special connector does not 'lock up' inside the lead under pressure, a common fault with ordinary swivels which can do so in the event of a crack off. The hooklength is invariably made from 12 to 15lb Kryston 'Merlin', although in truly snaggy conditions I will use a braid in a heavier breaking strain. The first half of the braid below the lead is stiffened with superglue to provide extra protection against tangles. The rig terminates in a spade-end Owner hook which has a hair coming off the back of the shank in line with the point. Whenever possible, I like the bait to just touch the bottom of the bend of the hook, and it is this rule which dictates the length of the hair.

My hookbaits are invariably boilies, and I will choose from normal sinkers, pop-ups and critically balanced baits. For summer use especially my favourite bait size is ½in (12mm) and my favourite rig involves using one pop-up and one sinker on the hair. Rather than 'pop' the baits up, I squeeze the air out of the buoyant boilie underwater until the weight of both baits just about sinks the hook. This is a deadly presentation and one that has led to the downfall of lots of carp. It is especially good in weedy lakes when traditional bottom tails can be obscured by debris or weed. Depending on the degree of pressure on the water, however, I might choose a bottom bait first before moving on to pop-ups and finally the double slow-sinking bait when the fish began to 'wise up'.

Sometimes it is necessary to use shock leaders, and if this is the case I will use a helicopter rig to ensure that the terminal tackle doesn't tether up a carp in the event of a crack-off. The problem with shock leaders is that they require a leader knot, and it can be difficult for rigs incorporating

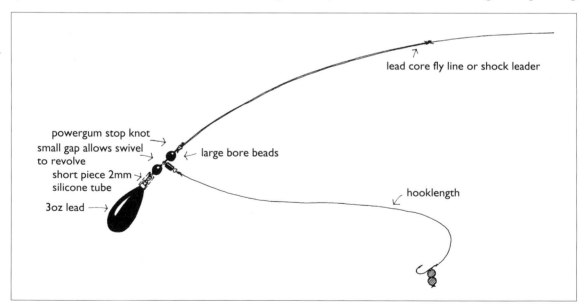

Fig. 49 *Dave Thorpe's helicopter rig.*

tubing to pass over the knot. My version of the helicopter rig appears in the diagram (*see* Fig. 49), and two points in particular are to be noted: firstly, I use a large-bore bead as the top bead, and it will possess a hole easily big enough to clear a leader knot; carp will be in no danger of getting tethered up on this set-up. Secondly, I might choose to use lead core fly line instead of a snag leader, especially if I think that the carp are wary of line rising up behind the lead. In either case the rig is perfectly safe for carp.

Baits

I have already stated my bias towards boilies as a hookbait, although sometimes I will use boilie hookbaits over beds of particles, particularly for close-range work. On other occasions I will use 'neat' boilies, choosing the size through personal preference, but also allowing the range at which I'm fishing to influence my decision. It's no good, for instance, trying to fish ½in (12mm) baits at 140yds (130m), because you simply won't get them there, and ¾in (18mm) baits would be a better choice in this situation.

As far as complexity of bait is concerned, my choice will be dictated by the amount of angling pressure that the fish have been subjected to. Invariably, a highly digestible boilie will be at the top of my agenda; whether it was a large or a small head of carp that you were pursuing, you would want them to clear up all the free offerings and keep coming back for more.

If the water was under serious angling pressure, I would choose a more complex bait which combined pure extracts and palatants, as well as base mix/flavour. But whatever my choice, I can assure you that it will deliberately be different to anything that is currently, or has been, in 'vogue' on the water. The same comments apply to size of baits: if everyone is on ⅝in (16mm) boilies I will go down to ½in (12mm) or maybe up as high as ⅞in (22mm) – anything to be different!

Being different is important, and it is vital that you build up your own ideas on big waters, rather than slavishly copy someone else. Learn to do your own thing, don't feel pressurized into getting early results, and be prepared to experiment.

GET ON TOP: FLOATER FISHING

At one time or another, most species of coarse fish can be tempted into taking the odd floater; I have actually witnessed barbel and tench feeding off the surface, but these are rare events and I wouldn't recommend a summer's campaign geared towards surface fishing for either of them. A number of other species are reliable surface feeders, however, including carp, rudd, chub, dace and orfe.

The degree to which surface feeding takes place depends to a great extent on the venue. Some lakes, for example, are tremendous floater waters, whereas others are decidedly poor. The key factor appears to be whether fish are used to finding food 'on the top'. Stillwaters that are surrounded by trees usually prove to be superb floater waters due to the number of bugs, moths and beetles that get blown onto the water off the nearby foliage. The most fickle lakes, in my opinion, tend to be clear-water gravel pits, and it sometimes takes a pre-baiting or 'education' campaign before the fish begin to respond to surface fishing tactics. This may be due in part to the amount of available food found near the bottom, since clear-water pits generally tend to be full of weed and consequently choked with all manner of sub-aquatic life.

I have also heard it suggested that the pH value of a water can have a direct effect on its floater potential. This may indeed be true, but I have no time for such theories, not because of their validity or otherwise, but principally because I don't believe that anyone in the angling world truly understands this complicated subject. It will take a lot more conclusive evidence to convince *me* to include some litmus paper in my tackle box! No, let us just accept that some stillwaters respond better to surface baits than others, and that there is indeed one conclusive thing which will prove its worth one way or another: it is called experience, and involves catapulting out a few floaters and using your eyes...

Rivers display similar characteristics, though here I can be more useful. Generally speaking shallow, clear rivers with some pace tend to make very good floater waters, whilst wide, deep, powerful rivers offer poor prospects. Small rivers, streams and tributaries usually make great floater venues – provided, that is, that chub are present in reasonable numbers.

Surface Baits

When the Mars food company invented Pedigree Chum, they could hardly have anticipated its popularity amongst anglers – indeed, I doubt whether they are aware of Chum's potential as a fishing bait to this day. Let's just hope that they don't estimate the country's canine population on the basis of Pedigree Chum mixer sales, otherwise some hopelessly misguided marketing executive will be trying to convince his board of directors that every British household has at least eight dogs living in it!

The fact is that Chum mixer has become synonymous with floater fishing, almost to the exclusion of any other bait. It can be used in its natural state, 'straight from the packet', and is a superb particle floater, being the perfect hook size, roughly round (for ease of catapulting), and very buoyant. Chum's natural meaty aroma is instantly recognized by fish as being edible, although the addition of flavours and colours can improve its attractiveness. A whole variety of flavours work well on Chum, my favourites being: 'Scopex' (Rod Hutchinson), 'Strawberry Supasense Oil Palatant' (Nash), and 'Sour Cream' (D.T. Bait Developments).

Oils also work very well. I like to combine Nash's oil palatant with some strawberry flavour, thus making the most of the strength of the flavour and the pulling power of the oil; oils float, so their distinctive aroma can be spread across considerable distances. My favourite oil for Chum is Dave Thorpe's 'Lump Liquid', a syrup-like product that can pull carp from considerable distances.

Dyeing mixers can be worthwhile. The most successful colour I have used is red although yellow, orange and green also work. I'm not sure that the dye makes much difference to the fish, but coloured mixers offer other advantages: against a bright background, for example, dark red mixers show up well, while dark backgrounds are tailor-made for yellow and orange – rather like choosing a float tip for maximum visibility. Green is used to fool waterbirds when fishing in weedy areas, a ploy that has a limited lifespan!

Chum can be used dry or soaked, though most anglers prefer to soak it because this makes the bait soft, rubbery and ideal for side-hooking. On pressured waters a change to hair-rigged dry, crunchy mixers can find favour with carp in particular. Flavouring is still a viable proposition.

Chum mixer is a great floating bait, but it isn't the only one. Other dog biscuits, for example, can be excellent, particularly if they are a different size/shape/colour to Chum. Just lately I've been using some large mixer biscuits at least twice the size of Chum, and the carp have been more than

Chum mixer, the greatest surface particle of them all, and four ways to present it on the hook. Left to right: side hooked, superglued to shank, hair rigged and bait-banded.

happy to 'wolf' them down. Take a trip down to your local petfood wholesaler and make your choice from literally dozens of dog and cat biscuits.

Bread crust is almost a forgotten surface bait as far as carp anglers are concerned, but it still catches plenty of fish. There is something about the smell and appearance of crust that attracts the immediate interest of fish, to the extent that single hookbaits often work very well indeed. I like to use it either on its own, or with a scattering of free crusts. In addition to being attractive to fish, it has a number of other advantages, being easy to hook and very easy to freeline at short range: it is altogether a superb bait.

Breakfast cereals make good floating baits, but they are difficult to catapult out unless you can get behind the wind when they can be excellent. Sugar Puffs are good for the smaller species, but my favourites are Corn Pops which have the added advantage of being delicious to eat if the fish aren't co-operating!

There are other baits, too: *floater cake*, for example, can be made to a precise recipe using a whole variety of flavours. *Floating naturals* such as flies, bees and moths have caught lots of fish over the years, while artificial flies used in conjunction with a fly rod set-up can be superb when coarse fish are taking fly life from the surface.

Techniques

There are a number of ways in which you can present floaters. From freelining to the beach-caster rig, surface presentations are as complicated as you want to make them. Personally I prefer simple methods, freelining being my favourite, but there are occasions when a more sophisticated approach is called for.

Bait Mounting

The way in which you attach the floater to your hook can have a critical effect on your success. Side-hooking is the most common method, and with bread crust at least it remains the most effective. Impale a lump of crust on a size 8, 6, 4 or even a 2, leaving the hook point exposed, and you have a deadly presentation that has stood the test

of time. The only additional comment that I would make concerns the preparation of bread crust: by leaving the crust to 'sweat' for a while in a sealed polythene bag, a much more durable hookbait will be the result; 'sweaty crust' is rubbery and it stays on the hook longer.

Particle baits such as mixers can be side-hooked too, but you will need to soak the bait first so that it is soft enough to be penetrated without fracturing into thousands of tiny pieces. A single mixer on a size 8 or two mixers on a size 6 will be a perfect match between size of bait and hook, the main consideration being that the hook point and the bend of the hook should be fully exposed. Nick the mixer as lightly as possible through the skin for maximum hookability. The major drawback with side-hooked mixers is that they will swivel round during a cast and mask the hook point. To avoid this, add a small dab of superglue to the shank of the hook so that the mixer stays locked in place.

Side-hooking is a very effective way of presenting mixers because it does two things: firstly, the hook and bait sit in the right position, with the hook hanging below the bait like a claw. Secondly, plenty of the hook is exposed which improves the chances of a successful strike. There are, however, alternative methods that improve these benefits still further.

Supergluing the bait to the back of the shank of the hook is the first way; this gives maximum exposure to the hook and entirely eliminates the risk of masking. To achieve the best results, cut a small, steep-sided 'V' into one side of the mixer, fill it with a dab of glue and push the shank of the hook into the cut. A short, firm press that lasts for approximately twenty seconds or so will secure the hook to the bait. Also on the market is the 'bait band', manufactured by John Roberts. Bait bands are hard plastic rings that possess a degree of elasticity; the idea is that you push the mixer into the band, whereupon the band can be transferred to the shank of the hook by pushing the hook point through a hole located on a small tab which forms part of the bait band design.

The other alternative is to hair-rig the bait, and this can be especially useful when fish become very wary of floaters. To be honest I have only ever found this to be a problem with carp, which is due, I suppose, to the popularity of surface fishing for this species. There are many variations to try on the hair-rig theme, but when I am hair-rigging I usually use two mixers on the hair. Presenting a double mixer has, in itself, a positive effect in overcoming the carp's suspicion.

Hooklengths

For most of my floater fishing I use mono hooklengths. Multistrand hooklinks have also proved to be successful when a degree of finesse is required in your presentation, without a loss of line strength. Combi-links, utilizing strong mono (usually 10, or 12 bs) and multistrand are very successful, not only in improving your chances of hooking and landing the fish, but also avoiding the tangles that usually result from using a hooklink made purely of multistrand. My favourite hooklength combination involves the final 2ft (60cm) being made of Multistrand, with a minimum of 4ft (1.2m) of mono. To join the two materials together, use a four-turn water knot, adding a touch of glue for extra security.

LONG-RANGE FISHING by Dave Thorpe

I am an angler who spends a lot of time on large waters, both at home and abroad, so fishing at distance has become something of a way of life. I do not fish at range for the sake of it – clearly if likely fish-holding areas exist close to the bank I will fish to them – but on many of the waters that I fish, presenting a bait between 60 and 140yds (55 and 130m) is essential.

How far is a long way? To some anglers anything over 50yds (45m) would be considered a long cast, while others talk glibly in terms of 100yds (90m) plus. However, most of the people I know who consistently brag about fishing at 140yds (130m) or more have no concept whatsoever of distance; they deceive themselves because, believe me, 140yds is a very, very long way and I have seen only a handful of anglers who can cast that far, never mind fish compe-

tently at it. Nevertheless, distance fishing might be considered to be any range beyond 70yds (65m), since this seems to be the point at which accuracy becomes difficult.

Rods, Reels and Line

One of the most important influences on distance casting is tackle. There is no point in trying to cast 130yds (120m) with a rod that simply cannot handle that sort of range, or indeed using a lead that is totally ill-matched to the rod.

Let us discuss rods first of all. For distances up to 100yds (90m), a 2¼lb test curve model is ideal, while distances between 110 and 140yds (100 and 130m) are better suited to a 2½lb rod. For casts regularly in excess of 140yds a rod of 2¾lb to 3lb test curve will probably be necessary. Personally, I am loath to go above 2¾lb and beyond a length of 12ft. I have experimented with 13ft 3lb test curve casting rods on a number of occasions, and I have found that I can't cast as far with them as I can with a 2¾lb. Now I am no weakling, either, and I genuinely feel that it is nigh impossible to get a 13ft 3lb test curve rod to its full casting compression; so I stick to 2¾lb.

As far as reels are concerned, for fishing beyond 70yds (65m) I use the Daiwa SS3000, which is now even better thanks to the new baitrunner devices I have fitted to the front of them. The size, shape, spool design and line lay of the SS3000 is tailormade for fishing at range. I couple mine with line between 8lb and 15lb, depending on how far I have to cast and how snaggy the swim is. For general fishing I like Berkley Trilene Trimax in 12lb, whilst in snaggy swims 15lb Big Game provides me with extra reassurance. On occasions, in open water, I will use 8lb mono where extreme distances are involved. This calls for the use of shock/snag leader, my favourite being Amnesia mono, a stiff, slippery black line that casts well and copes admirably with snags and bars.

Bite Indicators

Bite indicators play a critical role in all aspects of carp fishing, but never more so than when fishing at range. Indicators are required that will show

Dave Thorpe's distance fishing rig.

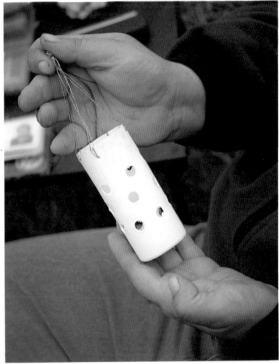

A 'spod' like this one is essential if you want to loosefeed particles at range.

both runs and drop-backs, with the emphasis firmly on the latter. My favourites are the tension arm type manufactured by Dennis McFetrich. Appropriately called the 'Wanger', these indicators are very sensitive, the short quiver keeping line under tension until a take occurs. Even a slow 'drop-back' causes them to fall rapidly, whilst a fast run produces a dramatic effect which cannot be mistaken for anything other than the real thing! The latest generation of 'Wangers', with an improved head and line clip, are as close to perfection as Dennis is ever likely to get.

Leads

Leads play a critical role in accurate distance fishing, not only in terms of their weight, but also their shape and their ability to minimize tangles. First you will have to decide the weight. With most rods a direct correlation between ounces and pounds produces maximum distance: for example, a 2½lb test curve rod is best matched with a 2½–3oz lead, whilst a 2lb test curve model achieves optimum casting performance with 2–2½oz. Similarly, a 2¾lb rod is best suited to a 3oz lead.

Shape is vitally important, firstly in respect of aerodynamics (to lessen wind resistance) but also in terms of neatness, resistance to tangling and the maximization of the 'bolt' effect. Once again I use a Dennis McFetrich product, this time his new 'in-line' lead set-up, which is brilliant: the shape of the lead is perfect for long distance, whilst the imaginative use of the tubing and semi-fixing device is the best that I have seen.

Accuracy at Distance

This is the single most difficult thing to achieve. When I talk about accuracy at distance I am not only referring to the positioning of the rig, but also the achievement of accurate free baits. Unless I am casting tight to a visible feature such as an island or an overhanging tree I always use a

Dave Thorpe with a 41lb leather from France, caught at extreme range.

marker float. The first purpose of the marker float is to pinpoint the exact position of the feature or area you are casting to; I like to position my rig within 2 or 3ft (60 to 90cm) of the marker, which is then used as a guide for positioning free bait.

Those of you who have fished in this way will realize that there is a risk of tangling your rig with the marker, but it is a risk I am prepared to take for the sake of pinpoint accuracy. After all, it takes only a few minutes to re-tackle but it can take hours to realize you are not fishing in the right place. I sincerely believe that accuracy is very important in carp fishing and I always try to create as dense and as tight a carpet of bait as possible.

When you exceed 70 or 80yds (65 or 75m) you are pushing your tackle beyond catapult range, and a throwing stick is the only answer; mine is specially designed and very accurate. Its range is somewhere between 100 and 120yds (90 and 110m), perhaps more with a following wind, but I can pass on no more advice other than to say practice makes perfect. To become competent quickly, purchase a throwing stick and practise baiting to a marker, preferably in an area you don't intend to fish; only when you become proficient should you contemplate baiting up at distance. You will find in practice that timing and technique are the keys to throwing stick success, and not brute strength.

Bait Size and Shape

A common mistake made by many anglers is to ignore the shape and size of their boilies. For long-range fishing, 'roughly round' boilies will not do; they have to be *very* round. Misshapen boilies will not only fall short of the mark, they will fly off in all sorts of directions, creating a loose spread of bait in an area that can be measured in hundreds rather than a few square yards.

The size of the bait will also have a direct bearing on the distance it can be thrown. Regardless of the size of the bait you would *like* to use, distance often dictates the choice for you, and at extreme range, ¾–⅞in (18–22mm) boilies are essential. Also on the market is Dave Thorpe Bait Developments' 'Heavy Bait Additive' specifically manufactured to help increase range from the throwing stick. It is a tasteless, odourless, environmentally friendly powder that can be added to your base mix, and its inclusion to the recommended level will increase the weight of boilies by as much as 15 per cent. Now that may not sound a lot, but when you consider that extra weight equals extra yards, you will appreciate that its inclusion in the mix can mean the difference between 'getting there' and falling short.

In Conclusion

Long-range fishing can be very effective, but it is important to remember that it is but one weapon in our armoury. The most important task on any water is to locate either the carp themselves or the features that hold them. That is where you must put your bait, and if it so happens that the best areas are a long way from the bank, so be it. Increasing range potentially means decreasing accuracy, so remember to keep everything tight and do not accept a compromise. And if you can't fish accurately at distance, don't try.

12 TENCH

The tench is arguably our most beautiful coarse fish species. Its olive green flanks give way to a buttercup-yellow belly, and its endearing little red eye provides a final, almost outrageous touch of colour. It is a powerful adversary too, with large, scallop-shaped fins and a broad tail that is more reminiscent of a paint brush than the comparatively dainty forked rudder of the majority of freshwater fish. Irresistible runs, dogged resistance and heart-stopping power are the trademarks of a fighting tench. It is little wonder then, that the tench is at the very top of the majority of summer anglers' priorities and has become synonymous with the early part of the angling season.

TRADITIONAL TENCH FISHING

If the tench is synonymous with summer, it is equally true that estate lakes are synonymous with tench and traditional tench fishing. Even the relatively recent development of swimfeeder and bolt-rig styles have done little to dent the popularity of float fishing for tench on stillwaters of this kind. But before we examine tench fishing styles, let us consider the key subject of location.

Location

Most estate lakes and ponds are relatively shallow, they contain prolific summer weed growth, and are usually bordered by a riot of bankside vegetation. Early in the season, tench will be found predominantly in the shallowest areas of the lake. Depths between 2 and 6ft (0.6 and 1.8m) will be favoured, particularly if there are reedbeds or rushes nearby to provide the tench with a spawning facility. Spawning usually takes place in early July, but hot weather in May or an unusually cool summer will disrupt this pattern. However, tench will almost certainly be found on or near to the shallows until early July at least. Estate lakes were created largely in the seventeenth, eighteenth and nineteenth centuries by the damming of feeder streams, and the water inlet area is the most reliable indication to the tench's spawning ground.

As the summer progresses, the tench will gradually drop back into deeper water. By mid-July, depths between 4 and 10ft (1.2 and 3m) are

Stewart Allum with a rare golden tench.

171

reliable, and the presence of features, either in the form of lily pads, reedbeds, other weedbeds or depth variations will often make the difference between a good and a bad tench swim. Some of the features will be obvious enough, especially weedbeds that break the surface of the water, but submerged features such as shelves and depressions in the lake bed will have to be located with the aid of plumbing tackle (*see* Chapter 4).

By·early autumn the tench will have migrated to the deepest areas of the lake. Sporadic sport can be enjoyed at this time, but by mid-September the tench fishing on this type of water will probably be well and truly over.

Feeding Periods

Feeding periods are important with tench, and on estate lakes and ponds they usually conform to a regular pattern. By far and away the most reliable time is dawn, with feeding commencing at first light and continuing for perhaps three or four hours. Later in the year, this phenomenon is less pronounced, and tench feeding spells become difficult to predict. Dusk runs dawn a close second on some waters, while on others it is nowhere near as productive. On most lakes and ponds though, an evening feeding spell can be relied upon, even if it is a short one.

All-day sporadic feeding is possible during the summer, particularly on heavily stocked waters, or on dull, overcast days when light values remain constantly low.

In summary, there is always a chance of tench at any time of the day, but the most successful tench anglers on estate lakes and ponds are usually either well disciplined early risers or insomniacs!

Baits

Although tench on traditional waters can be caught on modern baits like boilies (*see* Chapter 11), their use seems rather inappropriate, and in most cases unnecessary. Traditional and proven tench baits are therefore used.

Worms

Tench love worms of all kinds, and if I were restricted to just one tench bait for the rest of my life, it would be a big, fat, juicy **lobworm**. The great thing about lobs, in addition to the fact that tench seem to find them irresistible, is their versatility. A single lob on a size 6, a bunch of big worms on a size 4, or the tail half of a lobworm on a size 10 can be used to match the preferences of the tench on the day. To make them even more attractive, I like to 'nip' the tail off the worm, thus releasing their scent into the water.

An Estate lake tench, a shade over 6lb in weight.

Jim Gibbinson's favourite worm for tench is the **blue-head**, a medium-sized, tough, lively worm usually found in clay-based soil. Having used them, I can understand Jim's enthusiasm, and a bunch of three blue-heads on a size 8 takes some beating as a tench bait. The only drawback is their apparently limited availability.

The **redworm** is the third tench fisher's worm. True 'reds' as opposed to **brandlings** (a similar-looking worm with yellow bands around its head), make fine hook offerings. They are particularly successful fished in small bunches on a size 12 or 14 hook over a bed of casters and hemp.

Maggots and **casters** are mass baits, both equally productive as hookbait and loosefeed. Of the two I prefer casters, principally because I believe the tench favour them, but also because casters will remain on the bottom, giving the tench more chance of finding them, as opposed to maggots which are inclined to wriggle away! In any event, whatever your personal favourite may be, you can use it confidently, safe in the knowledge that you will catch plenty of tench as a result. The major problem with maggots and casters is that they are prone to the attentions of 'nuisance' species. For this reason, I tend to use them primarily as a loosefeed, or as an addition to groundbait, with a larger bait on the hook. Indeed, my favourite loosefeed combination for tench is a mixture of casters and hemp; this is a recipe that will keep them bubbling for hours!

Sweetcorn is a relatively recent discovery (as a bait, anyway), but it is now so widely accepted that it can be considered as one of the all-time great baits. At the beginning of the season, tench are usually happy to accept standard yellow corn, but as the season progresses, the bright yellow coloration can act like a warning beacon to them. Twitchy, unhittable bites, even on a single grain of corn become commonplace, in complete contrast to the bold bites that three grains on a no 8 hook would have produced earlier in the season. At this stage a switch to dyed and flavoured corn is in order. Of the Pescaviva fishing sweetcorn range my favourite flavours for tench are: cream caramel, cherry, sardine, tutti-frutti, strawberry, yoghurt and banana.

Bread, in the form of both crust and flake, is a superb tench bait; indeed, it is one of those baits that you should never approach a tench session without. Early in the season, a 50p-sized piece of flake or a chunk of crust on a size 6 hook will be gratefully accepted; later in the year a small 5p-sized pinch on a size 10 or 12 will probably yield more bites.

Amongst other well-established tench baits, **cheese paste** and **luncheon meat** are both instant and much liked by tench. They have the additional advantage of being relatively cheap, and are well suited to 'sensible'-sized lines and hooks.

Finally, **swan mussels** make superb pond and estate lake tench baits. Being very common in this type of water, they can be considered the most natural bait of them all, and tench will

Pescaviva sweetcorn – available in resealable cans, fourteen different flavours and three colours.

readily accept them. Hook the bait through the yellow 'foot' area on a size 2 or 4 hook, leaving plenty of mussel to give the tench a real mouthful. Don't worry about the seemingly oversized nature of the bait because it won't concern the tench one bit! It is simple enough to obtain swan mussels for the hook: a paddle and 'feel around' in the shallow areas of the lake should provide enough for a day's fishing. To extract the mussel from its shell, place a knife blade between the two halves and cut around the shell, making sure that you sever the hinge area at the back. Remember to throw in a few fragments of chopped mussel as an additional groundbait attractor.

Tackle

Tench are powerful fish, and generally speaking strong tackle is required to control them. Equally though, there is no point in using brutish equipment which will spoil your enjoyment of the fine sport that tench can provide. For float fishing a 'stepped-up' float rod of some 12 or 13ft is ideal. The action of the rod should be 'progressive', with plenty of speed in the tip but forgiving enough to bend through to the butt section when you need to apply pressure. Ideally, leger rods will possess similar characteristics, although a slight bias towards a 'through' action will provide a perfect combination of hookability, power and forgiveness. A rod with a test curve somewhere between 1lb and 1¼lb is ideal.

A good, fixed spool reel with a reliable slipping clutch is essential and you should choose a 'medium'-sized model somewhere between 'match' and 'carp'. Feeder or light baitrunner reels are a good proposition, but the ultimate reel will possess 'fightin' drag', a facility that is ideal for tench (*see* 'Reels' in Chapter 2). Make sure too, that the spool(s) of the reel can hold at least 110yds (100m) of 8lb line.

Rigs and Methods

There is no finer way of fishing for tench than with a float at short range in the idyllic surroundings of a beautiful stillwater, and the simplest style is a technique that has become part of tench fishing tradition: the 'lift' float method, which is as effective today as it was when Fred J. Taylor first publicized it over thirty-five years ago.

The 'Lift' Float

A piece of peacock quill is attached to the line with 1in (2.5cm) of silicone rubber, bottom end only. A single shot somewhere between a BB and an SSG is the only weight added to the line; this shot acts as a 'trigger', causing the float to rise from the water like a periscope (lift) when a tench picks up the bait. A strike should be made as the float begins to lift. In order to achieve this effect, the shot is located within a few inches (or less) of the hook; the closer the shot to the hook, the more sensitive the set-up (*see* Fig. 50).

To rig up a lift float, trim off a short length of peacock quill and attach it to the line. Begin by fixing the float under-depth and add the shot to the line. Cast out, and trim pieces off the quill until the weight of the shot sinks the quill very slowly. Now cast to your intended area, adding depth until the float lies flat on the surface. By slowly tightening the line, the float can be made to 'cock', and further fine adjustment will cause it to sink under tension until an inch or so of the tip is showing.

A modern alternative to this style is to add the quill to the line, followed by a sliding rubber float stop. Fox 'Supa-weight' putty is moulded around the stop and replaces the shot. Keep adding rig putty until the float sinks slowly as before. The lift float is a superbly sensitive method that is particularly suited to large baits such as bread, lobworms and luncheon meat.

Smaller baits are very effective under a float too, particularly for late season tench that have become wary of large offerings. This time the float rig is designed to show bites in more typical fashion, either by the tip 'sailing away' or lifting (in less dramatic style). An insert waggler is the ideal choice, made of peacock quill with a thin inserted tip. Floats carrying between 3BB and size 2 or 3 swanshot can be used to present a bait either in the margin or at a range way beyond the capabilities of the 'lift' method. This rig, also illustrated in Fig. 51, can be used just as effectively for big baits at range, by simply scaling up the hook size and the size of the tell-tale shot.

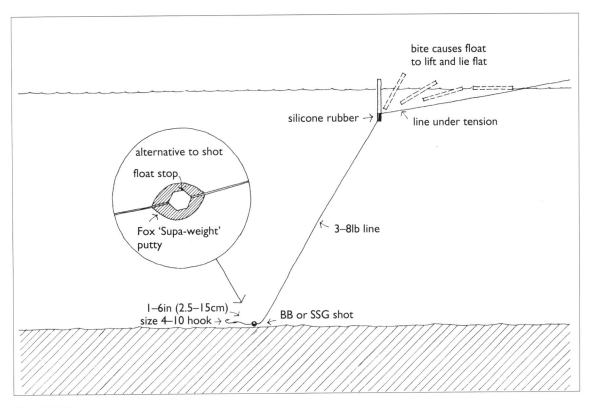

bite causes float
to lift and lie flat

silicone rubber →

line under tension

alternative to shot

float stop

Fox 'Supa-weight'
putty

3–8lb line

1–6in (2.5–15cm)
size 4–10 hook →

BB or SSG shot

Fig. 50 *Lift float*

Dull, windy conditions may be difficult to cope with, but they are nonetheless conducive to all-day-long tench sport, and the float is still a viable method provided that you use a drift beater. This specialist pattern will present the bait on the bottom, holding its position admirably on all but the stiffest breezes. Keep the shotting pattern simple for for maximum success (*see* Fig. 52), and use variety of baits for a stable and sensitive presentation.

Groundbait

Groundbait is only sometimes useful for tench. In some situations it can act as a very positive attractor, but in my opinion, on estate lakes at least, its use is rarely worthwhile if your fishing range is close enough to be able to loosefeed. At range, however, either as a carrier for loosefeed or as a plug for swimfeeders, it performs well. Indeed, there is nothing wrong with a fine carpet of groundbait at any range, I am just not convinced of its tench-attracting properties in its own right. For short-range gravel pit fishing I rate it very highly, but in the relatively coloured water of a lake or pond, I find it difficult to justify its expense, unless it is being used as a carrier. In short, if groundbait is going to be used, it should be of the finest possible texture, so that ideally it lightly 'dusts' the bottom, rather than coating it in a stodgy 'goo'. For feeder fishing I like the groundbait to 'explode' the loosefeed out of the feeder and I use a mixture of brown crumb, Sensas 'Explosive Feeder' (which contains a lot of crushed hemp) and 'Supercup' (a sweet, fine groundbait by Van Den Eynde). For short-range work I use a similar combination, dropping the 'Explosive Feeder' in favour of van den Eynde 'Expo'. I am more convinced of the role that groundbait plays as an attractor on gravel pits, and in particular about flavours and additives.

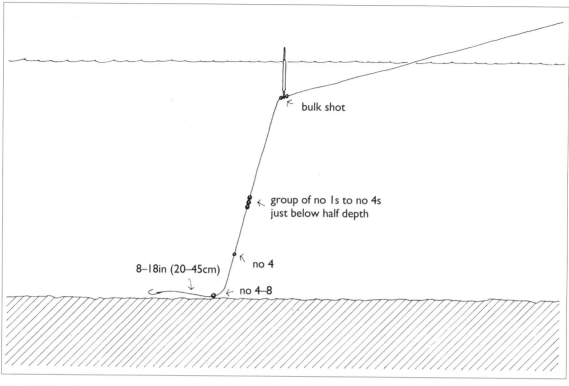

bulk shot

group of no Is to no 4s
just below half depth

8–18in (20–45cm)

no 4

no 4–8

Fig. 51 Waggler.

The Leger Rig

Legering is a less exciting method for tench, but a productive one nonetheless, especially for fishing at medium to long range. Simple leger rigs work well for tench, and the basic choice lies between running legers and fixed paternosters. Both methods are equally effective. Their construction is shown in Fig. 53. Legering for tench in traditional style is all about minimizing resistance. With a fixed paternoster you should use the lightest leger you can get away with; it is essentially a short- to medium- range method because the use of heavier legers for distance work tends to make paternosters less sensitive in my opinion. In theory, the tench should feel the resistance of your indicator before it encounters the weight of the leger, but tench bites can be dramatic in the extreme, often consisting of blistering runs that make it impossible to reach the rod before the indicator reaches the limit of its rise. When this happens, the only alternative is to engage the anti-reverse or baitrunner on your reel to allow the tench to run with the bait. Heavy legers are likely to result in dropped baits, because of the extra resistance involved.

Thus, for long range, a running leger is more appropriate, but for a leger to truly 'run' a weight of at least 1oz should be used; failure to do this will cause undue resistance since light legers have a tendency to 'plane' up off the bottom, whereas heavier leads remain in place, allowing the line to run freely. To improve the ability of the rig to slide still further, a Roberts' low resistance leger ring should be employed to link the bomb to the main line.

Another problem that may be encountered is the presence of soft weed, silt or debris on the bottom, all of which have the potential to foul a free-running set-up. To avoid the rig 'clogging up' it is important to make the sliding ring sit above the leger and clear of the weed and silt. Moreover, when the obstruction is particularly bad, the link

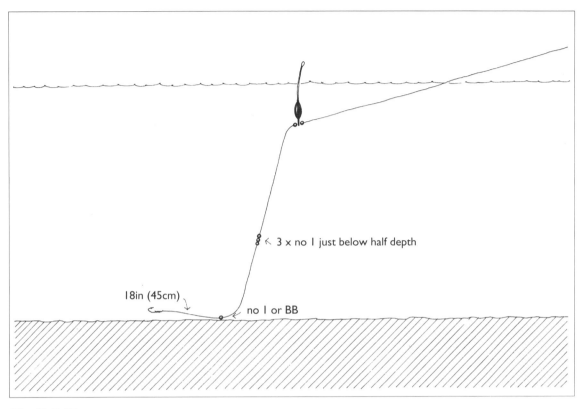

Fig. 52 *Driftbeater.*

3 x no 1 just below half depth

18in (45cm)

no 1 or BB

This picture shows the difference between a female tench (above) and a male tench (below). The male has longer ventral fins and a distinctive pelvic muscle.

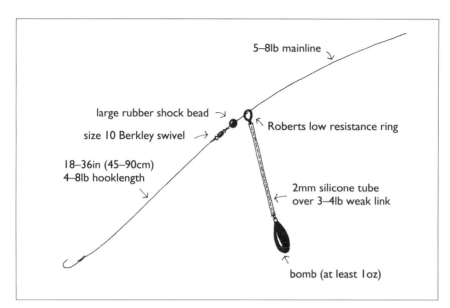

Fig. 53a Sliding leger.

5–8lb mainline

large rubber shock bead

Roberts low resistance ring

size 10 Berkley swivel

18–36in (45–90cm)
4–8lb hooklength

2mm silicone tube
over 3–4lb weak link

bomb (at least 1oz)

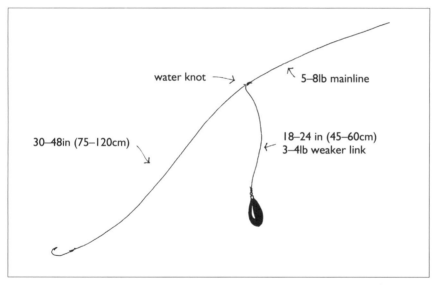

Fig. 53b Fixed
paternoster.

water knot

5–8lb mainline

30–48in (75–120cm)

18–24 in (45–60cm)
3–4lb weaker link

cannot be solely relied upon and a buoyancy aid of some description is required. The diagram shows how a small, semi-fixed polyball can be used to this purpose; note that the length of the link is adjusted so that the leger ring sits comfortably just above the weed and silt (*see* Fig. 54).

The Swimfeeder

One of the most effective tench fishing techniques is the swimfeeder. This cunning device allows the angler to create a tight carpet of bait in the immediate vicinity of the offering with the hook in it. Not only does this inspire confidence in the angler, it also gives the fish confidence too. Feeders are particularly useful for fishing with particle-sized baits such as hemp, corn and maggots, all of which can be delivered very accurately at range. Furthermore, feeder rigs can be tuned to produce a high degree of sensitivity. Filling the feeder with a mixture of groundbait and loose-

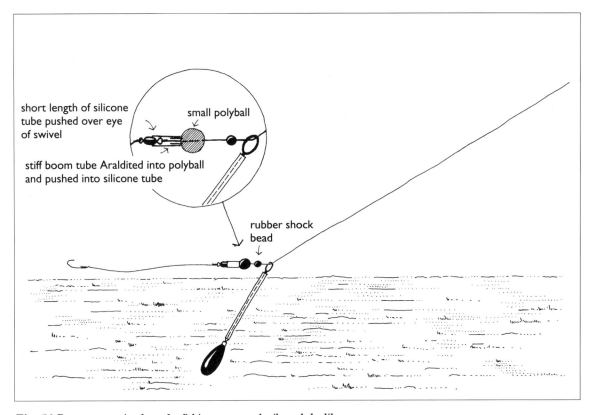

short length of silicone
tube pushed over eye
of swivel

small polyball

stiff boom tube Araldited into polyball
and pushed into silicone tube

rubber shock
bead

Fig. 54 *Buoyant running leger for fishing over weed, silt and the like.*

feed provides a considerable amount of casting weight, but when empty, a lightweight feeder will minimize resistance to a tench which picks up bait.

Open-ended swimfeeders are best suited to this style of fishing, and I always choose the lightest feeder possible and fish it 'fixed' rather than running style. My favourite set-up is an adaptation of the carp angler's 'helicopter rig', principally because it is superb for minimizing tangles and eliminating line twist.

Bite Indication

I use two types of bite indicator when I am legering for tench, in combination with electronic bite alarms. For this style of 'confidence' fishing, sensitivity is very important. On calm days, my preference is for a lightweight bobbin which is pulled down to give a 3ft (90cm) drop. This will give the tench plenty of resistance-free play before the bobbin reaches the limit of its ascent. If the water is slightly choppy, by simply adding SSG shot to the length of line below the bobbin, a precise balance can be achieved.

Very windy conditions or the presence of a side wind will make the bobbin redundant – false 'bleeps' and swinging indicators are irritating, to say the least. In these conditions I switch to a fixed arm indicator which has a sliding collar weight which can be used to counteract wind pressure, undertows and so on. Sensitivity is still imperative, and the perfect indicator will be very sensitive at its lightest setting and with a long enough arm to allow a 2–3ft (60–90cm) drop. My favourite is the Fox International Mark one Longarm 'Swinger', an indicator that possesses all of the qualities described, and is capable of taking an isotope for use after dark.

The author plays a big gravel pit tench hooked in the middle of the day. Gravel pit tench are late feeders.

MODERN TENCH TECHNIQUES

Many leading anglers believe that gravel pits represent the future of fishing, and the explosion of huge tench in pits over recent years provides evidence that their convictions are well founded. Since the early 1980s, the capture of tench from gravel pits weighing in at sizes that were previously unthinkable, has changed tench fishing almost beyond recognition. Gravel pit tench are not biologically different from their fellows, but they are very much harder to catch; this is because of the relatively low populations of tench stocks, the prolific weed growth and clear water, all of which contribute to difficult tenching. However, if you want to catch a really big tench, then gravel pits are undoubtedly the places to be.

Location

Most gravel pits tend to be large; moreover, a 50-acre (20-hectare) water may possess as few as fifty tench and finding them can be difficult. But it is surprising how misleading results can be. A good friend, John Everard, recently told me of a reasonably productive big tench water that was widely believed to contain hundreds of tench. When the water was drained, anglers simply could not believe that the total tench population for the lake was a mere forty-four fish. What does this tell us? Quite simply it means that tench favour certain areas of the lake, and that if you can find these areas, consistent success is assured. On any pit, tench will favour some areas very highly indeed, which means that even on a 50-acre water you might only be fishing a couple of acres or so – a strong incentive to learn the fundamentals of tench location.

The first area that should attract your attention is the marginal shelf. Gravel pit tench love to browse the margins, and if you did nothing more than spend a whole season exploring the margins of a pit, confining yourself to fishing within two rod-lengths of the bank, you would catch plenty of tench. My biggest tench, weighing 9lb 5oz, was caught in 2ft (60cm) of water, no more than 6ft (1.8m) from the bank; proof indeed that the theory is correct. I suspect though, that most anglers recognize the validity of margin fishing, but when it comes to putting it into practice, a mental block intervenes and they simply cannot resist casting at least 20yds (18m) out!

The most prolific tench-holding marginal areas will shelve away very close to the bank. Ideally there will be weedbeds present on the top of the shelf, while the slope area will possess clean gravel. Channels or holes in the weed are ideal since they provide the patrolling tench with security. Baits presented at varying depths from the top to the bottom of the shelf will produce at different times.

During periods of low light the tench will move into very shallow water; strong sunshine, on the other hand, is the sign to fish at the bottom of the slope. Baits presented on the incline work well too.

Gravel bars and plateaux are very reliable tench-producing areas, particularly if they are bordered by weed; certainly the fish appear to use bars as patrol routes or highways as they make their way around the lake. Tench like to browse, and contrary to popular opinion, they do not spend all of their time on the bottom. Patrolling fish often swim in mid-water or even on the surface until something catches their attention, which in turn causes them to investigate. Obviously, certain bars will be productive, while others will not, and the best way to narrow the odds in your favour is to watch tench rolling at dawn or dusk. To the experienced eye a tench roll is unmistakable: a slow, deliberate action that produces an almost black silhouette, characterized by large blunt fins. Frequently, rolling tench will also slap the surface of the water emphatically with their tails.

Having located a potentially good tench bar or plateau, investigate its possibilities by placing baits on the top and sides of the slope, and at the bottom too. Tench are very particular about *where* they like to feed, and within any 'hot' area there will be a small, even 'hotter' area, probably no more than a few feet square. Find this, and the number of bites you receive will increase dramatically.

Weedbeds are an obvious place to find tench. I like to fish near to weed which gives surface cover, but does not coat the bottom. Lilypads are an obvious example, but my other favourite is amphibious bistort with its tough, sapling-like stems and numerous long, thin leaves. Prolific soft weed and filamentous weed such as Canadian pondweed will also attract tench, but it is a nightmare to fish in – unless, that is, you find a clear spot that is surrounded by the stuff, in which case you may have found a tench fishing goldmine. Weed-free 'holes' are often areas that have been cleared by feeding fish, and it is far better to place a bait in a natural food larder than to attempt to create one.

Feeding Periods

This is an interesting aspect of tench behaviour, because in my experience, contrary to the habits of their traditional stillwater fellows, gravel pit tench are very sociable when it comes to feeding times. No two pits are ever exactly alike, but daytime fishing is a viable proposition on all the pits I know, and mid-morning from, say, 9.00am through to early afternoon appears to be the best time of all. On some pits, late afternoon and early evening can be exceptional while on others it will be a waste of time. Dawn will always produce the odd fish, as will the hours of darkness, although I have found the most reliable time to be within a couple of hours of first light rather than up to, say, midnight. The fact is that every pit you visit will possess its own little idiosyncrasies, but you can bet that mid-morning *will* be productive *wherever* you fish.

Even bright sunshine will not put gravel pit tench off their midday feeding routine; indeed on some pits it positively *improves* chances. Bright sunny weather and tench do not, in theory, go together, except on gravel pits. It doesn't worry me at all if the sun is already blisteringly hot by 9 or 10 o'clock in the morning because I know that the tench will still feed, regardless of the light conditions. It is one of the anomalies of gravel pit tench fishing that the worst conditions of all for traditional tench lakes can be so productive for pit fish.

Being somewhat nomadic, gravel pit tench are inclined to respond to the wind. I personally wouldn't place them in the same league as carp, but a big, warm summer southerly or south-westerly will often cause tench to populate a small corner of the lake heavily, and in the presence of such conditions it is a brave tench angler that ignores them. My good friend John Everard is a gravel pit tench expert, and he places great faith in the influence of strong, warm winds on tench.

Baits

Although gravel pit tench will readily accept all the classic tench fishing baits, there can be no doubt that boilies, pastes and particles play a much wider role in this type of fishing. Whenever I approach a new pit for the first time my initial reaction is to use large baits such as lobworms, bread and luncheon meat, but I will usually present these over beds of particles which will hold tench in the swim. Gravel pit tench like to 'browse', then having attracted them to an area in the first place, the only way to keep them there is to give them lots of small food items.

Maggots, casters and hemp are probably my favourites, with the emphasis firmly on the latter. Hemp is a tench attractor *par excellence*, and I rarely approach a session without it. My favourite feeding tactic involves laying down a bed of hemp along with a light scattering of my chosen hookbaits, and at regular intervals I will loosefeed maggots or casters in the swim to attract the attention of cruising tench. Additionally, it is just as well to vary the types of food item in the swim in order to prevent the tench becoming totally preoccupied with hemp alone.

I also like to include groundbait in the feed, introducing it in fine, cloud form at regular intervals so that the bottom is lightly dusted and there is always a touch of colour in the swim. Active groundbaits are best, and the types that include crushed hemp are my favourites. I usually mix the 'special groundbait' with traditional brown crumb, at a rate of 60/40 in favour of the brown crumb, and introduce a flavour; this is invariably Rod Hutchinson's 'Maple Cream', probably the finest tench attractor in the world. Liquid molasses is also good, being an exceptional natural sweetener and I usually include both types of additive in the mix.

When the tench become difficult to catch on traditional hookbaits, a change is called for, and several alternatives are available. The usual indication that a switch is required is when the tench continue to visit the groundbait, indicating their presence by giving line bites or by rolling, but takes dwindle away. The downturn in sport is usually quite dramatic, but the introduction of particle or boilie hookbaits will soon set your indicators flying again.

The first hookbait I would try is usually sweetcorn, standard yellow at first, and then dyed, flavoured varieties as results begin to taper off. Pescaviva ready-flavoured/dyed corn is one of my favourites (*see* 'Particles' in Chapter 3). The use of maggots and casters on the hook can also provide exceptional results where nuisance species allow, while cocktail baits can be even better.

Maple peas are the next logical step. Maples really are an exceptional tench hookbait, particularly when fished over hemp. To prepare maples, bring them to the boil, adding a couple of tablespoons of sugar to the water beforehand, and simmer them until they are soft enough to accept the hook. Half a pint of maples is quite adequate for a day-long tench session, and I confine freebaiting to a sprinkling on top of the hemp groundbait.

Other useful tench particles include chick peas, black-eye beans, tares and Aduki beans. Once again they are best used sparingly, in the same quantities as the maples, over a bed of hemp.

Finally, there are boilies and pastes, particularly useful when long session angling is involved. Once tench get a liking for boilies they can become very addicted to them, and results are often spectacular. The most devastating tench boilies will be particle-sized baits, usually in the $5/16$ to $1/2$in (8 to 12mm) size range. A bed of boilies of this size will attract and hold tench in the swim and are unlikely to be eaten by anything other than tench, bream and carp.

Most flavours will catch tench at one time or another, but my experience suggests that some are better than others. Here is my list of favourites:
Rod Hutchinson: 'Maple Cream', 'Mega Maple', 'Tench Attractor Spray', 'Tutti-Frutti', 'Autumn Harvest'.
Dave Thorpe Bait Developments: 'Strawberry Nectar', 'Juicy Peach', 'Sweet Damson'.
Solar Tackle: 'Pear of Bananas', 'Ester Pineapple', 'Esterblend 12', 'Caramel Toffee'.
Nutra Baits: 'Salmon Elite', 'Banana Nutrafruits', 'Pineapple Nutrafruits', 'Strawberry Nutrafruits', 'Raspberry Nutrafruits', 'Toffee Cream Elite'.

As you can see, I rate fruit flavours very highly indeed, but dairy-based flavours such as 'Maple Cream' and 'Caramel Toffee' are probably even better. Fruit attractors can be improved by blending, and I like to add a third of Rod Hutchinson's 'Scopex' to the main flavour in use, just to 'smooth it off'. As a general rule, tench will tolerate quite high flavour levels, but I never exceed the amount recommended in the manufacturers' instructions, and nor should you. Too much flavour will repel rather than attract. However, the addition of sweeteners will certainly improve the attractiveness of the bait to tench, and the types that I would recommend are liquid molasses and Dave Thorpe's 'Sweet Cream' palatant, 'Tastetone' sweetener or 'Magnasweet'.

Whether you make your own boilies or buy 'ready-mades', it is certainly worth either making or purchasing some 'pop-up' buoyant hookbaits too. These are particularly useful when fishing over soft weed. Home-produced 'pop-ups' undoubtedly score over 'shop-bought' ones for gravel pit tench; I make my own in the microwave, a process that allows me to control the amount of buoyancy in the bait by playing around with cooking times. As well as making truly buoyant baits which can be 'popped up' to hover up to 2 or 3in (5 or 7cm) off the bottom, I also like to produce baits that will sink slowly with the weight of the hook. These 'semi-buoyant' baits can be fished on long hooklengths to sit on top of thick weed, since the addition of rig putty to pop up a very buoyant bait can pull the offering down into the weed itself. Such critically balanced baits are absolutely deadly, being extremely responsive to a general 'suck' aimed at a group of baits by a tench. They are also excellent for attracting patrolling fish.

As far as base mixes are concerned, I tend to stick to milk-protein-based or yellow birdfood mixes. My favourite base mix at the moment is Dave Thorpe's 'Supercede', a highly digestible mix that is naturally a bright, vivid yellow in colour. Bright colours appeal to tench and I tend to dye my baits either yellow, red or orange. Excessive fishing pressure, however, can cause the tench to view bright baits with suspicion, in which case a change to a more subdued bait, without the addition of dye, provides the answer. Fishmeals are an obvious choice, being a dull reddy brown in colour, although I would tend to compliment them with a fruit, rather than a savoury or fish flavour.

Anglers who do not make their own boilies are well catered for by the ready-made boilie manufacturers. The foremost among them, Richworth Streamselect, produce some excellent tench flavours including 'Tutti-Frutti', 'Strawberry Cream', 'Plum Royale' and 'Salmon Supreme'. There are also two sizes: ¼in (6mm) 'Match Size' baits and ⅜in (10mm) 'Midis'.

Tackle

Big tench in weedy waters invariably demand the use of stepped-up tackle. For float fishing, a 'specimen'-type float rod between 12 and 13ft long is ideal. The test curve of the rod should be around 1lb 2oz which will enable you to use reel lines in the 3 to 7lb category. Couple the rod with a nice medium-sized fixed spool reel; my favourite is the Shimano Aero G.T.M. with its superb fightin' drag feature (*see* 'Reels' in Chapter 2).

For general leger work, a rod somewhere between 1¼lb and 1½lb test curve will suit most gravel pits. Obviously the strength of the rod you choose should be dictated by your favourite venue(s), the key influence being the amount of weed. However, I am increasingly persuaded these days that a 12ft 1½lb test curve rod with a progressive/through action is ideal, since it will cope with everything from general leger work to bolt rigging, while reel-wise a medium-size baitrunner reel is perfect. The baitrunner concept has revolutionized modern big fish angling; it is just a shame that Shimano have not produced a medium-size baitrunner with fightin' drag on it too!

The reel(s) should be loaded with spools of 6lb, 8lb and 10lb line. In weedy pits, a limp, castable reel line is not enough: it must be capable of resisting severe abrasion, too. My favourite line for this type of work is Berkley Trilene XT with its extra-tough outer protective coating. It will take a very special mono indeed to persuade me to change.

Rigs and Techniques

For information concerning traditional rigs, see the start of this chapter; all the methods discussed will work on gravel pits at one time or another. The key difference between modern and traditional tenching techniques lies in the use of particles and boilies, which have 'knock-on' implications in terms of rigs.

Dealing with Weed

The first consideration when fishing weedy waters should be tackle strength. We have looked at main lines, but what about hooklengths? On gravel pits the weed problem is inevitable, and I now use braided hooklengths almost exclusively – except, that is, when I'm stalking (more of this later). Braids, in my opinion, give a superior presentation to mono with the added advantage of greatly increased abrasion resistance. For float fishing at a close range, I prefer multistrand, a material which, due to its many fine fibres, gives a superb presentation and possesses excellent abrasion resistance.

The other problem with weed is that it tends to mask and obscure the bait. However, with a little forethought, it is possible to make baits sit on top of the weed, rather than sink into it. When I am side-hooking baits I like to glue a small piece of cork onto the back of the shank of the hook, which is invariably a Fox series 2 eyed variety. By nicking a small 'V' into a block of cork with a sharp knife and filling the cut with superglue, it can be made to sit securely in place. Trim small pieces of cork off with the sharp knife, and it is possible to get the hook and bait arrangement to sink extremely slowly so that it sits on top of the weed. Long hooklinks – from 18–36in (45–90cm) – will help this neat refinement to work to perfection.

Hair rigs can also be adapted to achieve the same effect, either by using a buoyant or partially buoyant bait (boilie), or by adding a buoyancy aid to the hair. The best material I have found for the job is rig foam, available in different colours to suit the bait of your choice. By sandwiching this foam between a pair of particles, or using a single particle and a piece of foam which is trimmed down to resemble the bait, the hookbait can be 'popped up'

or made to sink *very* slowly. Baits popped up some 1–3in (2.5–7.5cm) off the bottom can be very effective for tench, although I must admit that the slow sinking rig is my favourite.

If you are using traditional legering styles for gravel pit tench, one of the problems you will probably encounter at some point is the increased resistance imparted to the rig by weed clinging to the leger. The answer is to use a running leger set-up with an Arlesey bomb of at least 1oz in weight. This will stay firmly in place if a tench picks up the bait, and the addition of a buoyancy aid to lift the running part of the rig above the weed will allow it to operate in a resistance-free manner. A polyball or balsa-float body, fished on a link to match the depth of the weed, is ideal for achieving this effect (*see* Fig. 55).

There are two further methods that are absolutely deadly on gravel pits; both are close-range techniques which are best described as 'ambushing' set-ups. Gravel pit tench like to patrol the margins, and my favourite style of fishing for them involves presenting a bait either on, or just beyond, the marginal shelf. Before you begin fishing, prebait a number of likely-looking swims with a few handfuls of particles and then leave them to 'develop'. Your next task, with the aid of polarizing glasses, is to establish the presence of feeding tench. In clear water, you may be fortunate enough actually to *see* the tench themselves feeding in a couple of the baited areas. Provided they are not disturbed, the tench will work their way right up to the marginal shelf into incredibly shallow water, as shallow as 2ft (60cm) on occasions! For this reason it is advisable to groundbait in a 'line', so that some of the bait lies at the bottom of the shelf, with the rest distributed in a line, up the slope. Other signs of tench feeding further out include bubbling, colouring of the water, or debris drifting to the surface. If none of these signs are present, cast a float into each swim; you will soon establish whether tench are present or not.

For really close-range fishing I will freeline a visible bait such as bread flake or yellow sweetcorn. It is one of the greatest thrills in coarse fishing to watch a big tench tip deliberately forwards, its head downwards and tail waving in an upright

Fig. 55 Buoyant leger.

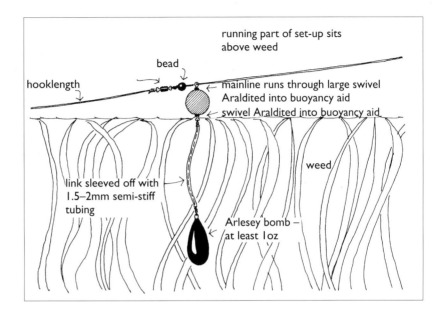

position, and then suck in your bait – try it and see!

For presenting baits to tench well down the marginal slope, I will float fish using the rig shown in Fig. 56. This is an absolutely deadly set-up that gives a very delicate presentation on surprisingly strong tackle. There are no weak spots in the rig, and it is perfectly suited to giving bold, positive bites. 'Liners' will cause the float to dip and bob, while a proper bite on this rig will be signalled by the float just 'sailing away'.

Bolt Rig Fishing

The other extreme is bolt rig fishing for tench with particles and boilies. We have already discussed with the hook-mounting of particles both hair and side-hooked style, but with boilies the bait is invariably mounted on a hair. The number of baits you place on the hair will be dictated, to an extent, by the size of the baits you are using; thus for ⅝in (14mm) boilies and above, a single bait works best, while for ¼–½in (6–12mm) boilies I will often

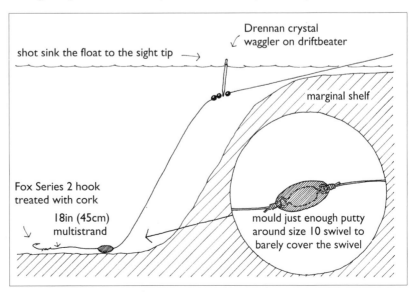

Fig. 56 Specimen float rig.

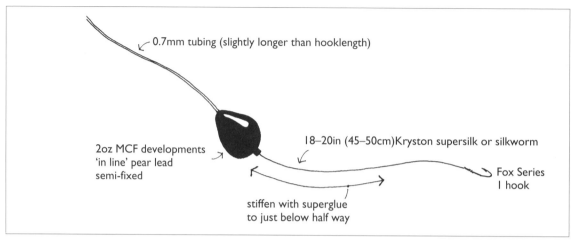

0.7mm tubing (slightly longer than hooklength)

2oz MCF developments
'in line' pear lead
semi-fixed

18–20in (45–50cm)Kryston supersilk or silkworm

Fox Series
I hook

stiffen with superglue
to just below half way

Fig. 57 *Tench bolt rig.*

vary the presentation between one and two. Both 'popped-up' baits and bottom offerings work well, but if weed is present in the swim it is advisable to use a buoyant bait of some description. My favourite set-up involves the use of either a single semi-buoyant boilie which has been microwaved so that it just sinks under the weight of the hook, or one pop-up and one sinker on the same hair. The buoyant bait is squeezed gently under water to expel some of the air until the whole arrangement sinks, very, very slowly. It helps, of course, to use long hooklengths to prevent the bait from being dragged down into the weed by the lead, and

I have found that this presents few problems with tench, who will still bolt, with an 18in (45cm) or even a 20in (50cm) hooklink.

The lead part of the set-up is a 'cut down' version of carp rigs, and for tench fishing I like to use a 2oz bomb rather than a really heavy 3oz or more model. Bombs in excess of this weight seem over the top for tench, and I always worry about damage to their mouths with a really heavy lead bouncing around in front of them during a fight. Besides, a 2oz version produces perfect bolt takes, sinks less easily in the weed, and makes less disturbance on entry into the water.

A fantastic gravel pit tench of 9lb 5oz caught on strawberry-flavoured sweetcorn.

13 PIKE

RIVER PIKE

In spite of the recent exceptional growth in carp fishing, pike are arguably still Britain's most popular big fish target. And whereas even the most prolific pike stillwaters do not receive anything like the angling pressure that 'circuit' carp waters do, anglers in the UK tend to carry out most of their pike fishing on lakes, gravel pits and drains. Sadly, pike do not cope well with angling pressure, and they are undoubtedly a species that thrives on neglect. Given this situation, it is surprising just how under-exploited river pike are. Admittedly, if you want to catch a truly exceptional specimen, large gravel pits offer the best prospects, but for sheer productivity in terms of numbers of pike, rivers win hands down in my opinion; so if I want to enjoy a busy day's piking I will head for moving water every time.

Location

In order to investigate the location of pike on rivers, you need to draw a distinction between fast- and slow-moving water. The influence of a strong current, or the lack of it, has a major effect on pike behaviour, and it is therefore impossible to give a 'blanket' guide to river pike location.

Fast-flowing Rivers

Pike are essentially a species that relies on ambush to capture prey fish. For this reason the most likely place to find them on a fast-flowing river is in a place that offers them cover and good ambushing prospects; and whereas they are quite happy to reside near to a brisk current, they do not enjoy living *in* one. Slack or slow-moving water which is adjacent to a streamier section is definitely favoured by pike. Nevertheless, the confusion and

under-water turbulence created by the pacey water helps to conceal the pike from its prey, and it will enjoy a comfortable existence by lying in wait near to an available food source. Invariably the margins of fast-moving rivers display these characteristics and offer the additional benefit of providing cover in the form of reed- and rush-beds, overhanging trees, undercut banks and marginal snags. On a major river certainly, I tend to regard the margins as one long pike swim.

It would be unwise, however, to ignore the other areas of the river. Mid-river obstructions, weedbeds and depressions provide the pike with plenty of cover, a gentle flow near to faster water, and therefore ample opportunities to surprise unsuspecting prey fish. Of all the spots on a river, bends tend to be the most heavily associated with pike, primarily because the inside of a bend is an enlarged slack area that can potentially harbour numbers of fish. Couple this with the fact that the outside of the bend will be moving at a relatively brisk pace, and you can appreciate that all those characteristics that appear to make a good pike swim apply once again.

The same criteria seem to be evident when we consider one of the other traditional pike hotspots, the weir pool. Weir pools are mysterious places, peppered with all manner of depth changes, often littered with obstructions, and generally synonymous with wide variations in flow rates. The turbulent white water present in weir pools contributes to the confusing underwater scenario and pike, being the great opportunists that they are, quickly learn to take advantage.

To sum up on fast-water pike: try to locate areas which possess steady water adjacent to a pacier current, and be especially alert for snags, obstructions and overhanging cove.

Slow-Flowing Rivers

To a large extent the rules governing the location of fast-water pike also apply to slow-water fish: namely cover and good ambushing prospects. But on a truly slow-flowing river – one which possesses a uniform flow no greater than a slow walking speed – there are many more areas which the pike find comfortable; without pacey water to contend with, slow-water pike can turn up almost anywhere.

Baits anchored in seemingly featureless areas in the middle of the river are frequently productive, but there will usually be one single, powerful factor governing their success – the presence of prey fish. In many ways the location of pike on fast-flowing rivers is much easier than on slow-paced rivers because most of the swims are more obvious, and generally speaking you don't have to cast beyond two rod-lengths from the bank. On canalized moving water, however, the location of fodder fish becomes all-important, and it is frequently necessary to present baits systematically in a number of areas until the pike are found. An obvious short-cut can be achieved by visually confirming the presence of prey fish, but more frequently it is necessary to 'cast around' in order to find the best areas.

Certainly I would never neglect the margins of the river, either on the near or the far bank; these are likely to possess the greatest amount of cover either in the form of rushbeds, overhanging trees or undercut banks, and on a largely featureless waterway these are important features offering the pike all-important ambushing opportunities. Slow-flowing rivers also present improved opportunities for decent far bank presentation. On fast-flowing rivers, baits presented at distance tend to get dragged out of position very easily, whereas on slow-moving venues they remain in place until they are eaten.

If you take a close look – and I mean a very close look – at a slow-flowing river, you will notice that flow rates which appeared at first glance to be totally uniform do in fact vary. Finding these varying flow rates, no matter how subtle they are, is very important. These areas, where slow water meets faster water are known as

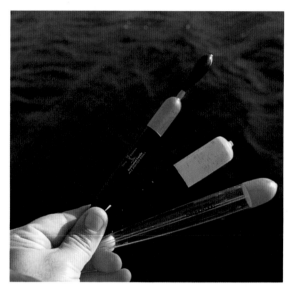

A selection of river pike floats.

'creases'; they operate as food conveyer belts, and predator fish tend to use them as such, by waiting for food to be swept down to them. And remember that on a slow-flowing river, the current is rarely too strong anywhere to bother a pike. This means that creases are very important pike swims, and should never be ignored. Bends are a typical example.

Finally, to state the obvious, any feature on a relatively featureless stretch of river is likely to attract pike. Even the most insignificant-seeming mid-river depression could hold one or a number of fish.

In summary, the key to slow-water pike location is to keep an open mind. Potential swims should be thoroughly explored, and you should never discount an area until you have presented baits across its full width. In fact, location of pike in rivers is far more important than any other factor: locate river pike, and to be quite truthful, catching them is usually easy.

Tackle

Choosing a rod for river pike is far easier than for stillwater fish. Casting distances become largely irrelevant because pike fishing at extreme distance is unnecessary. A good river pike rod will have a progressive action with enough 'steel' in reserve to bully a hard-fighting fish but with enough forgiveness to avoid tearing the hooks out of the pike's bony jaw. Rods with a test curve between 2lb and 2½lb are ideal, though if you intend to pursue pike on stillwaters as well as rivers a rod somewhere between 2¼lb and 3lb test curve is perhaps a better compromise. Personally I use the Shimano Diaflash carp rods, and am fortunate to possess both the 2¼lb and the 3lb models. The Diaflash has the best action I have yet to encounter for pike fishing, and its forgiving but powerful characteristics make the 3lb version a superb all-round pike rod for both stillwaters and rivers.

As far as reels are concerned, I would not be without my Shimano baitrunners. The AR GT 8010 is a superb carp and pike fishing reel, with excellent balance, precise clutch and superior line lay. When I am pike fishing I rarely use the baitrunner facility (except for trolling on trout reservoirs), but there can be no doubt that the 8010 possesses all the essential features of a good pike reel. The spools will be loaded with Berkley Trilene 'Big Game' in 15lb breaking strain, a line that simply won't let you down regardless of the conditions, and I usually lay at least 166yds (150m) of it on the spool (just in case I hook that elusive river giant).

A pair of good bite alarms is helpful, but not essential, for river pike fishing. There are times, especially on slow-flowing rivers, when I like to sit behind two legered deadbaits, and audible alarms provide a definite advantage on such occasions. More frequently, though, I prefer to float fish, even when I am using two rods, and a selection of 'cigar'-type pike floats is indispensable equipment.

Wire traces are vital for pike fishing. I make my own using Berkley Steel Strand and a combination of double and treble hooks. Invariably the hooks I choose will be semi-barbless, my favourite patterns being the Fox Pike Treble and the Partridge double.

Add to this collection a selection of beads, SSG shot and drilled bullets in varying sizes, and the essentials are covered – except for unhooking equipment. I always carry at least two sets of artery forceps, both of which will be at least 12in (30cm) long; and although I've never had to use it, I also carry a (John Roberts) 'deep throat' pike disgorger just in case I deep-hook a fish beyond forceps range (God forbid). A good unhooking mat, too, is more essential for pike than any other species due to their habit of refusing to lie still when you unhook them. The Fox International 'Classic' mat is my first choice since it is large enough and possesses ample padding for even the biggest pike; it is easy to carry and weighs next to nothing.

Finally, when I decide to retain a fish for photography my aim is to keep it out of the water for as short a time as possible; temporarily keeping it in the margins in the bottom of a large landing net will give it time to recover while I set up the camera. However, occasionally, a pike *will* show signs of exhaustion. The worst thing you can do is to place the fish in a standard sack. Carp sacks are far too restrictive for pike, and an open frame construction is much better; but the only safe option, in my opinion, is a pike/barbel tunnel and I recommend them without hesitation for emergency use. Peg out the tunnel in a steady current and allow the pike time to recover, keeping a watchful eye on its condition at all times; like this you should encounter few problems.

Baits

I do not rate bait choice as being of paramount importance with pike. Live- and deadbaits are very effective, although I would openly acknowledge that livebaits probably have the edge for sheer frequency of pike sport; medium-sized dace and small chub up to 6oz in weight are my favourites, since both species are hardy enough to withstand the stresses imposed upon live fish by moving water. Having stated this, on 'good' days livebaits rarely remain on the hooks long enough to justify worrying about longevity. Perch, roach and gudgeon will catch plenty of pike too, but it is my experience that deadbaits tend to produce pike of a higher average size. My favourites are whole herrings and sardines, both of which are 'punctured' prior to casting out in order to allow their attractive (to pike, anyway) scent to escape into the current. Smelts, mackerel and sprats will also produce plenty of runs, but large herrings and sardine are the best in my opinion, and they are relatively cheap, too. Certainly, if I was restricted to just one river pike bait for the rest of my life it would be a fresh herring of around 8oz or so.

Rigs and Tactics

If you want to catch river pike, forget about complicated rigs and concentrate your efforts on being mobile. In many ways it is better to use one rod rather than two, since your aim should be to carry the minimum amount of tackle. On fast-flowing rivers certainly, one rod is ample due to the fact that 90 per cent of the time you will be concentrating on marginal areas. I will rarely spend more than half an hour in an individual swim, and a fifteen-minute visit is more usual. It's always advisable of course, to revisit a productive swim after a suitable rest period, but in the meantime you can be exploring new swims. On slow-flowing rivers where baits can be presented at a variety of distances, the case for a two-rod approach is stronger; it is also my experience that this type of venue will produce numbers of pike. For this reason I probably spend a far greater period of time on average in a productive swim, though I would strongly advise moving every hour or so if runs are not forthcoming.

Without a doubt, my favourite river pike rig is the float fished deadbait (*see* Fig. 58). The bait is presented over-depth, with a double hook in the tail root and a treble along its flank. The anchor weight, which on slow-flowing rivers will be SSG shot and in pacey water a drilled bullet or barrel lead, is fished on the bottom and *just* enough weight is used to hold bottom to prevent the bait from being dragged out of position by the flow. Moving the bait every few minutes by lifting the rod tip and allowing the arrangement to bump downstream will enable you to cover a greater amount of water. This is an ideal technique for presenting a static bait in the margins of major rivers, or across the full width of the slow-flowing type.

The same rig, with a couple of important variations, can be used to 'stret peg' deadbaits down

an inviting run where the current is strong enough to trot a float. The method involves bouncing the bait slowly along the bottom and is most effective on faster-flowing rivers. This time the bait is mounted head first with the double hook fished in the lip and the treble down the flank; a slow retrieve at the end of the trot will sometimes produce a take when the bait is presented in this way. To fish this method effectively the bait should bounce across the bottom, but the weight on the line will either be just off bottom or not quite heavy enough to anchor the bait in the swim (*see* Fig. 59). With both the anchored and 'stret-pegged' deadbait, bites will be positive, with the float either lifting and shooting across the current or simply disappearing in dramatic style.

The same set-up can be used to present livebaits by simply shallowing the float up until the bait is clear of the bottom. Ideally the fish will be trotted some 1 to 3ft (30 to 90cm) off the bottom, and once again the bait is mounted head up trace. This time the double hook is again placed in the lip of the bait, with the treble lightly nicked into the dorsal area. Hooking livebaits in this manner will provide you with more trots per bait. Be warned, however: this is an absolutely deadly technique, and takes can frequently be instantaneous!

I am not a great fan of legered baits for river pike, but on a slow-flowing river I must admit that the two rod/buzzer approach sometimes has its advantages. Also, on fast-flowing rivers it is rarely possible to present a static bait on a float rig anywhere but in the margins. On the former type of venue, the leger weight will simply consist of a number of SSG shot which are carefully added and subtracted until the bait *just* holds its position, while on the latter a standard Arlesey bomb is used adopting the same principle. When adopting this approach the rod should be placed on a buzzer with the bail arm open and the line secured near the rod butt in a line clip. An indicator is useful since some of the takes may be of the dropback variety. On slow-flowing rivers I would advise the use of the traditional 'drop-off' sort, while on a fast-flowing river the Fox Swinger Mark II is superior since its heavy sliding collar weight can be balanced against the flow.

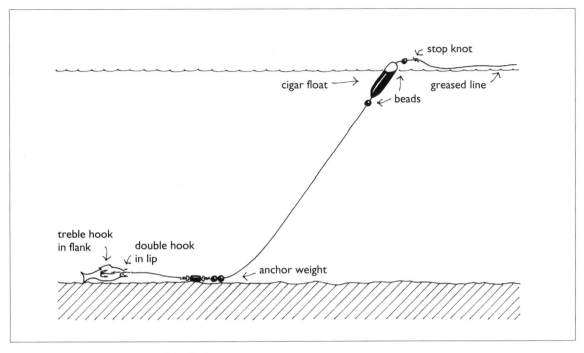

Fig. 58 *River pike rig. Anchored deadbait.*

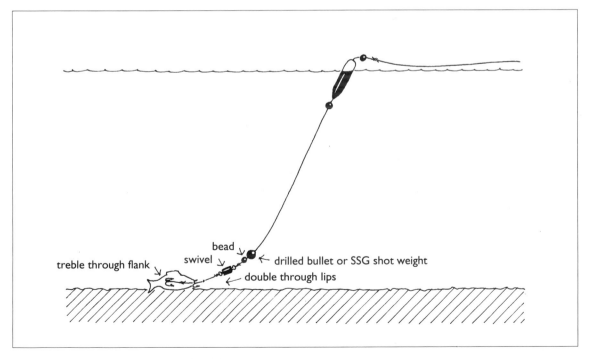

Fig. 59 *River pike rig. Stret-pegged deadbait.*

The final method described here is the sink-and-draw technique. This is especially deadly in slow-moving water but it is equally productive in slack areas on fast-flowing rivers. The beauty of this method is its simplicity, and since it is only possible to fish with one rod when 'sinking and drawing' it also encourages mobility. The sink-and-draw technique is virtually a freeline method involving the bait being mounted head up on a wire trace. Depending on the flow, you may wish to add some extra weight, either in the form of an SSG shot or two, or a light barrel lead. The key point is that the bait sinks to the bottom and does not 'plane up' to the surface on a tight line.

Begin by casting the bait out, and allow it to sink to the bottom. By retrieving the line in short bursts the bait will dart upwards for a few seconds, then flutter invitingly back down again. This stop/start method is superb for provoking an angry reaction from pike since it imitates the behaviour of an injured prey fish. Casts should be made in a fan shape around the fishing position so that as much water is covered as possible. Sink-and-draw can produce some amazing catches of pike.

Feeding Periods and Seasonal Factors

I regard the pursuit of river pike as an exclusively winter pursuit, and in the summer I prefer to concentrate on other species. However, there can be no doubt that warm water piking is both worthwhile and fun. If you are interested in summer pike fishing I suggest that you immerse yourself in the world of lure fishing and follow the excellent advice given in numerous articles and books. But be warned: you will be tampering with one of the most addictive styles of angling, and your 'other' fishing may be abandoned, so consuming is the art of lure fishing.

Nevertheless, even if, like me, you regard pike as essentially a winter quarry, you cannot expect to hook pike all day long on every session. Despite the fact that river pike are less prone to strict feeding periods than stillwater fish, they nonetheless have their preferences. Early morning is always a prime time, especially in the early winter period up until January. Dusk can be good too, especially towards the back end when a 'double feed' is common. On the right day, however, – which is usually mild and overcast with a little wind – sport will continue sporadically through-

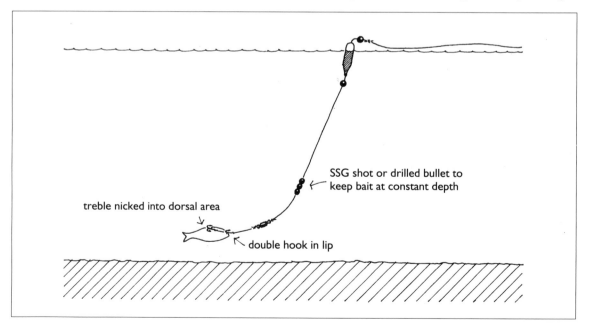

SSG shot or drilled bullet to keep bait at constant depth

treble nicked into dorsal area

double hook in lip

Fig. 60 *River pike rig. Float-fished livebait.*

out the day. It is my belief that because river pike live in a current they are not prone to the bouts of lethargy associated with their stillwater cousins. For this reason a river pike is always susceptible to a well presented bait. And remember, the key to successful river piking is mobility: so, if it's not happening – make it happen!

GRAVEL PIT PIKE

It would be easy to believe that every water in this country holds at least one monster pike if you were prepared to accept local gossip at face value. Stories of gigantic pike which terrorize the local duck population, cause match anglers nightmares and regularly consume small children or dogs who have been foolish enough to stray into the water, are common place. Experienced pike anglers know, however, that big pike are quite rare and that the number of waters that contain a healthy head of 20lb-plus fish are even rarer still. Waters that contain 'thirties' are almost priceless, and are the closely guarded secret of a few fortunate anglers. The best prospects of a truly gigantic pike, and here I'm talking of venues which contain fish distinctly over 30lb, are undoubtedly the trout reservoirs and giant Irish/Scottish stillwaters. Access to this type of fishing is restricted for most people because of the considerable cost involved in terms of travel, fees and specialized equipment such as boats, fishfinders, trolling motors and so on. My good friend John Watson, from Kent, is an expert in this style of fishing and I am grateful to John for sharing his knowledge with us (which appears in the next section of this chapter).

For the majority of anglers in this country, though, gravel pits probably offer the best prospects of big pike. Despite folklore, most lakes in this country are not capable of regularly producing specimen pike. By and large, big pike thrive on neglect and the fishing pressure associated with club waters and popular day ticket venues usually takes its toll on specimen pike populations. Big fish need room, too, space in which to grow and lead largely untroubled lives.

Finally, a good head of food fish is absolutely essential to promote maximum growth and whether this is provided by shoals of medium-sized bream, thousands of roach and perch, or by the artificial introduction of trout, it's a fact that pike do not become large unless there is plenty for them to eat. There are, however, some fisheries that I know which have low stock densities of fish and yet possess some *very* large pike. Invariably, though, the head of pike will be low and they will have access to a stock of prey fish which offers them high growth potential – 3–4lb tench, stillwater chub, 1lb-plus perch or 3–4lb bream. It's all relative really, and like all specimen fish, ultimate growth potential is dependent on stock density versus available food.

Gravel pits tend to match the list of requirements for growing big pike quite well. Fishing pressure, especially by occasional anglers, is generally scarce; pike populations are often relatively low and there is plenty of space in which pike can thrive. Since gravel pits are readily accessible to most of us, I suggest that you give them a try (if you haven't already).

Tackle

The sheer size of most gravel pits and the prospect of relatively slow sport means that equipment needs to be fairly specialized. If you want to catch lots of pike on simple tackle, I suggest that you go river piking instead.

Rod wise, you should not contemplate tackling gravel pit pike without a rod which possesses a test curve rating less than 2½lb. Personally I use 3lb models – rods which are 'beefy' enough to punch large deadbaits considerable distances and yet are forgiving enough not to tear hooks out of a pike's tough, bony jaw. Forget about fast taper rods for this type of fishing; not only will you gain less enjoyment from playing big pike on them, but you'll lose plenty of fish too, through hook-hold failures. Rods of the right calibre are rare and I would recommend the Shimano range wholeheartedly because they are built to play fish on. Yes, I know that I'm a consultant for the company, but take my word for it, Shimano make the best pike fishing rods I've ever used.

A tough, reliable reel with a large spool capacity is a must for gravel pit fishing, since tackle abuse and misuse is a hallmark of piking at distance with big dead- and livebaits. A baitrunner feature is not necessary and you should concentrate instead on a big reel that has a large line capacity. Any reel that you choose should be capable of accepting at least 250yds (230m) of 15lb line. It almost goes without saying that the line you choose to fill the reel with should be strong and extremely durable, but it's surprising how many anglers I've seen with inadequate mono. A minimum line strength of 12lb is essential, while 15lb or even 17lb is better. The use of lighter monos offers no advantage (except for increased casting distance) but the key point is that if you leave a rig in a pike it will probably die. The best line I have found in this respect is Berkley 'Big Game' in 15lb breaking strain, a product that is reliable, relatively cheap, available on bulk spools and as tough as old boots.

Traces will inevitably be made of wire and I would recommend that you use wire with a breaking strain of at least 20lb. Try to choose a brand that is easy to twist, does not 'kink' readily and is available on bulk spools. Usually I use Berkley wire and it has never let me down, although PDQ trace wire, available via the Harris Angling Company in Norfolk, is also extremely good.

By now you'll have realized that the key requirement when buying tackle is to choose quality, strength and reliability. The same maxim applies to hooks and swivels. Dealing with the swivels first, I use Berkley products in size 7. They have never let me down and I use both the standard and cross-lock variety, the latter when I need to employ a link swivel in the set-up. I and a few friends have experienced some disastrous failures with the snap link-type swivels and nowadays I *never* use them on the hooklink.

Hookwise, I like three patterns – the Fox International Treble, Drennan flank treble (when large hooks are needed) and the Partridge VB double hook. Naturally, I use all three patterns semi-barbless and if barbless versions are out of stock I always squeeze down the barbs on all but the bait-holding points of the hook before using them.

A drop-off indicator is also essential equipment for gravel pit piking. The idea behind these ingenious indicators is that they provide minimum resistance to pike and give a very dramatic indication that the bait has been taken. When set up properly, both runs and drop-backs cause the indicator to fall to the ground. If the pike runs with the bait, it pulls line out of the clip and the drop-off indicator falls away. Because the set-up involves the bail arm of the reel being open, the pike is free to take line with minimum resistance. A drop-back take, caused by the pike running toward the angler, will also cause the indicator to fall back.

There are two styles of drop-off indicator available – electronic and standard. AVA Systems make a superb electronic model which emits a continuous ear-piercing screech in the event of a take. Last year I managed to 'drop off' (forgive the pun) to sleep whilst piking on a local pool. A 6in (15cm) drop-back caused the indicator to create the most hellish racket imaginable and I was startled into a state of alertness immediately. A rude awakening maybe, but well worth it when the culprit proved to be a near 20lb fish!

Electronic indicators are just another example of the increasing expense involved in big fish angling. If you already own some electronic buzzers for carp fishing, you can save yourself some money by using them in conjunction with a pair of standard drop-arm indicators, which cost just a few pounds and are available from most tackle shops. They operate in precisely the same way as the electronic versions, delivering visual confirmation of a take to support the audible indication provided by the buzzer. Remember, though, that a drop-back take might only cause one or two bleeps from the buzzer – so investigate everything.

Finally, it goes without saying that proper unhooking and weighing equipment is essential for all forms of pike fishing. A good pair of artery forceps, at least 12in (30cm) long, should be carried at all times, along with a John Roberts 'deep throat' disgorger as a back-up in the event of emergencies. A pair of long-handled wire cutters are just as important in case, God forbid, you need to cut through trebles or wire in the event that the pike is very deeply hooked.

An unhooking mat is almost as important and I use the Fox International 'Classic' mat, which is big enough to cope with even the largest pike and is also suitable for boat fishing. Similarly, boat fanatics might also like to consider another Fox product, the short, boat landing net handle on their specimen landing net – it's tailor made for the job.

A good sling is also vital and you need to purchase one that will cope with long as well as heavy fish. There are plenty of good slings around and I recommend that you choose one with 'monster' in its title!

As far as other items of tackle are concerned, I will cover things like floats, polyballs, beads and so on later in the section.

Locating Gravel Pit Pike

Many of the anglers I see fishing on gravel pits employ a single style of angling, which involves mounting a half mackerel or other deadbait onto a trace and then hurling it to the limits of their casting ability. They catch the odd pike too, but they invariably suffer a high proportion of blanks and I cannot help but think how much more difficult my own pike fishing would become if these people employed a bit more thought into locating pike and enjoyed bigger catches as a consequence. It's all too easy to think of pike, all pike, as aggressive hunters who spend the majority of their time scouring the water for food. But they don't! Invariably, feeding periods will be restricted and whilst some pike are quite nomadic, just as many are not. On any lake, certain areas will be more favoured for feeding than others. These places are known as 'hot spots': find them and the result will be highly improved catches. Remember though, that while some 'hot spots' are regular pike producers, others will be temporary and the fish often abandon them as a result of climatic influences, the movement of prey fish or, most frequently, angling pressure. Pike, despite their ferocious reputation, seem more susceptible to angling pressure than other species.

Before we move on to considering specific features, let's pick up on the feeding period theme for a moment. As I said before, pike do not feed continuously and one of the most notable features about gravel pit pike is that they display quite rigid adherence to fixed feeding times. I do not mean by this that they feed every day at 2.04 pm for instance, but there can be no doubt that it's possible to allocate approximate time scales to their feeding habits. Sometimes these will be several hours in duration, while at other times of the year they might be measured in minutes. Feeding habits also vary widely from water to water and on every gravel pit that I know, change in duration and timing according to the time of year. On most of my local gravel pits for instance, from mid-autumn through to early winter, most feeding takes place between an hour after dawn and eleven o'clock in the morning. Takes later in the day are very rare. After mid-winter, however, an afternoon as well as a morning feed is common place, the two hours prior to dusk being the best period. At the back end, when the pike are getting ready to spawn, takes can be sporadic throughout the whole course of the day.

Friends of mine have detected similar trends on their local pits although they have also pointed to waters where the timing of the feed is *quite* different. I know of a couple of waters that fish very well at night, for instance, while most that I know are a waste of time during darkness. The earliest or latest (whichever way you want to look at it) that I've caught a gravel pit pike is at 2 am and it seems that the best night waters are ultra-clear, since the examples that I'm thinking of possess remarkable water clarity.

Anyway, the point is that you need to discover the prime feeding periods on your local water, noting how they vary according to the time of year and so on. Be reassured, too, that just because gravel pit pike tend to feed within limited constraints, this is not always the case and it's always worth having baits out between periods to catch the occasional fish that inevitably defies the rules!

The first area in which I suggest you look for gravel pit pike is in the margins. The majority of pike anglers neglect marginal swims; when referring to the margins I'm specifically targeting an area within two or three rod lengths of the bank. On many gravel pits this distance happens to coincide with the first 'drop off' or marginal shelf, an area which the pike are fond of patrolling. Indeed, bars, gullies, plateaux and other depth variations are reliable pike-holding areas wherever you find them. Pike use these features to ambush their prey and by using the feature-finding techniques discussed earlier in the book to pinpoint their position, you'll enjoy better results than by adopting a 'chuck it and chance it' approach.

Other prime pike-holding areas include weedbeds, which offer all predatory fish the opportunity to conceal themselves and ambush prey fish. Marginal reedbeds are always worth a try as are areas that contain sub-surface weed further out in the lake. Many anglers are afraid of presenting baits on top of weed, but it's my experience that pike are capable of rooting baits out in these areas, and a slow sinking deadbait nestling on the surface of a weedbed will produce takes. Better still, if you can find them, are natural 'holes' in the weed and in many ways, the smaller the clear area the better. Friends who have taken boats out onto gravel pits have reported the sighting of groups of pike lying in holes in the weed, and it's obvious that these areas are potential 'hot spots' wherever you find them. Sub-surface snags, too, such as sunken trees, abandoned machinery or dumped cars, attract pike and it's always worth placing a bait in the immediate vicinity of features like these.

Finally, one of the most reliable pike-attracting features in any gravel pit will be the shallows. At the back end of the season, particularly, the shallows can harbour large numbers of pike as they congregate to prepare for spawning, but I would not dismiss them at any time of the year, including mid-winter. The attraction to the pike will be the opportunity to hunt for large concentrations of prey fish and a number of friends and I have all caught pike in water as shallow as 2 or 3ft (60–90cm) even when there has been ice in the margins of the pit.

Baits
It is inevitable that the subject of livebaits versus deadbaits will raise itself in this section, so let's tackle this emotive subject at the outset. It's my

opinion that, to catch pike from gravel pits consistently you will need to use both 'lives' and 'deads'. This is not to say that if you are morally opposed to the use of livebaits you will not catch gravel pit pike. You will.

Inevitably though, your catches will be nowhere near their optimum level and the well equipped gravel pit piker will carry both types of bait. If I did not genuinely believe that this is the case I would happily use deadbaits exclusively. The fact is though, that there have been days when livebaits have produced pike runs when 'deads' have been steadfastly refused. It's impossible, of course, to be dogmatic about when this phenomenon will occur, but generally speaking, I've found that on cold, bright days (usually associated with high pressure) livebaits work best, while 'deads' are more productive during low pressure periods. It also has to be said that I know some pits where deadbaits are largely a waste of time during any conditions and vice versa (although this is the rarer of the two examples). What I am trying to do here is to reinforce the point that a selection of dead- and livebaits should be carried on the majority of pike trips in order to cope with the preferences of the pike on your pit on the day in question. Do not, however, run away with the idea that deadbaits are inferior to 'lives', because this is not the case, and I can recall a number of sessions when deadbaits have produced the majority of runs. My usual tactic is to start off by using both types of bait, establishing the preferences of the pike on the day and then switching all of my rods onto the 'winning' method.

Livebaits
Roach make good livebaits because of their visibility and activity. I like to use roach in the 3–10oz class and certainly no larger – not because pike won't take a big roach but because I can't bring myself to deprive one of our fisheries of a decent specimen. The problem with roach is that they will not withstand frequent casting.

Dace are better than roach in my opinion, being livelier, more durable and more streamlined in shape for casting. Dace in the 3–6oz class make superb livebaits.

Perch make surprisingly good pike livebaits, being relatively tough, lively and reasonably durable. Better than roach, but not as good as dace, chub, trout and carp in my opinion.

Chub have to rank as the best livebaits of all. Tough, lively and able to withstand recasting, chub will 'work' for hours. Fish in the 4–12oz class are ideal.

Trout are the toughest, liveliest and most durable livebaits but their 'wiriness' can work against them. Pike find it difficult to hold onto trout sometimes, but nonetheless they can be excellent where their use is allowed; 4–8oz baits are ideal.

Carp Small mirror and common carp, up to 8oz in weight, make ideal livebaits. Durable and lively, they'll work for hours, although they tend to have 'bursts' of activity.

Tench I'm told that tench make super livebaits, but since I've never used them I can't really comment.

Rudd are similar to roach, except that they have a tendency to tangle rigs up due to their habit of swimming high in the water. Worth using when you cannot obtain other, superior baits though. Before I conclude this section, let me issue a word of warning regarding the general use of livebaits. Some fisheries do not allow anglers to bring their own livebaits to the water, and if this is the case, my suggestion is that you stick to the rules. The transfer of fish from one water to another can cause disease and on commercial fisheries it is only fair to respect the wishes of their management for this and moral reasons.

Deadbaits
Deadbaits are universally allowed and a healthy stock of deadbaits in your freezer provides a cheap and convenient source of pike baits. Try to freeze baits individually, with each fish wrapped in cling film. Store them flat, for 'kinked' frozen deadbaits are difficult to cast, awkward to hook and probably less attractive to pike.

Mackerel are one of the universal pike baits. Use either whole or in half sections. When the mackerel rod is away it's often a sign that a bigger than average pike has picked up the bait. Baits between 8oz and 1½lb are ideal for pike fishing. Immature or 'Joey' mackerel are difficult to get hold of, but well worth the effort – they are a super bait. Richworth Streamselect sell frozen, vacuum-packed Joey mackerel.

Herrings A fresh whole or half herring is probably the best deadbait of all where this prolific pike catcher has not been over-used. My favourite baits are small 8–12oz whole herrings.

Smelt There is something about the smelt that pike find very attractive. Oddly shaped, unappetizing-looking fish with a distinctive cucumber smell, smelts will often produce runs when other deadbaits fail. Difficult to obtain, but well worth the effort.

Sprats are cheap, universally available and very popular. Fished either static or sink-and-draw style, sprats catch plenty of pike. Personally, I rarely use them due to their fragile nature and their tendency to produce lots of jack pike. Some big pike have been caught on them, though.

'Exotics' Unusual species such as red gurnard, snappers and horse mackerel can be very productive when other, more traditional deadbaits have been hammered. My favourite is the horse mackerel, a round, plump, oily fish with a tough outer skin.

Naturals Dead coarse fish can be very productive, especially on waters where deadbaits are widely used. Roach, rudd, chub and carp all make super deadbaits.

Trout I don't rate dead trout very highly. They lack both a strong scent and a highly visible appearance. Some anglers swear by them, though, and they are a good stand-by bait.

Eel sections I've never used eel sections, but I'm assured that pike love them, especially on pits

Smelts are superb pike baits.

that contain healthy eel populations. Even on those that don't, eel sections can be a nice change bait when deadbaits are widely used.

Tips for Improving the Effectiveness of Deadbaits
Most anglers are content simply to mount a deadbait on a snap tackle and throw it out. The most innovative technique they employ is to cut the bait in half, which helps to release much of the fish's scent. There are other small but important edges that can be employed, though.

Puncturing Deadbaits rely on the attraction of smell as much as appearance (in contrast to live-baits, whose attraction is purely visual and vibratory). Cutting the bait in half is one way of releasing the bait's scent, the other being to puncture it with a baiting needle if whole baits are being used.

Injecting flavours and oils This is a method that can be used to boost the scent attraction of the deadbait. Using a complementary fish oil, for example, mackerel oil in mackerel, or herring oil in herrings, is my favourite technique, although the use of alternative oils sold by carp bait companies such as red salmon oil, capelin oil, fish feed-

inducing oil and so on can produce the goods. Another additive that appears to produce genuine results is Rod Hutchinson's 'Compound TF', a natural amino acid with a ridiculously strong fishy aroma. This is one half of the highly successful 'monster crab' flavour. A word of warning though – open it in a confined space at your peril!

You will need to purchase a syringe if you want to inject deadbaits, but be warned – the injection of an air bubble into your bloodstream is fatal. For this reason:
1.   Always store the syringe with a needle guard on it.
2.   Always inject the deadbait on a hard, flat surface, well away from your fingers – a tackle box top is ideal.
Whether injecting deadbaits produces significantly improved results is open to question. Certainly, in coloured water, where scent attraction is vital, it's obvious that a boosted aroma will be more easily detected by pike. Personally, I feel confident using injected deadbaits, and this fact in itself is ample justification for the practise in my book. Besides, the appearance of a big oil slick on the surface as the pike chomps the bait prior to setting off the drop-off alarm, is one of the truly exciting sights in pike fishing!

Popping-up Deadbaits can be made fully or semi-buoyant by the injection of air into the skin of the bait, or the insertion of a buoyant material such as balsa wood sticks, foam, polystyrene and so on. Partially buoyant baits can be made to sink slowly so that they rest lightly on top of weed or silt, while fully buoyant deadbaits can be popped-up, carp boilie style. The latter method increases the bait's visibility to pike although it tends to enjoy a limited lifespan since pike will eventually wise up to the method. Specialized products, notably deadbait floater sticks and pop-up foam (sold with a special punch), are readily available via specialist tackle shops.

Wobbled deadbaits The practice of 'wobbling' deadbaits to impart movement to a lifeless bait has a great deal of merit to it, especially static baits are not producing the goods. It's also a good technique to use on venues where livebaits are banned. The other technique used to impart movement to deadbaits is 'sink-and-draw', which involves retrieving the bait in short erratic bursts before allowing it to flutter down to the bottom where it is left for a few seconds at a time. Both of these methods will often produce bonus pike and allow deadbait anglers to cover more water.

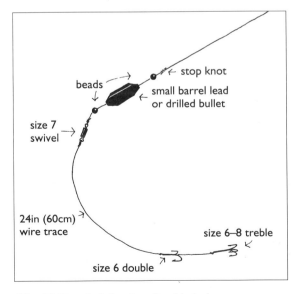

Fig. 61 Gravel pit legering. Dead bait rig.

Methods and Techniques

Let's begin by examining the mounting of pike baits and the various ways of presenting them on the hooks for gravel pit fish.

My standard approach for pit pike is to incorporate both a single and double hook on the trace. Both will be semi-barbless with the barbed point inserted into the bait for greater security. The double hook is positioned at the top of the trace, a method I prefer to using an extra treble because I believe that the double is both easier to remove and gives an improved hook-hold. This is often the hook that ends up in the pike's 'scissors' and the large 'hooking' single part of the hook is, in my opinion, better than two points of equal size. And when the strike is timed properly, the hook should find a good hook-hold in the pike's jaw, the treble improving the chances of a good hook-hold over a double. Other anglers prefer different hooking arrangements and there is nothing wrong with using two trebles or two doubles – the choice is yours and by experimenting you'll be able to form your own conclusions.

The simplest rig to use for pike is the legered deadbait. Most of the anglers I see on the bank use a running leger set-up for presenting deadbaits, but I prefer to fix the lead, either in the form of a small drilled bullet or barrel lead, directly onto the line. There is plenty of casting weight in a deadbait and I can't see the point in adding an extra ounce or two for the sake of it. The reason for this is twofold. Firstly, most of the gravel pits that I fish are weedy and the weight of the bait tends to drag the lead into the weed. This prevents the leger set-up from 'running' in the first place and the use of a lighter leger weight will help the set-up to rest on top of, rather than among, the weed. I use just enough weight to tighten up to, and something between ⅜oz and ½oz is usually ample. The second reason for not using a heavy leger mounted 'pendulum' style is that it creates an imbalance during flight which inevitably reduces casting efficiency. In any event, mine is a simple set-up that catches plenty of pike and produces positive takes.

The deadbait is mounted head down the trace, with the top hook nicked into the tail root of the

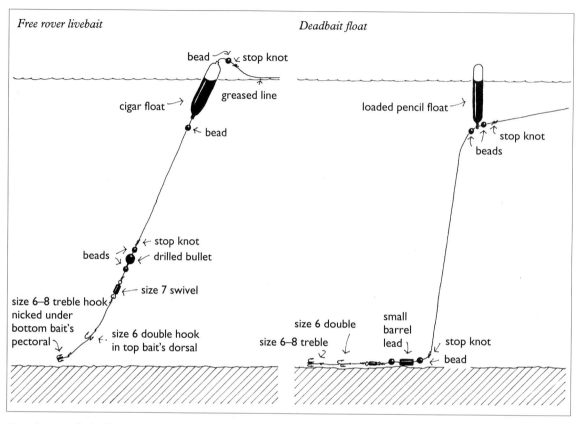

Free rover livebait

bead — stop knot

greased line

cigar float →

← bead

← stop knot
beads → ← drilled bullet

← size 7 swivel

size 6–8 treble hook
nicked under
bottom bait's
pectoral

← size 6 double hook
in top bait's dorsal

Deadbait float

loaded pencil float →

stop knot
beads

size 6 double

size 6–8 treble

small
barrel
lead

stop knot
bead

Fig. 62 *Gravel pit pike float rigs.*

fish and the bottom treble inserted into its flank. This is a better casting shape and delivers improved distance. When 'wobbling' the deadbait I dispense with the leger weight altogether and mount the bait head up the trace so that when it is retrieved it comes back naturally, that is, head first. For all static deadbait presentations, I'll mount the bait using the former method (head down the trace).

The float-fished deadbait is little more than an adaptation of the legered method. The only difference is that a loaded pencil float is added to the set-up to give a visual indication. The float is attached to the line bottom end only and allowed allowed to slide freely on the line. The depth is fixed via a stop knot, which is set to fish the rig a couple of feet over depth. Because the float is loaded it will 'self cock' with as much as half of the float's sight tip proud of the water. Takes will

cause the float either to submerge, or 'dither' on the surface before tilting over and lying flat. This is a super method for presenting deadbaits because it gives a visually dramatic indication that a pike has taken the bait. It's especially useful for anglers who do not possess electronic alarms, but for pikers everywhere there's something about watching a float that justifies its use wherever possible.

When I'm livebaiting on gravel pits I use three presentations which can be considered as short-, medium- and long-range, namely the float-fished livebait, the sunken float paternoster and the drifter float rig. In each case the bait is mounted in the same way, with the top hook inserted just in front of the bait's dorsal fin and the bottom treble nicked into the area around its pelvic fin. This allows the bait to swim as naturally as is possible, although there are occasions, especially on heavily fished waters, when I put the top hook into the bait's tail root and the bottom treble into the dorsal area. This causes the bait to work in 'bursts', swimming away from the float and creates a more 'erratic' effect.

The Float-Fished Livebait

Let's start with the free roving livebait. It's the oldest presentation of them all, but deadly wherever it is used nonetheless. A cigar-style float is used with the line threaded through its central bore. A stop knot fixes the depth, which can be anywhere between a couple of feet below the surface and a foot or two off the bottom. The idea is that the bait will rove around and find the pike for you. The signal that this has indeed occurred is usually a dramatic increase in the bait's activity as it senses the pike's presence and attempts to leave the area. It's important to grease the line above the float, otherwise line drag will impede the bait's freedom of movement and since the idea behind this rig is that it searches a wide area of water, this would defeat its purpose.

The other way to use the free rover is as a short-range drifter. A few seasons ago I was fishing a shallow local pit whose only distinctive feature is a pronounced marginal shelf about three rod lengths out from the bank. Many of the pit's pike patrol the bottom of this marginal slope and I managed to devise a way of drifting a bait in a constant line parallel with the base of the slope. This enabled me to present baits over considerable distances in an area highly favoured by the pike. The rig was a free rover, fished a couple of feet off the bottom. To make the rig work properly, a wind blowing either left to right or right to left (as opposed to away from or directly into the fishing position) parallel with the bank was necessary. Using a heavily greased line, the bait was cast out level with the shelf and a large bow placed in the line. By walking slowly along the bank in front of the float, and manipulating the bow, I found that it was possible to drift the bait parallel with the drop-off for some 60 or 70yds (55–65m). The result was impressive catches of pike at a time when others (including me up to that point) were struggling, and I managed to bank fish to over 20lb.

The Sunken Float Paternoster

The next rig, the sunken float paternoster, is ideal for presenting baits near to known or suspected pike-holding areas. The bait is allowed restricted movement, continually working a confined area and, hopefully, attracting the attentions of resident pike. The other benefit of this type of rig is that while free roving baits might be ignored by a pike not in a feeding mood, the paternoster is a constant reminder that a meal is available for very little effort and is therefore ideal for 'provoking' takes.

The sunken float paternoster, as the name suggests, incorporates a sunken float to keep the bait away from the bottom and constantly working. The beauty of this rig is that it can be cast into any depth of water greater than 3ft (90cm) and it will be functional. The bait's movement is restricted by the presence of a 2oz lead, which holds it in position. The main line is clipped onto a 'drop-off' style indicator, with the line clip adjusted so that the actions of the bait are not quite strong enough to free the line. When a pike picks up the bait, the line pulls free from the clip and spills off the spool, thus minimizing resistance to the taking fish. After a few seconds' delay, a positive strike should be made to set the hooks.

When making sunken paternosters there are two important considerations – avoiding bite-offs and tangles. Fortunately, Neville Fickling's 'Pike Safe' paternoster boom solves both problems. This 24in (60cm) long length of semi-stiff boom tube incorporates attachment points for a bomb link, short wire trace (up to 18in – 45cm – long) and main line. An up-trace and anti-tangle boom rolled into one, it's highly effective and I no longer bother to make my own up traces. If you want to purchase one of these excellent products, contact the Tackle Box at Gainsborough, Lincolnshire.

To ensure that the paternoster works effectively, use a bomb link that is approximately 18in (45cm) longer that the short wire trace; this will keep the bait off the bottom and working constantly. Also, after casting out, tighten up to the bomb and then pay out a small amount of line so that the float can rise up to its stop knot, a practice which will also prevent the bait from reaching the lake bed.

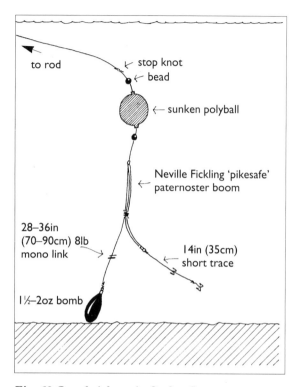

Fig. 63 Gravel pit leger rig. Sunken float paternoster.

The drifter float works best with greased line – note also the 'auto-regreaser' which plugs into a rod ring and automatically greases the line.

The Drifter Rig

The third livebaiting technique that I frequently use is the drifter rig, incorporating a large, vaned drifting float, which is capable of carrying the bait considerable distances (up to 200yds – 180m – or more). By using a greased line, and positioning yourself so that the wind is blowing over your shoulder, the bait can be drifted to cover a huge amount of water. To search a very wide area effectively, it pays to close the bail arm on your reel periodically, which will cause the float to swing in an arc.

Experienced drift float pikers can control the float to such an extent that it will cover a large area of water. With practice, the rig can be made to drift in a zig-zag pattern, which adds breadth as well as distance to the drift and improves the chance of a 'snap-up' still further. It also pays to vary the depth at which the bait is fished, although wherever possible, a couple of feet off the bottom seems ideal. You may also find that at some point during the drift, the float refuses to progress any further. This means that you have found a bar, plateau, weedbed or shelf and this is a signal to place a paternostered bait to fish in the proximity of the feature.

Conclusion

The fact that the number of gravel pits is slowly increasing with each successive year in this country, and the fact that gravel pits are readily accessible, suggests that these prolific fisheries could be the pike waters of the future. I would never describe pit fishing as easy, but most gravel pits of a reasonable size usually hold at least a few specimen pike. Master the techniques required to crack these challenging fisheries, and you are well equipped to tackle pike on just about every type of water likely to contain this fascinating species.

TROUT RESERVOIR PIKING — by John Watson

When the trout reservoirs, so long out of bounds to coarse anglers, began to open for pike fishing back in the 1980s, a whole new concept of pike fishing was also opening up for anglers who had

John Watson with a 37lb 8oz pike from Bough Beech reservoir – proof indeed of the potential of trout waters for pike.

maybe in the past yearned to fish such places. The likes of Llangdegfedd, Ardleigh and Bewl presented the angler with waters which had the potential to throw up huge pike and also perch, and the enlightened attitudes of people such as Ian Taylor and Ken Crow, at Weir Wood and Bough Beech respectively, provided memorable days for anglers such as myself. Some, of course, have gone on record indicating that such fishing is not for them, branding the style artificial, but these same people are often happy to fish a small river for 6lb stocked trout, where fish under 1lb are the norm. It is also said that success on such waters comes easy, but try telling that to those who have had limited catches and there may be an interesting response. However, as I have said, these waters can provide significant memories – and there is no denying that a 40lb pike is magnificent, is there?

So how does an angler unfamiliar with boat fishing for pike go about the job?

Well, first and foremost, safety in a boat is of paramount importance. It does not, I hope, need to be emphasized to anyone that falling into 30ft (9m) of cold water, fully clad, in the midst of winter can seriously affect your health to the point

that you may never go fishing again. Obviously, a lifejacket is an essential piece of kit that should be *worn*, and not left at the other end of the boat. A boat should be kept tidy, with a minimum of clutter, and it is worth working out what you are going to do should you hook a good fish, before the event actually takes place. If you are sharing a boat, it should be a simple matter to work out between the two of you who will do what and when, although the person playing the fish will obviously be occupied with one task. A boat must have a suitably padded area to lay fish on, to safeguard them from damage; a piece of old carpet laid on the bottom of the boat, whilst providing a splash of colour, also reduces vibration.

As far as equipment is concerned, I have pressed into service some 2¼lb test curve pike rods, and know of friends who have been successful with 1¾lb models. A big pike on a short line – you may have less than 50ft (15m) of line between you and the fish when you initially make contact) – is not something that I have ever wished to do battle with on a heavy rod, and a forgiving action is, if not essential, then certainly useful. Indeed, Simon Marshall took his 40lb 2oz fish from Bough Beech on a 1¾lb tool. Don't feel, as some do, that a heavy rod is necessary to get a big pike off the bottom, since once you get above a fish, it is surprising how with steady pressure, it can be coaxed into the net. These waters are generally snag-free, and it would be advisable to use a light rod in situations where the fish may need to be bullied away from an obstacle of some sort.

I personally use Shimano baitrunner reels which can be useful if, when on the move, a second float-fished bait is used (but I will cover this at a later stage). The reels are loaded with 15lb Berkley Big Game line, and a 20lb Berkley Steel Strand wire trace of at least 24in (60cm) is used in conjunction with Drennan or Terry Eustace treble hooks, in sizes 6 and 8, with Berkley no 10 swivels.

Having stipulated that a tidy boat is a requirement of this form of fishing, it should be said that a landing net is designed to do just that: to land fish. Thus the short handle advocated by some may be convenient when stowing gear in the boat for a day's fishing, but it may be a drawback when a big fish nears the boat and needs to be dealt with cleanly and efficiently. Some friends swear by the use of a circular net, but I cope quite adequately with a 42in (106cm) triangular one with a handle of 7ft (2.1m) in length. Care should be exercised when using the net as it may 'billow out' in the water, and there is the chance that a loose treble will catch on its outside.

Livebaits are retained in a livebait cage, and while I have heard it said that anything hung over the side can affect boat control in windy conditions, I personally have not experienced any problems. My cage was obtained from Taylor Engineering and is excellent for the job.

While it may not always be the best method on the day, I thoroughly enjoy trailing a bottom bait. The rig used is a simple sliding link leger which is lowered to the bottom, and with, in my case, the use of an electric motor powered by a deep cell leisure battery, a lot of water can be covered. The link should be a 'rotten bottom', and it is useful to incorporate a drilled bullet held in place by a split shot. In using this, if the link does get caught on the bottom, it is highly likely that a little pressure will cause the shot to slip, releasing

the bullet and hopefully the line. This should prevent baited hooks being left in the water. When lowering the bait to the bottom, light pressure is applied to the edge of the spool to feather the line and prevent tangles.

An area of reservoir is fished almost at a 'crawl', thoroughly, speeding the boat up intermittently to inject some additional movement, if necessary, into the bait. I like to hold the rod, but some friends prefer to use boat rests and wait for the rod to bend. I watch the rod top for any indication and, holding the line round a finger with the reel bail open, release the line when a take is registered. The bail is then engaged, and a firm steady pull drives the hooks home. Some claim to 'touch leger', but I invariably sit with the rod at 50° to the trail line, and feel that any action will be absorbed by the rod tip before it reaches my often numb fingers. Perhaps I am just an unfeeling person! I would suggest keeping rigs as simple as possible, placing emphasis on the need to safeguard pike stocks, and I have no use for attractor blades, bearing in mind the speed at which I generally operate the boat, or any other paraphernalia including polyballs.

I occasionally put out a second rod on float tackle and leave this in a rest using a baitrunner reel. Once more the set-up is as simple as possible, taking into account an additional wire trace above the weight to prevent potential 'bite-offs'. You also need to take into account that there will be a certain amount of 'blow back', depending on the speed at which you are trailing, and the depth the bait fishes should be adjusted accordingly. A float lock may be used, otherwise the bait may rise in the water, and you could see your bait on the surface as you motor or row around the reservoir.

Alternatively, and a potentially better method, is to use a run clip on the side of the float and slip the line into this before going on the move. I sometimes find that a lock can become clogged with line grease and will not slide down the line whilst playing a fish. This can present a problem should the float arrive at the tip ring and refuse to budge any further, while you are left with a pike on the end of 20ft (6m) of line. To overcome this I use large floats which carry a lot of weight and keep the baits down where I want them.

On the subject of line grease, butt greasers are available, although when I have used them I find that lumps of the stuff are pulled out of the greasers when line is pulled from the reel. Perhaps I am doing something wrong, but I find it more effective to cast a fair distance, pack the reel spool with grease and then reel in. The pressure of the line returning to the spool forces the grease to the surface and each coil is coated. This method certainly works for me, and the line remains buoyant for several sessions.

Over the last few years trailing as a method seems to have been most productive when water clarity is reasonably good. Having said that, on the occasions when I have fished waters that have had visibility seriously affected by an influx of dirty water, the reservoir seems to have switched off completely, or has been productive only when using deadbaits. Such baits, fished almost in the margins, have been productive for some when the action slows.

Let us assume, however, that visibility is good and the fish are keen to respond to baits. Trailing with lures can be an enjoyable diversion, and many of the deep-diving and mid-water patterns can be employed with some success. In the case of plugs, the tackle can be kept to a minimum with a wire trace incorporating a swivel at one end and a wide-gape cross-lock clip at the other. Many swear by the use of glass rods for this form of fishing as the rod is not always hauled over, and little knocks on the rod top can be seen. (There are specialist operators in the UK who import all sorts of lures, and the Harris Angling Company will be able to help with any enquiries which you may wish to make.)

Drifter fishing can be a useful method to use, and as long as it is conducted sensibly, no problems should arise. Please bear in mind, however, that you may not be overly popular should you cut off half the width of the reservoir with a couple of drifted baits.

The subject of fishfinders is one which often prompts interesting conversations. The non-angler will say that it is cheating to use such a piece of kit, but I respond by saying that if I see fish on the screen I just become more frustrated in that I can 'see' fish but still cannot catch them! Experienced anglers have stated that they feel it is unethical to use a finder to locate shoals of fodder fish and then to fish around the edges of these shoals for predators. They are, however, happy to find fish-holding features and fish these areas for other species as well as pike. My view is that a shoal of fry is simply another feature. Spinning around such a shoal can be productive and is well worth the effort.

The general misunderstanding of the capabilities of finders can often be witnessed and as an example I can refer to an angler who motored out from the margin at speed, without his baits in the water, and having seen the depth drop away on his screen, dramatically announced to everyone that he had found a drop-off which he hadn't seen there on any other occasion. In fact if he had motored out at a slower speed, he would have seen the gentle slope that everyone knew was there. I am not referring to this incident so as to ridicule the angler in any way; the purpose is to emphasize that the readings of a finder can be open to misinterpretation, and it is worth familiarizing yourself thoroughly with the capabilities of any machine which you may acquire.

Fish symbols supposedly indicate the presence of fish, and are another interesting facility. My machine illustrates such a symbol, or when this feature is switched off, a dot or series of dots. However, on one occasion on a clear Scottish loch whilst in a boat floating 4ft (1.2m) above the bed, I experienced fish after fish passing across the screen. Peering into the water revealed nothing, and we discovered that suspended silt can often give a convincing dot reading also. Nonetheless, such machines are of great value, and I use mine primarily for depth readings, showing contours and various features.

In strong wind conditions, drifting with a drogue is another option, as the drogue will allow you to drift whilst offering control of the boat; alternatively, should you wish to trail in the direction that the wind is blowing, you can use an outboard in reverse to achieve a more controlled effect.

When to hit a take is something which always raises conflicting views. For my part, once I engage the bail I generally switch off the engine if conditions allow, as this prevents any other lines becoming entangled with the propeller (and stops me going round in circles); I stand up, tighten to the fish and pull the hooks firmly home. Others hesitate for a few seconds and then strike, whilst some of my friends who fish with rods in rests wait for the tips to bend round, as I have already mentioned, and then strike immediately. They comment that although on most occasions all the fish are well hooked, sometimes the hooks are only lightly embedded at the front of the mouth; these same friends never deep-hook fish. Their view is that when the bait is taken by a large pike it is initially engulfed, but is then passed forwards to the teeth where it is killed, and only then is it swallowed; if this is the case, it goes some way to explaining why those that delay their strike only hook the pike lightly in the bony part of the front of the mouth. Just a theory of course, but a chance to speculate, and an interesting guess at how these fish hunt. You will, of course, follow your own method, but an excessive delay should not be encouraged, and quite obviously deep-hooking should be avoided at all costs.

As far as location is concerned, on the big waters that I have fished no patterns of any relevance have arisen. On one particular reservoir, during its early availability it could almost be guaranteed that fishing the shallows during November and December would result in small fish hitting the bait. However, big fish, it seems, can come out of almost any area.

A mobile approach is an obvious method to employ on a new water, and will help you to get to know the place quicker. If this method is ineffective, static fishing with deadbaits can be productive, moving the position of the baits and boat regularly until fish are caught. Your positions can be recorded by noting landmarks. Slowly wobbling a deadbait around the boat can also be effective when the pike are not actively hunting.

If you decide to tackle a big reservoir, bear in mind that whilst the pike in such waters may be magnificent, they will undoubtedly be susceptible to damage. Do not put a fish into a sack and head for the shore at speed unless you feel that it is absolutely essential to weigh it and photograph it there, as in the case of a record fish, maybe. If you must head to the shore, do it in a steady manner, and if there are two in the boat, the second angler should keep an eye on the fish. If the fish is taken to land, an area of substantial padding must be provided to lay it on; similarly the boat should have a suitably padded area, and it is worth considering putting a big fish into a sack after unhooking to allow it to recover a little before weighing and photographing. Remember that it may be quite lively when taken from the sack. The advantage of releasing a pike from the boat in the area in which it was caught, is that it does give the fish the opportunity to dive straight down; releasing it from the bank can result in the fish appearing to be disorientated as it flounders in the shallows. Deal with all of these procedures quickly and efficiently. There is no excuse for keeping a fish out of the water for an unacceptable period of time.

Lastly, if you are new to this branch of the sport, go fishing if you can with an experienced pike angler; although there is nothing to be concerned about, some people are likely to become nervous when dealing with pike, and the fish may suffer. If you need guidance it is worth contacting the Pike Anglers' Club, a body which is always most helpful, since both the pike's safety and yours whilst boat fishing, are of maximum importance.

If you consider all these things carefully before you tackle reservoir piking you will, I hope, get the most out of the sport. There are some superb fish to be caught, and hopefully, more forward-thinking reservoir managers will adopt a more enlightened view towards the pike, rather than just seeing it as a trout-munching machine. Proper control of the pike stock, instead of indiscriminate removal, could lead to a useful winter-time income for owners, whilst at the same time ensuring that the water does not produce predominantly small pike. Who knows, in the future we may see more waters becoming available to us all. Let us hope so.

Good piking!

INDEX